WRITERS
IN
LOVE

Mary Kathleen Benet

MACMILLAN PUBLISHING CO., INC.

New York

Macmillan Publishing Co., Inc.

866 Third Avenue, New York, N.Y. 10022

Collier Macmillan Canada, Ltd.

Library of Congress Cataloging in Publication Data

Benet, Mary Kathleen.

Writers in love.

Includes bibliographical references and index.

1. Women authors—Biography.   2. Women authors—

Relationship with men.   I. Title.

PN481.B4   809'.89287   76-25560

ISBN 0-02-508900-5

First Printing 1977

Printed in the United States of America

FOR JULIAN

ACKNOWLEDGMENTS

I would like to give special thanks to Antony Alpers (whose definitive biography of Katherine Mansfield is almost completed), Herma Briffault, Maurice Goudeket, Colin Middleton Murry, Richard Murry, and John Wolfers; to the members of my family who provided me with room, board, baby-sitting, and moral support during the final stages of work; and to Amanda Vaill for the kind of editing that few writers are lucky enough to receive.

CONTENTS

Introduction: The Female Genius   3

Part I: Katherine Mansfield & John Middleton Murry

1 / Apprenticeships   21
2 / The Two Tigers   40
3 / Murry Post Mortem   76
4 / The Art of Katherine Mansfield   89

Part II: George Eliot & George Henry Lewes

1 / Each Alone   113
2 / Partnership   138
3 / The Works of George Henry Lewes   159
4 / The Novels of George Eliot   170

Part III: Colette

1 / Sido   187
2 / Willy   198
3 / Jouvenel   213
4 / Goudeket   227
5 / The Style of Colette   237

Conclusion: The Muse at Work   255

Notes   263
Index   271

INTRODUCTION

The Female Genius

A weak ego does not gain substantial strength
from being persistently bolstered. A strong
ego, secured in its identity by a strong society,
does not need and in fact is immune to any
deliberate attempt at artificial inflation.
Its tendency is toward the testing of what
feels real, the mastery of that which works,
the understanding of that which proves necessary,
the enjoyment of the vital, and the overcoming
of the morbid.

—*Erik Erikson,* Identity, Youth and Crisis

For a writer to receive help and inspiration from a woman is a common occurrence—so common that language is full of clichés of the "behind every man . . ." or "cherchez la femme" variety. Wives, mothers, secretaries, and other female acolytes have throughout literary history devoted themselves to shielding the creative man from the arduous necessities of daily life and to preserving the tranquil atmosphere that he demanded for his work. Far less attention has been paid to the reverse situation: to men who provided the necessary working and living conditions for gifted women. The obvious reason is that this situation is so rare. Women writers have generally had to do without the kind of help men got from their wives: their choice lay between marriage and work, and the ones who chose work also chose spinsterhood: one thinks of the Brontës, Jane Austen, Emily Dickinson.

But a few women writers have found men who were content to spend much of their lives furthering their wives' careers. These unusual cases indicate unusual qualities in the people involved. Women who receive this kind of devotion often inspire it by extraordinary brilliance; the men who respond to such women have a humility and insight that may be rarer still. George Eliot, Katherine

Mansfield, and Colette all established this kind of relationship with men, and the literary reputations of all three confirm the suspicion that their exceptional lives were the results of exceptional qualities. Today, when relations between men and women, between women and work, are being so closely scrutinized, the lives of these women have more to tell us than do the stories of those who accepted a kind of defeat by renouncing one part of life or the other.

In *Seduction and Betrayal*, Elizabeth Hardwick describes such "women behind men" as Dorothy Wordsworth and Jane Carlyle; and parenthetically she touches on the reverse situation:

> George Lewes, one of the most lovable and brilliant men of his day, gave the same kind of love to George Eliot and to the creation and sustaining of her genius. A genuine dedication has a proper object and grows out of a deep sense of shared values. It is not usual because the arts, more than any other activity, create around them—at home, with those closest, in the world, everywhere—a sense of envy.[1]

This is only part of the explanation. It is also true that there are few geniuses, male or female, who can be a "proper object" for the life-long devotion of anyone but a damaged and dependent human being. Which comes first, the devotion or the genius? I began by thinking that it must be the devotion; if other women had had such help, such sustenance, what could they not have achieved? But the more deeply I explored these three lives, the more certain I grew that the genius came first—and that part of the genius was the ability to choose an appropriate partner, one who would respect and not hinder the task that this gifted female ego had set itself.

Genius, of course, is a romantic word, and there can be no final agreement on its application. But during the period spanned by these three writers, it said something about how creative people viewed themselves and their ambitions. Part of the definition in the *Oxford English Dictionary* is "instinctive and extraordinary capacity for imaginative creation . . . often contrasted with *talent*." The quotation they give from Thomas De Quincey develops this contrast in ways that are relevant to our purpose:

Talent and genius . . . are not merely different, they are in polar opposition to each other. Talent is intellectual power of every kind, which
acts and manifests itself . . . through the will and the active forces. Genius . . . is that much rarer species of intellectual power which is
derived from the genial nature—from the spirit of suffering and enjoying—from the spirit of pleasure and pain. . . . It is a function of the
passive nature.

How close these descriptions are to the truisms about masculinity
and femininity! It has often been noted that there is something
feminine about genius—artistic men do not conform to masculine
stereotypes—and yet women of genius who have realized their potential are often considered to be violating received notions of femininity. This paradox has been the torment of many creative
women, and the solutions to it represented by these three lives
seem to me to be worth examining today more than ever.

The three women in this book, so apparently dissimilar, all
needed to be closely and happily in touch with life in order to do
their best work; they could not live alone, and each gradually
learned what sort of man could give her the sympathetic help she
required. All had happy country childhoods, and all seem to have
acted out the frustrated ambitions of strong mothers to whom they
were close. All were the objects of passionate adoration from other
women, and all relied heavily on female friendships in periods
when they lacked the right kind of male support. All rebelled
against a domestic role, but remained intensely feminine in sensibility.

The men they chose also show similarities. Far from being the
rocks that might be thought necessary to bear such weight, all were
idealistic, insecure, and sensitive—they needed the women at least
as much as they themselves were needed. Mutual dependence,
mutual help—this was the key to the happiness of these women in
love.

But this book is not simply a description of one kind of woman,
one kind of relationship. It is also a polemic. It began as a reaction
against two current ideas—one put about by feminists, one by antifeminists. The "feminist" idea (which, of course, I am not

suggesting that all feminists share) is that playing the traditional female role, getting married—or indeed having any relation with men—is detrimental to the development of a woman's talents. Her role will necessarily be subservient—if there is literary creation to be done, the man will do it. Did not F. Scott Fitzgerald use the material that belonged equally to Zelda, and was she not certified insane partly because she demanded the right to use it too? Did not Jane Carlyle and Dorothy Wordsworth, enormously gifted as they were, produce only letters and journals while serving the needs of their male geniuses?

Ideally, such feminists admit, a choice between love and work should not be necessary, as it is not necessary for men. But as things are, women who hope to develop their creative gifts would be better off opting for lesbianism or independence. The famous literary spinsters lend some credence to this view—but there is another type of woman writer who seems to exemplify it, and who has had a great deal of influence in forming concepts of this kind.

Virginia Woolf and Sylvia Plath are two who tackled the literary heights, married colleagues, and committed suicide after exhausting themselves in the attempt to conquer lives of unbearable strain. The interior monologues they carried on with themselves in their books reveal their inner loneliness, their feeling that death and madness were the only safe retreats.

Were these women killed by the conflict between love and work, in spite of the efforts of supportive men who tried to help them combine the two roles? Was the conflict too profound to be solved by a therapeutic marriage? In both, the suicidal abnormality is evident very early, in their own descriptions of their young lives; as adults, they were racing against time, hurtling toward what they felt to be the inevitable result. Certainly Leonard Woolf was the savior of his wife in a very literal sense—and in this sense, her books would certainly not have been written without him. Like George Eliot, she began writing novels only after her marriage. This is why, though she is of a different psychological type from the women in this book, she emerges as a constant source of comparison with them. She, too, felt their conflicts, different as the outcome was in her case.

Sylvia Plath implies in her poems that she identified her husband, colleague though he was, with her father—and that the dominant male was crushing the life out of her. A. Alvarez, in his essay on suicide, says that the breakup of her marriage reenacted her father's death when she was a child, with fatal results. Ted Hughes had his own work to do; perhaps a more self-sacrificing man could have saved Sylvia Plath's life temporarily; but no reader of her work can be in much doubt about the inevitability of the final result.

The lives of these two women are too pathological to take as indications of any kind of general rule. They were modernists, and their alienation seems to mirror that of the modern movement as a whole. They have become heroes of feminism because their plight is a drastic example of the conflict so many women feel between love and work. Virginia Woolf, indeed, was saved by her husband, and thus superficially seems not to belong to this category—but in her suicide note, she said that she was killing herself as an act of mercy to him, rather than again trying to save herself at his expense.

We cannot take the alienation and despair of such examples as the inevitable consequence of female genius, any more than we can take the alienation of Sartre and Beckett as the inevitable consequence of artistic genius faced with the modern world. Writers must create monuments of dislocation, despair, alienation, barrenness, if that is what the age presents to their view. No one would suggest that the great moderns were disqualified by their point of view from being great artists, or that the books they wrote should not exist. But in every age, there are writers who manage to connect, to feel and express the surge of the life force. It seems to me that this is the more difficult, triumphant, and admirable achievement.

The women who broke themselves on the wheel of modernism clearly felt that being female was part of what destroyed them. Being a working-class writer used to present the kind of suicidal problems that being female contained more recently—one thinks of some of Alvarez's other famous suicides: Clare, Chatterton, even Keats. And in modern times, being an intellectual seems to have been, especially in America, as alienating as being a woman: Lowell and Berryman have an obvious kinship with Sylvia Plath.

But to say that these conflicts are inevitable, and that any serious woman writer must suffer them or keep to her solitude, is to my mind a false turning. It has been necessary for the self-preservation of many women writers who were not strong enough to face and accept a complex human existence; but their work has been seriously flawed by the limitations placed on their emotional lives. Remoteness, intellectualism, coldness; or, at the other extreme, febrile emotionalism and overactive fantasy—these are the pitfalls that lie in wait for the woman who dedicates herself to her work at the expense of life.

This is not merely a matter of preference between artistic styles or schools; it is a distinction between those who have been tragically tortured and defeated by their lives and those who, through greater psychological strength and other more favorable circumstances, have succeeded in a healthy struggle. That is why the category of women writers treated in this book seems to me to be so vitally important. The health of their art is rooted in the emotional strength and optimism of their lives; they show that living well and writing well are not opposites, but two aspects of the same thing.

Though feminism played only a subsidiary role in allowing these lives to happen and these works to be written, it seems to me that these three writers do have a message for feminists. The message is that renouncing human life in favor of any political ideal—whether feminism or another—produces an arid and neurotic art; that there is enough strength in the "female genius" as it has actually existed to give comfort to any feminist; and that a revaluation of this art is a more vital task than the creation of something more narrowly political.

To my mind, all three of these stories show not only that love and work were not at war, but that love was the absolutely necessary precondition for work. These women reversed the Zelda Fitzgerald situation, the Dorothy Wordsworth situation. Their cases may be unusual, but manifestly they are not impossible.

The argument of the antifeminists is more absolute and more difficult to deal with. It states that there has never been a woman literary genius, and even that such a thing is theoretically impossible. Why extend to women the privileges allowed to genius, since their work will always be second-rate? Physical creation takes the place, for them, of artistic creation. Why don't they stick to it?

There can be no arguing over this point of view. I must simply confess that I do not understand it. If there is a reader who does not find genius in these three women, there is nothing I can do to convince him of it. I can only hope that greater familiarity with their work will by itself change his mind. I say "his" mind because I am certain that the writings of these women have always been more admired by women than by men. Men tend to deplore the sensuous richness of Colette's style, and to complain of its lack of hard thought, of philosophical underpinning. The subtlety with which she presents her argument leads them to think that she is presenting no argument at all. They consider Katherine Mansfield a miniaturist—very sensitive and touching, but of no real consequence. George Eliot, with her "masculine" mind, is not so easily dismissed; but can one not accuse her of prudish moralism, of schoolmistressy sententiousness?

Naturally these writers are not above criticism; naturally their very virtues, in moments of exaggeration, can become defects. But while men are lining up these objections, women are finding in all three of these writers a reflection of their own experience. In a time when respect for the female experience is growing, and when men are listening more closely to what women say, perhaps they too will find greater truth and interest in these works than they ever suspected were there. The literary revaluations required by feminism are of this order: just as a more egalitarian age discovered the merits of Blake and Clare, and the alienated moderns rehabilitated Donne, so the greatest delineators of the female mind will gradually assume their rightful place in literary history.

I do not believe that genius is a pathological state. Nor do I believe that, for women, Freud's great criteria of mental health—love and work—are incompatible. The three women in this book held up their own love affairs as examples of human happiness at its most complete. If one must have an axiom about female genius, then "The best writers were also the best lovers" seems to me an acceptable suggestion.

Katherine Mansfield and John Middleton Murry wrote to each other some of the most famous and beautiful letters in the English language. Her last letter to him, to be opened after her early and tragic death from tuberculosis, said, "I feel no other lovers have walked the earth together more joyfully." The elopement of George Eliot and George Henry Lewes became one of the great romantic legends of Victorian England—and George Eliot herself said that without his sustaining love, she would never have written a single novel. Colette is a more complicated case: all three of her husbands were in some sense her impresarios, but her ambivalence about love was exacerbated by the tyrannies and infidelities of Monsieur Willy and Henry de Jouvenel. Finally, the young Maurice Goudeket elicited from her the romantic, passionate love that enabled her to write the serene and profound books of her later years.

To speak of these lives as romantic legends makes them seem exemplary, heroic. But can biography ever be an act of judgment? Can one really say to every frustrated or antagonistic woman, "Throw off your ideology and follow them?"

My most serious doubts on this score revolve around the much-debated question of the ego of genius, of what should be allowed to the artist that is ordinarily denied to people attempting to live harmoniously with each other. The tendency nowadays is to consider this kind of license a branch of male chauvinist piggery—to feel sympathy for Tolstoy's wife, Joyce's wife, the many women involved with Lawrence, and to say that the works of many such men are less pleasing to us because they were fed with the lifeblood of victimized women.

Can the personality type of genius really be recommended, for men or for women? Have these women simply reversed the situation, producing an emotional setup no more attractive even though the other partner is now on top? This accusation has at one time or another been hurled at each of them. They took it seriously, and would have considered themselves moral failures if it had turned out to be true. It is interesting to trace the line of defense that each took up.

George Eliot liked to approve of herself, to feel that she was doing what she thought was right. She presented all her life's choices in a moral guise. Her work, therefore, became a duty, its justification the fact that people found it edifying. Her flight with Lewes was presented as the rescue of *him* from an adulterous wife and an arduous career in literary journalism.

Colette argued that the betrayals of men had thrown her back upon the use of her own talents for her support—*she* was the last person in the world who ever intended to be a writer, until she needed to earn money and found that she was untrained for anything else. Thus she had to claim that the sexual infidelity of her husbands was the cause of both her divorces; like George Eliot, she believed, and tried to make others believe, that her choices in life were forced upon her. Only by the time of her happy third marriage was she confident enough to take full responsibility for her own choices.

Katherine Mansfield lived in a place and time when the ambitions of women were more permissible. She escaped her conventional family without binding herself to a fixed role in European society; the freedom given by her colonial origin, and the feminism that already existed in literary bohemia, enabled her to make and to declare her own choices. She admitted that she herself had chosen her ego's task, and defended it against all attempts at subjugation, though this very defensiveness about her own freedom was often in conflict with her need for love.

The most interesting aspect of these women's self-justification was in their choice of partners. Lewes, Murry, and Goudeket never would have allowed it to be said that they were exploited and subjugated by the strong women they had chosen: all three argued that they themselves had joyfully immersed themselves in the business of nurturing, serving, and publicizing the female genius. Far from feeling restive under the yoke, they felt that their rather aimless, insecure, and haphazard lives had been given shape and meaning by the opportunity of service. Women, too, chose to serve each of these geniuses, demonstrating that the magnetic fields of their personalities extended further than the conjugal bond. Their solution to the ego problem was that though they received much, perhaps they gave even more: all were charismatic enough for those in their aura to feel that life had suddenly been made exciting and meaningful.

This care in personal relations indicates that the lack of public tolerance for female ambition forced it to follow socially acceptable paths—and therefore to form loving relationships not always achieved by more indulged egos. Being allowed to get away with less in the way of selfishness did these women a great deal of good, and forced them to be more humane than their male counterparts. Without arguing that the charm of femininity is its weakness, or that the suppression of female ambition has produced qualities more valuable than untrammeled egotism—in other words, without trying to justify the structure of oppression—one can certainly relate the disguising of ambition to such literary triumphs as, say, George Eliot's elevation of altruism, Colette's direct and unliterary treatment of love, Katherine Mansfield's unequaled spontaneity. "Femininity," with all that that implies, prevented these women from indulging in the excesses, the solipsism, the egomania and obliviousness to other people, that have so often marred the works of the greatest male geniuses. This has to be counted a gain. To be a genius and yet to relate to other people—to make the two things work together, instead of warring—this has been the contribution of the greatest women writers, and this is why they are so deeply fascinating to read today.

It is impossible to say, as perhaps one would like to say, that had they not been handicapped by being female in a time when that was indeed a handicap, their genius would have fulfilled itself even more splendidly. All one can do is to trace the relation between what they were and what they did, and to say that in an age when they were something different, they would have done something different—but not necessarily better.

Every writer has the task of using what he is to the limits of its usefulness. Every set of circumstances contains the materials of art. You would not catch Joyce saying, "If only I had not been Irish, that oppressed race." Burns, Hardy, and Lawrence celebrated their working-class origins. Katherine Mansfield even said that her pain and illness had been "a great privilege." This argument has its dangers—one would not like to suggest that Wilfred Owen should have been grateful for the Great War that so staggeringly developed his talents. Nonetheless, it shows that human experience, in the artistic sense, is not cumulative (whatever the case may be in science). It shows the way around at least one current fallacy, which goes, "If only George Eliot had had the feminist consciousness of, say, Kate Millett, she would have been a much better novelist." The patronizing quality of this line of argument was shown up by Shaw when he said, with provocative irony, that he was greater than Shakespeare because he stood on Shakespeare's shoulders.

Naturally, being female has been a limitation and a handicap for many writers—it is a handicap that feminists have often compared with being poor or black or foreign. And, like these handicaps, it is not fatal to an artist—on the contrary, one is sometimes tempted to say. And just as the greatest writers from other difficult backgrounds have achieved their greatness by explaining, celebrating what it means to be them and to belong to their world, so the greatest women artists have explained and celebrated the female experience and never attempted to deny it.

Being a literary genius means, of course, being an exceptional member of whatever group one belongs to. It creates problems with accepting the female role, true enough—but it also creates problems with conventional families, earning a living, being patriotic, and other possible sets of expectations. The biography of every writer who fulfilled his gift is the story of his war against whatever barriers were set in his way, and the biographer must probe to find the sources of such exceptional strength.

This exceptional creative impulse is not, as so many Freudians have tended to believe, necessarily pathological, a sublimation or diversion of frustrated sexual and emotional energy that rightfully belonged somewhere else. Instead it may justifiably be analyzed as a powerfully productive interplay between the individual and society. The post-Freudian "ego psychology" associated with the name of Erik Erikson seems to me to provide a useful framework for understanding these lives. The ability to transmogrify life into art, and the artist into a symbolic personage who sums up certain things about a given society, is to the Erikson school a sign of unusual health, a kind of superhumanness. True enough, there are writers, as everyone knows, whose creativity seems to be pathological, who seem to be compensating for real or imagined sexual failure, repeatedly struggling with Oedipal relationships or whatnot. Neurosis and madness have, particularly in our century, been closely linked to the arts—or perhaps more easily comprehended and accepted by creative people. But the personality type represented by the three women in this book is of another order, and shows an outstanding ability to solve the dilemmas presented by various stages of the life cycle. Each woman, in fact, seems to especially represent one phase of this cycle: youth, maturity, and old age.

The freedom and brilliance of youth is the stage we associate with Katherine Mansfield, because she never lived to outgrow it— though at the end of her life, she was struggling for the kind of deeper commitment, in love and in art, that would have marked the beginning of full maturity. Erikson's words seem meant to describe her:

> The singular loveliness and brilliance which young women display in an array of activities obviously removed from the future function of child-bearing is one of those esthetic phenomena which almost seem to transcend all goals and purposes and therefore come to symbolize the self-containment of pure being—wherefore young women, in the arts of the ages, have served as the visible representation of ideals and ideas and as the creative man's muse, anima, and enigma.[2]

This is certainly related to Katherine Mansfield's feeling about herself and her life, though complicated by the fact that she was the creative person as well as the muse. The "self-containment of pure being" is what she expressed in her pervasive flower imagery. Her tomb bears her chosen motto from Shakespeare: "Out of this nettle, danger, we pluck this flower, safety"—and safety for her was her identity as a beautiful young woman, the inspiration as well as the executor of her own work. The threatened loss of this identity may have been one of the underlying reasons for her early death, which she almost seems to have desperately sought.

In fact, coming to terms with the loss of youthful beauty is one of the most difficult tasks for the female, whether muse or artist or both; many never manage to transcend this stage. George Eliot solved the problem by the radical means of asserting that she had never been youthfully beautiful, and by dissociating herself from women who possessed these gifts. Her novels assert that they are poisoned gifts, and that only those denied them can develop the far more valuable attributes of character. This is why it is so easy to associate her with the stage of maturity, again as described by Erikson:

Generativity, then, is primarily the concern for establishing and guiding the next generation. There are, of course, people who, from misfortune or because of special and genuine gifts in other directions, do not apply this drive to offspring of their own, but to other forms of altruistic concern and creativity which may absorb their kind of parental drive. And indeed, the concept of generativity is meant to include productivity and creativity. . . .[3]

The sense of fecundity in George Eliot's novels, the richness and prodigality of her creation, belong particularly to this stage of life. It is noteworthy, too, that she had the most conflict-free conjugal life of the three: her generativity seems almost to have required the fertilizing presence of a sexual partner.

Colette began to anticipate her ultimate role as the old wise woman at the very beginning of her literary career; she almost seems to have waited, through all three marriages, for the moment when she would begin to act out her appointed and anticipated role. This is not to say that the works of her old age are necessarily her greatest (though many have held that view), but that throughout her oeuvre one senses the desire to finally renounce love, the longing to put on the mantle of sage, witch, magic grandmother. The androgynous personae of her early books, the boyish Claudine and the Vagabonde, helped her to avoid too close an identification with youthful sexual roles, and to save her deepest commitment for the phase in which she felt most at home. Another part of her solution to the youthful identity problem was to associate herself with the characteristically French notion that a woman's beauty and fascination mature as she ages, and that youth in women, as in wine, is flat and uninteresting. Thus acceptance of the inevitability of age and death, identification with her own mother, and other difficult tasks of the mature ego, were eased for her by association with a powerful national ideology.

To examine the kind of man who entered the lives of these women is to establish another psychological type. Romantic, idealistic young men, attractive to women (who often felt like mothering them)—this describes Lewes, Murry, and Goudeket when they met the women who represented their destiny. Most significantly, all three felt like outsiders. Lewes was sketchily educated in England, France, and Jersey; his rivals in the fast, competitive world of intellectual journalism were almost all well-off university men. More intelligent and capable than all but a few of them, Lewes was outraged by the unfairness of the "old-boy network," and spent his life trying to establish a meritocracy in its place. He and Marian Evans were both outside the class from which litterateurs usually came; the provincial woman and the slightly disreputable journalist banded together against the conventional and philistine.

Murry was an even more extreme example of meritocracy: the first scholarship boy to enter the famous Christ's Hospital School, and one of the first to go to Oxford, he left his narrow petit-bourgeois origins far behind. Isolated by his massive intellect and social insecurity, he sought refuge with the confident, audacious Katherine Mansfield. She also was outside conventional literary life, and equally far from the bohemian aristocracy of Bloomsbury. But her provincial origins gave her the assurance of being a big fish in a small pond. She may have been on the periphery of English life, but her father, director of the Bank of New Zealand, was right at the heart of his own society. George Eliot felt that the question of whether a writer came from the center or the edge of a country was of great importance in determining his literary personality. She, too, was an outsider in the literary world, but she could and did feel that her Warwickshire, not parasitic London, was the heart of England.

The same was true of Colette. A provincial in Paris, she was an outsider in terms of the conventional Jouvenel, for example, or of the literary mandarins of the Academy, but she was far more representative of France than they. Her Burgundy became everyone's natal province; her childhood everyone's childhood. For Goudeket, trying to escape his Jewish commercial background, Colette represented the magic world of literature as well as essential Frenchness. A bizarre bohemian like Willy was too self-absorbed to be interested in furthering someone else's career, though he was willing to exploit them; the confident Jouvenel was much too arrogant to do so. Only Goudeket, thrown off balance by his own position "between two worlds" (as Murry called his autobiography), had the imagination to immerse himself in the life of another.

Cultural centrality may well be one source of the extraordinary sexual mana or charisma that all these women undoubtedly possessed. The men drawn into their magnetic field were those searching for some contact with a central identity; they were not so much representatives of declining groups, as people without a fixed adherence to any group whatsoever. Free-floating planets looking for a sun to revolve around, they had been cut adrift from whatever sources of identity most people have to depend on—family, class, nation.

Provincial females, outsiders on both counts, who turn out to be sure of their central place in their national mythologies; insecure men, caught between humble origins and the intellectual aristocracy to which their talents and ambitions entitled them—this is the pattern carried out in all three stories. And it is no coincidence: the social wounds suffered by these men made them fierce egalitarians, ready to recognize the claims of intellectual women in a way that the more conventional refused to do. There were sound emotional reasons, deriving from their own experiences, for their choice of role as these women's companions and champions.

This is not to say that such stories delineate the only kind of woman who can reach the heights of literature; or that this kind of man is the only one a creative woman should have anything to do with. As social and sexual egalitarianism becomes more marked, new patterns are appearing and will appear.

These stories indicate one way it has been done, a way that I believe will continue to be important, because it indicates solutions to problems that women will continue to face. The kind of wholeness achieved by these women—the organic unity of love and work—is something that many women, not only those with creative ambitions, are attempting to achieve today. It took genius to show the way, to establish the pattern—but now it is there for all of us to learn from.

Katherine Mansfield
&
John Middleton Murry

CHAPTER 1

Apprenticeships

The Soul selects her own Society—
Then—shuts the Door—
To her divine Majority—
Present no more.

—Emily Dickinson

On a tall gray house in Hampstead, facing the Vale of Health, is a round blue plaque saying:

Katherine Mansfield
1888–1923
writer
and her husband
John Middleton Murry
1889–1957
critic
lived here

The placing of their names on the plaque in this order reflects present estimates of their relative importance. Murry is described as "husband" and "critic"—the implication being that hers was the creative activity, his the supporting role. In his lifetime, he was also novelist, poet, editor, political propagandist, and utopian farmer. But even his most dazzling literary criticism, the best of its age, is no longer reprinted, and his reputation has vanished with the disappearance of the audience that read the *Athenaeum* and the *Adelphi* during his editorship. The reputation of Katherine Mansfield, on the other hand, has never been higher: her stories, letters, and journal are being rediscovered by a new generation of readers, and it now seems certain that they are permanent books.

Because of the autobiographical nature of these books, and because of Murry's confessional style of journalism, their relationship has, over the years, drawn at least as much attention as their literary works. And rightly so: they are both writers in whom it is next to impossible to separate the "works" from the "life." Murry built his entire critical credo around the kind of genius he perceived in Katherine's writings, and she maintained that their love was the source of her creative energies. In a sense, all their works are joint achievements.

This is the view put forth by Murry himself. He draws a picture of their relationship as a romantic literary love story: the beautiful, delicate genius isolated in her tower of suffering, and her champion defending her cause in the tournament of literary journalism. Certainly it is true that few writers have had such an advocate: he founded magazines in order to publish her stories, edited her letters and journal, wrote and lectured about her work, and evolved a theory of romantic literature that places her in the direct line of Shakespeare and Keats.

Paradoxically, however, many of Katherine Mansfield's acolytes see Murry as the villain of the piece. Her letters to him are full of accusations of betrayal and abandonment, which have been taken as the literal truth by her defenders. Murry's self-abasement in his autobiography, and the fact that he published and promoted her letters while neglecting his own, have added fuel to the flames. Which leaves us with a puzzling situation to unravel: how can they be the protagonists of one of the great literary love stories if their marriage is a tale of lonely suffering on the one hand, and emotional nonsupport on the other?

It is a tribute to the peculiar magic of Katherine Mansfield's style, and to the compelling aura of her personality, that Murry is now unquestioningly believed to have failed her, and that what he contributed to her art and her reputation goes unnoticed. It is also a function of Murry's unpopular beliefs and intellectual courage, which in the Thirties lost him the support of his more conventional contemporaries. The simple fact is that Katherine Mansfield died of tuberculosis at the age of thirty-four, that her doctors advised her to spend winters in the south of France (advice that she was more than happy to accept, as France provided her preferred working conditions), and that Murry was prevented by his work (and by the travel restrictions during World War I) from joining her. Her despairing, accusing letters were written during these inevitable separations, under the influence of her fatal disease. It is a story of great pathos, even tragedy, but not of villainy.

The true story of what they gave to each other, artistically and emotionally, is far more complex and interesting than the simplifications of her followers would suggest. They were both people who experienced life acutely, who had to prove things "on their pulses," in Murry's phrase. Outsiders in literary London—Katherine Mansfield was a New Zealander, Murry from a petit-bourgeois family— they perpetually saw themselves as "babes in the woods," and were bound together by their need to affirm a fragile, innocent, romantic love that would oppose the cynicism and brutality of Europe at war.

Katherine Mansfield is perhaps the purest type there has ever been of the female romantic artist. Murry continually compared her to Keats, and with some justice. The achievement of both was small and pure. Early death from consumption prevented the full flowering of their genius; but their letters reveal the writers as greater than the work they have left. Their appeal to us is as exemplary lives, "heroes of humanity," as much as writers. Love, suffering, and early death are inextricably twined together in their histories, and their best works have the luminous intensity of a fevered vision: the feeling is inescapable that they were literally consumed by their art.

Keats's letters spell out the credo of the romantic poet: that love is essential to his vision of beauty. But Katherine Mansfield was not only a romantic artist; she was a woman. For her as for all women, there was the risk that love would prove to be the enemy of work. If her genius and her craving for love were to be fulfilled, she had to choose a man who idolized the romantic artist in her while he loved the woman, a man capable of humility and generosity.

Murry had these qualities, and he had something more: a formidable intellect that made his advice and criticism as valuable as any she could have received. To her original wit and insight, he added consciousness of the tradition in which she was working, her relation to other writers and to her own time, that helped her to become the symbolic figure she has remained for everyone who discovers her work. This sense of herself as the incarnation of a romantic sensibility, working with an acute perception of modern life, deepened and enriched her work and helped to save her from the cynicism and sentimentality that were her two worst stylistic enemies.

This symbolic capacity, which Murry and Mansfield touched off in each other, has a tendency to make every development seem inevitable, to structure every aspect of childhood into a pattern of significant beginnings. What particular elements in her origins made Katherine Mansfield what she was? Not even the most painstaking biographer can, ultimately, answer that question; but a fruitful way to approach it is to trace the elements that she herself saw in this way once she began to think of herself as someone marked for a special destiny.

Katherine Mansfield was born Kathleen Mansfield Beauchamp, into a family of strong, go-getting, paternalistic men. Indeed, to call someone a "Pa man" was the highest form of Beauchamp praise. The Original Pa Man, the founding father, was a London silversmith called John Beauchamp. His son Arthur, Katherine Mansfield's grandfather, was one of five brothers who emigrated to Australia. Arthur, known in family lore as the *True* Original Pa Man because he was the founder of the antipodean dynasty, followed his fortunes to New Zealand, where, as he said in a line that Katherine found "very Pa," "the umbrageous hills kissed the waters of the South Pacific." There her father Harold was born.

Katherine's maternal great-grandfather, John Dyer, was a stern and slightly morbid Baptist minister. When he died, his son left England for Australia, where he married a Sydney girl called Margaret Isabella Mansfield. This was Katherine's beloved Grandma, whose last name she was to take as her own. Margaret Dyer, after raising her own nine children, was pressed into service to bring up her daughter Annie's girls. Annie had a heart condition, and the pain and difficulty of childbirth seemed to have spoiled her ability to enjoy her children.

Kathleen (Katherine) was the third daughter. Grandma looked after her, while Annie accompanied Harold, a rising man with an import firm, on his first business trip to England. Kathleen was secure in her grandmother's love for two years. But then another sister was born, and for the three months of its fragile life it took all of grandmother's attention. Then followed another little sister, and finally Leslie Heron, or Chummie. The first son born into the patriarchy, the little boy was the family idol.

The fastidious, withdrawn Annie and energetic, self-made Hal appear in many guises in Katherine Mansfield's stories—most notably as Linda and Stanley Burnell in the New Zealand series that centers on "Prelude" and "At the Bay." The relation of their character to their social circumstances is emphasized by Katherine's biographer, Antony Alpers:

> In the blunt opinion of acquaintances who disliked her social manner, Annie Beauchamp was simply a snob. . . . She thought there could still be a middle class in a country that had no upper class and was bent on having no lower. . . . Annie had to have babies against her will, and to suffer from the illusion of privilege in a self-levelling colony.[1]

In photographs, Annie's small, regular features are firmly set, with one eyebrow slightly, contemptuously raised. Hal is large, good-looking, and prosperously dressed, but his air of self-importance seems to derive not so much from snobbery as from the ultrapatriotism of the colonies and undisguised pleasure in being part of a boom economy. Annie seems to have enjoyed his wealth while condemning the drive that produced it as philistinism; this ambivalent attitude toward her husband created a pattern that her daughter, in her own way, was to follow.

When Kathleen was five, the family moved out of Wellington to Karori, to a beautiful, rambling country house with a veranda, a large wild garden, and an enormous aloe beside the drive. In "Prelude," the story that describes this move, the aloe becomes a potent symbol: it is about to bloom, something that happens only once in a hundred years. This house became for Kathleen the lost earthly paradise of childhood. It lasted only five years, during which the Beauchamp children roamed the garden and the surrounding New Zealand bush as a band of companions, while their grandmother provided the warm, domestic center of the house. The lack of neighbors meant that social stratification was impossible: they were in contact with every other family that inhabited this semiwilderness, and the contrast between their comfort and others' hardship was painfully obvious, with none of the insulating layers of habit and physical distance that muffled class-consciousness and the guilt of affluence in Europe.

The Beauchamps moved back to town in 1898, to a much grander house, for Hal had just become a director of the Bank of New Zealand. Annie was able to increase the distance between her family and their poorer neighbors, and her rigid conventionality was increased by the sense that they were surrounded by provincialism, frontier manners, and other threats that must be kept at bay while her girls became young ladies. Kathleen at school was remembered as being plump, moody, and difficult, in contrast to her pretty and docile sisters. Her form of rejection of the mother who had rejected her was to pose as a bohemian intellectual, a despiser of the bourgeois conventionality her parents were trying to impress on her.

There were a few intellectuals in Wellington, with whom she allied herself and who introduced her to the intellectual currents of the European *fin de siècle*. They also provided other possible channels for her desire to be artistically creative: the Trowell family, in particular, impressed her as a model. They were respectable enough for her parents, because they represented Culture; they were artistic enough for Kathleen, because their two attractive sons were musicians—Arnold Trowell, in particular, was a child prodigy who was about to leave for Europe to continue his study of the cello. Kathleen, too, began taking cello lessons from Arnold's father, and perhaps it was from him that she got the idea that education in Europe was within the realm of possibility.

The Beauchamps were receptive to the idea—sending their daughters to be "finished" in England appealed to their snobbery as well as to Annie's desire to wash her hands of troublesome adolescence. The girls' unmarried Aunt Belle could chaperone them, and there were cousins in England who could keep an eye on them there. In February 1903, Kathleen and her two older sisters set sail for England.

Queen's College, Harley Street, was a pioneering establishment in the serious education of women. But to Kathleen, it represented freedom and friendship rather than academic possibilities. She admired the German teacher, who invited her to his intellectual evening parties, and she developed rather emotional friendships with several of the girls; most of all, she explored the new sensations of life in a European capital, and the sense of her own energies in contact for the first time with a civilization to which she could not feel superior.

> My college life, which is such a vivid and detailed memory in one way, might never have contained a book or a lecture. I lived in the girls, the professor, the big, lovely building, the leaping fires in winter and the abundant flowers in summer. The views out of the windows, all the pattern that was—weaving. Nobody saw it, I felt, as I did. . . .[2]

Kathleen seems to have seen as little as possible of her sisters and her cousins; she was trying to wash her hands of everything that reminded her of home and of the conventional role for which she was presumably being trained. Like so many other families, the Beauchamps had tried to buy the best education for their daughter, not realizing that this contact with a larger world, as well as being the last word in status, contained within itself the seeds of alienation from them: and the already rebellious Kathleen was fertile ground for the seeds to take root.

At first, she was cautious and observant, as Alpers reports:

> Kathleen took to college life with perfect ease. Having command of the family manner, which could be formidable on occasion, she evidently used it freely towards anyone she did not like, and she showed herself in no hurry to choose her friends. She had her cello, and she was writing to Caesar (Arnold Trowell), who went to Brussels that summer; her first

term had nearly ended before she opened her heart to anyone. Then with a sureness and deliberation that now seem uncanny, she chose a friend who was to be hers, and hers absolutely, to the end of her life.[3]

The friend was Ida Constance Baker, the daughter of an Indian Army doctor who had returned to practice in London. Vague, self-effacing, and motherly, the tall, fair-haired Ida was a perfect foil for the dark, witty Kathleen, who immediately took the lead in their friendship. The first thing she did was to change both their names. Ida was to be Lesley Moore. Moore was Ida's mother's maiden surname, and Lesley a feminized version of Chummie's real first name—the companionship of the two friends was apparently to be modeled on the childhood companionship of the brother and sister. Kathleen was changed to the more sophisticated Katherine, and Beauchamp was dropped in favor of Mansfield. Katherine was clearly trying to get rid of her family name as she was trying to get rid of her family, and to assert her grandmother's primacy in her feelings over her mother. Perhaps, too, the Englishness of "Mansfield" appealed to her—she was always to experiment with this kind of nuance, signing herself "Schönfeld" when studying German, and "Ekaterina" during her Chekhov period. She had, one might even say, left the *beau champ* of childhood, and entered a "man's field."

During her time at Queen's College, Katherine was turning gradually from music to writing as her preferred means of expression. Perhaps one influence in this direction was the fact that a Beauchamp cousin, now the Countess von Arnim-Schlagenthin, had written the 1898 best seller, *Elizabeth and her German Garden*. Katherine Mansfield was to respond to "Elizabeth's" influence when she began writing seriously; now she responded to the influence this event had on the family pride. Writing took on a new luster in the eyes of the Beauchamps when it was shown that it had money-making potential. The dramatic possibilities of writing also appealed to her: she developed a habit of trying out poses and observing their effect on the other girls. She was discovering her ability to manipulate people's emotions, and to perceive the results. These abilities were so strong in her that once she discovered them, she ran the danger of assuming so many masks that she completely lost touch with her real feelings. The witty Katherine, the sensitive, withdrawn Katherine, the bitter Katherine, the gay, hilarious Katherine—which was really her? The game that had begun with her scarcely unusual adolescent desire to shock her family, and to attract attention, was beginning to get somewhat out of control.

Katherine's struggle with her own developing personality was rudely interrupted, however, by a more immediate practical struggle. In October 1906, education officially over, the girls sailed for New Zealand. Katherine had to confront the fact that no matter how she saw her future, she still had somehow to impress this vision on those who controlled her life, and who thought that she had been allowed quite sufficient freedom already.

By the New Year, the eighteen-year-old Katherine was writing, "I feel absolutely ill with grief and sadness here—it is a nightmare. . . ." She had decided that if she made herself sufficiently objectionable, her parents would allow her to return to London and the *vie de Bohème* she longed for. She turned her room into her idea of an artist's atelier, read the diaries of the rebellious young Russian Marie Bashkirtseff, and wrote endlessly—stories, journal entries, and letters to the friends who had been caught up in her orbit. Arnold Trowell and his brother Garnet were still her romantic idols, but at this point she seems to have been even more interested in intense friendships with girls. Their admiration of her adventurousness pleased her, and an interest in homosexuality was one of the shockingly "modern" ideas she had picked up in London.

Just as the impasse with her family was coming to seem insoluble, she was given a new weapon: the *Native Companion* in Melbourne accepted several of her sketches, and then a longer story. The check and the editor's astonishment at her age were almost as flattering to her father as they were to her, and he accepted them as evidence that he could no longer stand in the way of her budding career. Perhaps, too, his decision was influenced by some leaves from her notebook that her parents found and read. The romantic incidents they described, whether real or imagined, made them feel that the family respectability would be seriously compromised by keeping Katherine unwillingly in New Zealand. Thus her emotional experimentalism was encouraged by the fact that it seemed to have paid off: not only did it provide her with literary material, but it helped to open the gates of freedom.

The young ingrate wrote in her journal, in a vein that was to be all too characteristic later in her life,

> I shall certainly not be here much longer. Thank Heaven for that! Even when I am alone in my room, they come outside and call to each other, discuss the butcher's orders or the soiled linen and—I feel—wreck my life. It is so humiliating.[4]

In July 1908, aged twenty, she left for London. Her round-faced youthfulness was already beginning to give way to the pale, delicate look she was trying to cultivate, and which made her large dark eyes and chestnut hair more striking than ever. Her capacity for role-playing was ready to test itself against the anonymity of London. She wanted to seem older and more sophisticated than she really was, and usually she succeeded.

In 1907, the colony of New Zealand had become a dominion. Perhaps it is not too fanciful to suggest that New Zealand and its greatest writer were simultaneously losing their provincialism, and that Katherine's sense of her own importance owed something at this time to identification with her country. The moment was right for her, and she knew it.

But perhaps because she so outdistanced the society from which she came, her mistake was overconfidence, a feeling of invulnerability. She was ready, indeed eager, to experience pain and disillusion, because to her these were still only words.

Soon after her arrival in London she wrote "The Tiredness of Rosabel"—the earliest story in her collected works, and the first example of the adult Mansfield style. The subtle use of time perspective, the ironic contrast between the tired shop-girl and the selfish rich couple, the vivid physical details—all are precursors of her mature manner, which was not to appear again for several years. Her acute social consciousness is here, and she identifies strongly with the poor, anonymous Rosabel, with the secrecy of her private perceptions. Katherine, too, wanted to lose herself in the crowd, to be just like anyone else sitting in a London bus looking out at the rain, were it not for the hidden flame of her sensibility and her capacity for imagining herself into other situations.

The first exuberance of her release soon wore off, however, and she began the ordeal by experiment of which she later tried to destroy all trace, burning such letters as she could recover (those to LM, for example) and doing away with what she called her "huge complaining diaries." At a students' hostel in Paddington coincidentally called Beauchamp Lodge, where her parents had arranged for her to stay, Katherine embarked on a series of experiments in personality, turning a different face to each of the several worlds she inhabited. Her school friend LM was in one compartment; the Trowells (now living in a large, welcoming house in St. John's Wood) in another. A third was inhabited by a singing teacher eleven years older than herself called George Bowden. She had met him at a dinner party, but concealed from anyone else the fact that she continued to see him. Perhaps the original of Mr. Reginald Peacock in the story by that name, Bowden was apparently a mild and pleasant man quite baffled by Katherine's emotional vagaries. But she fascinated him, and on March 2, 1909, she went to Paddington Register Office and became Mrs. Bowden. Ida Baker, her only witness, recalls that she was dressed entirely in black. Bowden himself was astounded that night when Katherine exhibited a sudden and complete frigidity. She left him the next morning. Apparently she had found a loving note from LM concealed in her carefully packed suitcase, and realized that though she had entered marriage as just another pose, things were rapidly becoming all too real.

In her reaction to her failure to go through with the drama of marriage, she turned to her childhood friend Garnet Trowell, now playing in the orchestra of a traveling light-opera company. Katherine joined the chorus, and lived with Garnet for a couple of weeks, though it is difficult to be sure about the scanty evidence from this confused period of her life. She returned to London to meet her mother, who was on her way from New Zealand in response to the startling news of Katherine's hasty marriage. Katherine knew, though whether or not her mother shared her knowledge is unclear, that she was pregnant with Garnet's child. Mrs. Beauchamp was haughty and disdainful, and none of the other relatives assembled on the station platform spoke to the disgraced Katherine. Her mother took Katherine to a convent in Bavaria, where she was meant to get over the affair and keep out of the way of family gossip. Left on her own, Katherine soon moved to a pension at the Bavarian spa of Wörishofen. There she had a miscarriage.

She saw Bowden again when she got back to London, a meeting that had one positive result: he suggested that she take her stories to A. R. Orage, the editor of the *New Age*, at that time London's liveliest intellectual weekly. Katherine was taken up by Orage and his lieutenant, Beatrice Hastings, and they began to publish her stories. The first to appear was "The Child-Who-Was-Tired," an adaptation of Chekhov's "Sleepyhead." Katherine had probably begun reading Chekhov in German translation in Bavaria; he was just beginning to be translated into English, and the original of Katherine's story was unknown to Orage and his readers. Its "shocking" theme—the overworked child servant who smothers the baby in order to stop its crying and get some rest—appealed to the sophisticated *New Age*; but the close observation of the children in the story, and the contrast of their innocent brutality with the knowing brutality of adults, was neither Chekhov nor Orage, but pure Mansfield.

The other stories published by the *New Age* were drawn directly from the Bavarian experience—in their bitterness and horror of sexuality, they reveal something of what that experience had done to temper Katherine's longing for "life." She was damaged not only emotionally, but physically: she had been in pain ever since her miscarriage, and soon she entered a nursing home for an operation for peritonitis. LM took her, convalescent, to rented rooms in Sussex, where she evaded her husband's attempts to find her. LM recounts,

I did not know then that George Bowden thought I was KM's lesbian friend, and the cause of her leaving him in the first place. Indeed, I did not know then what a "lesbian friend" meant. . . . After a long time she was patched up, although the trouble was not correctly diagnosed nor was she fully cured until many years later in 1918 when Dr Sorapure took charge of her. He told her then that the pains she had suffered from almost continuously since this time in Rottingdean, and had always called her "rheumatiz," were the result of a disease that she had contracted before she was taken to the nursing home. [5]

LM does not say what the disease was; the consensus of evidence now suggests that it was gonorrhea.

When Katherine returned to London, a painter friend lent her his flat on the Chelsea Embankment. She furnished it with candles stuck in skulls and shining through yellow chrysanthemums; she and LM indulged in an orgy of dressmaking. It was time for a new image—this time, an "arty" one. She had another love affair, which left her pregnant again—and under the influence of the cynical Beatrice Hastings, she had an abortion. Her need to prove her attractiveness to men, and to assert the primacy of her own free will, were still stronger than whatever cautionary lessons she had learnt. When the owner of the flat came back, she moved to Clovelly Mansions, Gray's Inn Road, where she furnished one of her rooms with nothing but two black-covered couches and a large Buddha image.

In the autumn of 1911, *In a German Pension* was published. It was a success, appearing at a moment when anti-German feeling was sweeping the country. When Katherine's parents arrived in England for the coronation of George V, their daughter felt somewhat vindicated in their eyes by the fact that she had managed to emulate the achievement of "Elizabeth." But she was having a hard time living on her meager allowance of £100 a year, and she described her father as "the richest man in New Zealand, and the meanest." During this visit she made friends anew with Chummie, who wrote rapturously to LM, "Her work is conquering London." In the three years since Katherine had left New Zealand, he had crossed the line separating childhood from young manhood. The sweetness his sister had loved in him was still there, coupled with a new desire for sophistication—somewhat like Katherine's own— that made him the most susceptible of all the family to her recently acquired cosmopolitan glamour.

Katherine was already trying to shed her sophisticated *New Age* persona, and to write more simply and openly: in the last of the stories to be written for her book, "A Birthday," she introduced for the first time the characters who were to become the Burnells. In many ways, she was ready to start a new chapter in her life. The experience she sought had been painful and wounding as well as liberating; the veneer of "decadence" that had been her very youthful armor against life had worn thin. Her natural romanticism was asserting itself, now that the long struggle with her parents was no longer her primary emotional concern.

Katherine had shown herself to be in many ways ahead of her time. To have a period of sexual freedom between leaving one family and creating another was, much later, to become normal for girls as well as for boys, but in 1911, it was far from usual. Her experiments were damaging largely because society was not ready to allow her to make them—thus she had to bear the consequences alone and in secrecy, and the consequences included disapproval and ostracism as well as illness and unhappiness. It was not only as a developing person that she needed experience; it was as a developing artist. But experience, for a girl of her class (especially in terms of the rigid morals of the colonies), was shameful; she was an embarrassment to her family, and had no one (except perhaps LM) to whom she could tell everything that she had been through. Perhaps the most painful effect of her feeling of alienation at this time was that it went against a natural tendency to idealize love, to believe in a romantic union of souls that would make anything but truth and frankness impossible. She was forced into the bohemian world by the fact that she could not get what she needed in the conventional world; but she was never again to feel really at home in either one.

Finding a new market for her stories was one way of making a break with the immediate past. Orage was already criticizing her for not maintaining the brittle sarcasm of the first stories she had submitted to him; and when she heard of a new little magazine called *Rhythm*, founded by two idealistic Oxford undergraduates, she was immediately interested.

One of the editors of *Rhythm* was John Middleton Murry, the man she was to choose as surely and uncannily as she chose LM, and who was to be the other emotional pole of her existence. His isolation and idealism were at this moment parallel to her own; but he had traveled an entirely different route in arriving at the same place.

Murry's grandfather and great-grandfather were carpenters in the

Royal Navy shipyards at Sheerness; his father taught himself to write, and lifted himself out of the proletariat into a clerk's post at Somerset House and into impoverished married life in Peckham. Throughout his life, he was obsessed by the fear of sinking back into the working class, and determined that his son should rise even higher than he had done. The class obsessions of the time meant that anyone who moved an unusual distance upward felt perpetual anxiety—the cost of becoming middle class was paid in terror of debt and unemployment, fanatical insistence on genteel behavior, amounting to a preoccupation that now seems pathological. Murry says of his grandfather, the old shipwright, "I knew him as a lion; but I also knew that he would never dart his paw on me." But this calm, masculine certainty was divided in his father into a tendency to fawn on his superiors at work and persecute his victims at home. Murry's son Colin, describing a childhood visit to this terrifying grandfather, related that he confiscated teddy bears and pocket money, and that minor infractions of the rules made his neck go turkey-red with rage as he beat his small grandson into submission. Katherine later suggested that Murry should have confronted him more directly and drew up the following scenario:

> JMM (quite quietly): "You know, Dad, you're a horrid bully. Nobody loves you." [6]

But the young Murry's technique was to seek refuge with his mother and her indulgent sister, and ever afterward to prefer the company of women to that of men.

Throughout his life, Murry was to lament the loss of an "organic" society—the chaotic, postmedieval world was, he felt, responsible for the existence of people like his father: the craftsman alienated from his craft. His father had "the writing of a thwarted craftsman"—a statement that could well have been made of Murry himself—but social dislocation and the struggles it entailed led him to rob his son of his childhood. John must not only remain in the middle class; he must obtain a rank in it that secured him against the risk of falling. He must become a gentleman.

At the local school, John was continually cramming for the scholarship examination that would eventually admit him to the world of classical education and social mobility. His time was spent with books, not with other children. By the age of eleven, his aunt described him as "a little old man."

His friend Max Plowman was to speak of "that allegory of our time: the spiritual history of JMM." The allegory began in 1901, when he was one of the first six scholarship boys to enter Christ's Hospital School. The century of social transition had begun, and with it the transition of Middleton Murry into worlds ever further removed from his origins. His new uniform, the long blue coat that gave the school its nickname of the Bluecoat School, was the wonder of the neighbors on his increasingly rare visits home; he had already decided to follow in the footsteps of Coleridge, the school's most famous "old boy," and try for a university scholarship.

In 1908, Murry won the coveted scholarship to Oxford, and entered Brasenose College. He read Classics, joined the Pater Society and the Milton Society, and could not understand why the young aristocrats complained about the food, which to him seemed excellent. He had entered into one of the worlds of his dreams; his holidays in the country, previously almost unknown territory, showed him another. And in the Christmas vacation of 1910–11, he went to Paris.

Murry and his friends at Oxford had developed a lively interest in Fauvism and Symbolism, the artistic currents that were sweeping Paris. He and two other undergraduates, Frederick Goodyear and Michael Sadleir, sought out the Scottish painter J. D. Fergusson, whose work they admired for its doctrine of "rhythm." Murry explains:

> No man could be a professional artist. By profession he might be a painter, a writer, or equally well a boxer or a boot-black; whether he was an artist or not depended on what he was in himself. Art was a quality of being—an achievement of, or an effort towards integrity.[7]

The unity of all the arts was something Katherine Mansfield was also to express, when she called Van Gogh one of her writing-masters. And the notion of the artist as a hero, a symbolic person, not just the creator of his works, formed the cornerstone of Murry's aesthetic. In pursuit of these developing ideas, he sat in Left Bank cafés, visited artists' studios, talked and smoked all night, forgot to eat, and got propositioned by prostitutes who were so taken by his clean profile and spaniel eyes that they offered to go to bed with him for free. He fell in love, or thought he did, with a country girl not long in Paris called Marguéritte. Nothing is known of her except his feelings for her, which were compounded of gratitude for his sexual initiation and alarm at the commitment it seemed to entail.

The Oxford trio made plans to found a magazine called *Rhythm*—with Fergusson, the originator of the term, as art editor. *Rhythm* was to be the organ of Modernism, by which Murry meant Bergsonism in philosophy, Post-Impressionism in painting, and "yellow Syndicalism" in politics. The determined young men gathered a list of contributors ranging from luminaries like Picasso, Derain, and Van Dongen to such future friends as Anne Estelle Rice and Francis Carco.

Murry had to stay at Oxford, having no other means of support and no other way to make *Rhythm* a success. But when the magazine appeared as a quarterly in June 1911, its audience was not confined to the university; indeed, its cosmopolitanism helped to draw Murry away from his college and toward such Meccas of "real life" as Dan Rider's bookshop in St. Martin's Lane, where Frank Harris, Hugh Kingsmill, and other rakish literary lions held court. The young Alfred Knopf was so impressed with its ambience—and with meeting "real writers" like Murry and Mansfield—that he decided after his first visit there to become a publisher.

Rhythm published reproductions of the Post-Impressionists, and introduced new French writers to England. The first Post-Impressionist exhibition had just been held at the Grafton Gallery, and of it Arnold Bennett had written in the *New Age*:

I have permitted myself to suspect that supposing some young writer were to come along and do in words what these men have done in paint, I might conceivably be disgusted with nearly the whole of modern fiction, and I might have to begin again. This awkward experience will in all probability not happen to me, but it might happen to a younger writer than me.

It did happen to Murry and Mansfield, and to the part of their generation that thought of itself as modern. Indeed, it was happening to them at the very moment that Bennett was writing. Shaw, Wells, Galsworthy, and Bennett himself were just then coming into the sights of the young Mansfield, Lawrence, and Murry, who were to do their best to blast them off their preeminent perches.

To others, the Murry of this period could appear energetic and purposeful; to himself, he seemed lost and without direction. Marguéritte expected him to marry her; but when he arrived in Paris during his summer holiday, it was only to turn tail for England without seeing her or telling her that he would not be back. Guilt over Marguéritte added to his natural hesitancy in approaching other women; he wanted to leave Oxford but had no prospect of earning a living. All these circumstances combined to produce a sensation of drifting with the tide, unaware of where it would take him next. His neglect of such practical matters of food and sleep added an air of martyrdom and ill health to his natural good looks. His shyness made him hold his head on one side and look at people as if he was not really seeing them. His biographer says, "He was perfectly ill-at-ease in every walk of society."

Katherine Mansfield was to call Murry a monk without a monastery; sociologically, he agrees, he was a cleric without a church—the church that gave a social frame of reference to people like himself in the Middle Ages. The old avenues of intellectual advancement had disappeared; what were the new ones to be? The world of letters was inhabited by gentlemen; and part of what Murry tried to do in the name of Modernism, and in his later championing of D. H. Lawrence, was to win it for the aristocracy of talent.

What he felt most keenly was that by cutting him away from his roots, his education had made him a disembodied intellect, incapable of the harmony of mind and body that he found in Greek statues. "In touch with life"—"immediacy of contact"—this is the kind of phrase that was to haunt Murry's writings throughout his life, and the quality he found so irresistible in Lawrence and, above all, in Katherine Mansfield. The novel he wrote about these early years is called *Still Life*, with unintentional, ironic application to his own sexual paralysis at the time. It is dedicated to Katherine and her brother; the character based on Chummie, who finally gets the girl, says:

> But you don't tell us how to get to the harmony. . . . Or is it enough to find it in somebody else and experience it that way?

This is the experiment that Murry was soon to make.

CHAPTER 2

The Two Tigers

But at my back I always hear
Time's winged chariot hurrying near;
And yonder all before us lie
Deserts of vast eternity.

—Andrew Marvell

Mansfield and Murry made each other's acquaintance through their work. *Rhythm*, with its reputation for political radicalism, attracted Katherine, who was beginning to experiment with a new kind of realistic story, one that dealt with characters and themes foreign to the literary middle class. This was part of her change of heart, her search for authenticity. The first story she sent to Murry was "The Woman at the Store," a violent tale of madness and murder set in the savage New Zealand bush country. Murry was immediately interested in the new contributor who "expressed, with a power I envied, my own revulsion from life."

They finally met at a literary dinner party. Katherine was cool and poised in dove-gray chiffon, and Murry was fascinated by the way she held her hands: very still, palms upward, slightly cupped. Sour cherry soup, a Bavarian dish, was served in honor of the *German Pension*. But the talk revolved around Russian writers unknown to Murry, and he felt shy, gauche, and out of his depth. He walked home rather than sharing Katherine's taxi, because he was embarrassed to admit that he didn't have the money to pay for it—but before she left, she invited him to tea at her flat.

Katherine was enjoying her moment of triumph as the sophisticated young writer, but inwardly she was searching for something that all her "experience" had not brought her: an innocent, idealistic young love. Murry's youthful gaucherie, good looks, and obvious intelligence seemed the thing that could save her from her self-destructive games.

To Murry, Katherine seemed like a person utterly without the insecurities and self-doubt that were preventing him from realizing his abilities. She was capable of assuming any number of poses, from waif to rich girl to bohemian; but there was an underlying sense of truth: he might have described her in the words Truman Capote used for Holly Golightly in *Breakfast at Tiffany's*: "The kid's a *real* phony, though—she really believes that stuff she believes."

To others, they were an amusing and touching pair. They looked like brother and sister, and the barmaid in one of their local pubs was convinced that they were a music-hall couple down on their luck. But beneath the comradeship of the ardent young litterateurs, there were discrepancies in experience that were to color their whole life together. The fact is that neither of them had broken with the past as completely as they thought they had—something that was perhaps true of the modern movement as a whole. Katherine was still haughty, prudish, and used to deference; her commitment to her work made constant war against her inability to accept the life that that commitment entailed. Murry still saw himself as a jumped-up member of the lower orders, precariously poised while he awaited being found out and toppled from his new perch. She had chosen him because he was so unlike her father; she then could not forgive him for *not* being like her father. He, in turn, could not believe that she really loved him—that the whole thing was not just a mirage that would vanish as suddenly as it had appeared.

It was Katherine who suggested that Murry should be her lodger at Clovelly Mansions, and that they should become lovers—the latter had to be suggested several times before he accepted. Jack, as she called him, suggested in turn that she should help him to edit *Rhythm*. Previous loyalties were quickly pushed aside, as LM reports:

I did not know anything of Murry's plan and was happily looking forward to that week-end, as I was free to spend the whole of it with
Katherine. Alas, on my arrival I had to help Katherine fill his cupboard
with good things to eat—hiding a £5 note among the provisions, since
we knew that he was penniless. Then, forlornly, I returned. . . .[1]

Not for the first or last time, LM blamed Murry for pushing her
out, when in fact the plan was Katherine's.

Murry got a job reviewing books for the *Westminster Gazette*,
and on the strength of it, Katherine persuaded him to leave Oxford.
Rhythm was losing money, but the extent of its indebtedness was
not clear to them until the publisher (who also published *In a German Pension*) absconded, putting an end to Katherine's book royalties and leaving them with a printer's debt of £400. Instead of trying
to evade this legal (but scarcely moral) responsibility, for example
by filing for bankruptcy, they earmarked Katherine's allowance to
pay off the printers, and tried to keep the magazine going, changing
its name to *The Blue Review*. Their joint articles were signed "The
Two Tigers," and in the fierceness of their self-confidence and en-
thusiasm they called each other "Tiger"—Katherine was "Tig" or
"Wig" for the rest of her life with Jack.

Prevented from marrying by Katherine's position as Mrs. Bowden
(she claimed that he would not give her a divorce; he, that she
never asked him for one), they soon started referring to themselves
as the Murrys. They made friends with several new contributors,
the sculptor Henri Gaudier-Brzeska and D. H. Lawrence among
them. They seemed ready to become the embodiment of all that
their generation meant by the romantic artist and the romantic
young couple, as the Fitzgeralds were to embody it for Americans a
few years later. They were invited to Garsington, Lady Ottoline
Morrell's country house, and soon were on familiar terms with
Bloomsbury as well.

It was Lawrence who attracted them most of all their new
friends. He was living with Frieda Weekley, a German aristocrat
who had left her professor husband for him the year before. Their
anomalous status, and consequent trouble with landladies, was one
bond with the Murrys; another was Jack's capacity for hero worship,
brought out by Lawrence's desire for acolytes to whom he could

preach his doctrines of spontaneity, sexuality, and hatred of the modern world. He urged them to go with him to Italy, in search of the simple life of the instincts. But to Katherine and Jack, Paris was still the promised land, and they were saving their meager income for the flight. The editor of the *Times Literary Supplement* held out a vague promise about reviews of French books; in the meantime Katherine made money by giving drawing-room recitations and acting as an extra in silent films. In spite of their efforts to live cheaply, they could not keep the *Blue Review* going; it finally closed down in July 1913.

The Murrys hoped for a child, and at this time it still seemed possible that they would have one. But Katherine seems to have had one or two miscarriages, after which they realized that it was not to be. Murry was much the least sexually experienced of the two, and Katherine was trying to annihilate her own past: she destroyed the "huge, complaining diaries" she had kept for the three previous years, and never told Jack the full story of the adventures that had left her weakened in health and unable to bear children. In fact she seems to have let him believe that their childlessness was his fault: something he was all too ready to attribute to the sexual ineptitude of which she constantly made him conscious.

They left for Paris in December. Francis Carco, under the impression that Murry was "Paris correspondent of *The Times*," met them and helped them look for a flat. Another friend recalls,

> At that time in Paris, Katherine seemed very happy. I remember her gaiety, the way she would flounce into a restaurant and sweep her wide black hat from her bobbed head and hang it among the men's hats on the rack. I remember a group of men at a table running their tongues round their lips saying, "Oh la la," and her little muted laugh, delighted with herself.[2]

But within two months, their idyll in the Rue de Tournon was shattered—the book reviews were returned by the *TLS*, and they had no means of support. Murry finally faced bankruptcy proceedings on their return, and was taken back by the *Westminster*, this time as art critic.

In July 1914, the Murrys were witnesses at the Lawrences' wedding, an event that made them feel all the more keenly their own precarious place in life. In August, war broke out. The age of innocence was over for Europe; but the response of Katherine and Jack was to value their own innocence all the more highly, and to be drawn closer together by estrangement from the hysteria and violence all around them.

This impulse was paralleled in Katherine's writing. Her *Rhythm* stories had moved from the realistic ("The Woman at the Store") to sophisticated, satirical sketches of London life ("Bains Turcs"), to the beginning of her preoccupation with her New Zealand childhood. In Paris, she had written a longer story, "Something Childish but Very Natural." In its delicate portrayal of a childlike, trusting love that turns out to be a mysterious dream, she expressed her agonized sense that what she valued most was too fragile and insubstantial to last. And indeed life had confirmed this suspicion: she had experienced the liberating effect that France (or more accurately, escape from England) was to have on her talent, only to be rudely brought back to the reality of a London bankruptcy court.

Murry's own development as a writer seemed to be at a standstill. His work for the *Westminster* was dwindling as the paper retrenched to meet wartime austerity; his novel, *Still Life*, brought him £8 10s in royalties and cost £9 for typing. He was ready to become the acolyte of Lawrence, whose blandishments he had so far refused, but whose genius for fiction as for life was so much more assured than his own. Perhaps it is surprising that Lawrence, not Katherine, brought out his tendency to be the eternal consort; but part of Lawrence's propaganda was that to give this kind of deference to a woman was unnatural and unmanly. And Katherine, by no means established as a money-making writer, was still looking to him for some kind of a lead.

Katherine, however, was by nature the idol rather than the adorer, and Lawrence appeared to her as a threat. Her own acolyte, LM, had just left for a two-year visit to her father in Rhodesia. The *Journal* that Katherine began keeping at this time records her complicated feelings about LM—guilt and gratification mixed up together.

Have I ruined her happy life? Am I to blame? . . . She gave me the gift of herself. "Take me, Katie. I am yours. I will serve you and walk in your ways, Katie." I ought to have made a happy being of her. . . .

Content to stand outside and bathe and bask in the light that fell from Katie's warm bright windows, content to listen to the voice of her darling among other voices and to look for her darling's gracious shadow.[3]

This is the kind of passage LM had in mind when she described her own reaction to the published *Journal*:

I have read parts of the *Journal* and find a picture that faintly nauseates me, because it is negative. This was Katherine's old habit of elaborating on a feeling, in order to make it up into a picture.[4]

Katherine knew that she was already dependent on Lesley, and that the relation was not as one-sided as she pictured it in the *Journal*. LM records that Katherine invented, to describe their relationship, the image of LM as the high green pillar, and Katherine as the white bird that flew away to have adventures, but always returned to the pillar.

Murry was seeking a pillar of his own, and the charismatic Lawrence seemed—if not exactly static—at least strong enough to be a perch for any number of wandering birds. Both Murry and Lawrence were unfit for conscription—Murry had pleurisy, and the doctor who examined him recorded "query TB." The two couples found cottages in Buckinghamshire near each other—Murry's and Katherine's had the idyllic name of Rose Tree Cottage. Murry, Lawrence, and a young Irish barrister called Gordon Campbell (later to become Lord Glenavy and the father of the witty Patrick Campbell) spent their nights in furious intellectual discussion of, to paraphrase Campbell, the Male principle of Knowing and self-consciousness and mental love, and the Female principle of Being, self-mortification, and blood law. These were the "great Dostoevsky nights," when "Mansfield was always at her worst,"[5] when her resentment of the young men's absorption in what she saw as puerile intellectualism took the form of icy reserve, withering sarcasm, and occasional flight to London.

Katherine was not ready to undergo a Lawrentian "female self-mortification," although it sometimes appeared to her that she was being forced into it. As she had written a little earlier,

So often this week, I've heard you and Gordon talking while I washed dishes. Well, someone's got to wash dishes and get food. Otherwise— "There's nothing in the house but eggs to eat." Yes, I hate hate *hate* doing these things that you accept just as all men accept of their women. I can only play the servant with a very bad grace indeed. It's all very well for females who have nothing else to do . . . and you calling (whatever I am doing) *"Tig,* isn't there going to be tea? It's five o'clock," as though I were a dilatory housemaid.[6]

The egotism of these young men was as hard for her to take as was the conventionality of her own family; to both groups, she had to assert her claim to consideration as someone with serious work to do—and part of her commitment to her work was the fact that this seemed to be the only thing that would free her from the obligation to play traditional roles.

Lawrence's philosophy, however, held no place for the woman who was also a serious artist. His advice had been expressed in a long letter to Murry the previous autumn—advice that was very sensible as far as Jack's own insecurity was concerned. He saw Katherine's dissatisfaction as the result of Murry's failure to be master in his own house, not at all as a crisis in her self-realization.

If you work yourself sterile to get her chocolates, she will most justly detest you—she is *perfectly* right. She doesn't want you to sacrifice yourself to her, you fool. Be more natural, and positive, and stick to your own guts. You spread them on a tray for her to throw to the cats.

If you want things to come right—if you are ill and exhausted, then take her money to the last penny, and let her do her own housework. Then she'll know you love her.[7]

Between these points of view, what accommodation could there be? But in April, Lawrence wrote Murry another letter that Katherine would undoubtedly have agreed with.

Yes, you *do* need to write your own personal stuff, otherwise you can't be yourself. And if you can't be yourself, how can any woman love you? [8]

Equally, Katherine could not be herself without writing *her* own personal stuff—but Lawrence refused to take her work seriously, referring to it as "her little satirical sketches." There was no room for another genius in his world.

Katherine, in turn, was scathing about his obsessions: as she wrote much later,

> When he gets onto the subject of *maleness* I lose all patience. What nonsense it all is—and he must know it is. His style changes; he can no longer write. [9]

Beneath this tension, however, Lawrence and Katherine were much alike. Both outsiders in the conventional world of English literary life, both were to seek escape from England and all that it implied, and to try to reach out to life in a spontaneous, direct way that seemed to them embodied in the peoples of the Mediterranean. Both were to criticize the intellectualism of Murry, and to find acolytes of their own sex. Their similarity created a bond that was never to be entirely severed; but it also made them competitors. To the end of his life, Lawrence was fascinated by the pattern he saw in the quartet of Katherine and Murry, himself and Frieda. Which man was the stronger, which woman the more submissive? Was it better to choose a submissive woman, or to wring submission from an independent one?

The ascendancy of Lawrence was one factor in Katherine's unhappiness at Rose Tree Cottage. Her own work was going badly, and the one sure way she knew to restart the flow was to look for a new external stimulus. Two men, both slightly in love with her, represented the alternatives she weighed at this time.

S. S. Koteliansky and Francis Carco represented Russia and France—the two realms of experience that tempted Katherine when she was feeling trapped by her English life with Murry. To both she represented herself as a free spirit attempting to break the bonds of domesticity.

Koteliansky, in particular, was her secret friend and ally to whom she could confess her disloyal thoughts about Jack. She translated the letters of Chekhov with him, and they met for glasses of tea and feasts of brown bread with cherry jam.

> Every time I drop a piece of lemon into a glass of tea I say "Koteliansky." Perhaps it is a kind of grace.[10]

Kot, as his friends knew him, was a Russian émigré with a great bush of black hair who looked like a prophet and talked like a Dostoevsky character. Gordon Campbell's wife Beatrice said that Kot was Katherine's comfort, though "Kot's way of comforting was to say, 'There is no comfort, you must face it.' "[11]

But Koteliansky was too much a part of the London circle that included both Katherine and Jack for her really to envision him as a means of escape. Francis Carco, on the other hand, by now an established young writer (*Jésus-la-Caille*) and denizen of the literary bohemias of Paris, was writing her letters that awakened her longing for France and adventure. Carco later remembered that he and the "belle jeune anglaise silencieuse" shared a taste for

> la poésie de la nuit, de la pluie, des existences absurdes et dangereuses,—en un mot, d'un certain romantisme plaintif où l'exotisme se mêle au merveilleux avec une nuance d'humour, de désenchantement.[12]

> (the poetry of night, of rain, of absurd and dangerous existences—in a word, of a certain plaintive romanticism in which the exotic and the marvelous blend with a touch of humor, of disenchantment.)

He adds that he and Katherine were both born in remote countries—in his case New Caledonia. She inspired what he thought of as his best piece of writing—the character of Winnie in *Les Innocents*, a rapacious but charming writer who cold-bloodedly uses her friends and lovers as material.

Carco, a protégé of Colette's, was perfectly at home in the rather *louche* Parisian atmosphere that Katherine found so liberating after the anxious moral strivings of life with Murry. He became the model for the neat, quick, epicene young Frenchman in "Je ne parle pas français," Katherine's final statement of disenchantment with this world. But at this time, she was still eager to experience what freedom it had to give—and, incidentally, to feed her taste for reality by a glimpse of the battle lines.

When her brother Chummie arrived in England on his way to the army, he gave her the money to go to Paris. After a perilous journey to the front to spend two days with Carco, Katherine returned to England. The clandestine sexual adventure (though she describes it excitingly and warmly in her *Journal*) had turned her back to Murry; and though she went to Paris twice more that spring, staying in Carco's empty flat on the Quai aux Fleurs, it was in quest of work rather than love. Her conversations with her brother had brought New Zealand vividly back to her memory; the light of Paris worked its magic; and she began the first draft of "The Aloe," which later became "Prelude."

On her return, Katherine and Murry moved to a house in Acacia Road, St. John's Wood. For the first time they had a real home, charming and—it seemed—reasonably permanent. There Chummie visited them, and their long conversations ranged over the whole of their New Zealand childhood.

But in September, Chummie left for the front; and on October 7, he was killed during a demonstration of grenade-throwing. The war had finally come home to them, making the peace and security of their life together seem an illusion. In November, they left for the south of France, fleeing the memories contained in Acacia Road. Katherine's grief excluded Murry; she wrote to her dead brother in her *Journal*,

> To you only do I belong. . . . You know I can never be Jack's lover again. . . . I give Jack my "surplus" love, but to you I hold and to you I give my deepest love. Jack is no more than . . . anybody might be. [13]

Chummie represented the lost paradise of childhood which she was trying to recapture in prose, and he had been an emotional alternative to her increasingly difficult commitment to Jack. Carco was not a real alternative; he awakened all the revulsion that followed her violation of her own innate puritanism. But the trusting love that she and Chummie had shared, innocent of sexuality, seemed to her an ideal that she could never capture in real life.

Jealous and ashamed of his jealousy, Murry returned to London. But soon Katherine's letters recalled him, with their promise of a deeper love than she had ever felt before:

> You have written me such wonderful letters. It is strange. I feel that I only really know you since you went back to England. I feel as though a miracle had happened to you and you are rich and bathed in light. While I sit here writing to you time is not. I am one with our love for ever.[14]

What miracle had happened? It seems as if already Jack had begun to take Chummie's place—soon she started calling him "Bogey," a nickname she had first used for Chummie. Just as she began to write in an idealized fashion about Chummie after his death, the absence of Jack made her see him in a romantic, ideal light, difficult to sustain when he was actually there. Her longing for him grew, and she tempted him with descriptions of the house she had found for them:

> If you *should* come, I have found a tiny villa for us, which seems to me almost perfect in its way. It stands alone in a small garden with terraces. It faces the "midi" and gets the sun all day long. . . . It is very private and stands high on the top of a hill. It is called the *Villa Pauline*.[15]

In these letters, written long before Katherine was ordered abroad for her consumption, all the themes of the later, agonized letters appear. Waiting for Jack's letters, reviling him for neglecting her and then turning on herself for her misplaced accusations, sexual jealousy, blissful descriptions of France alternating with desolate feelings of exile—and above all, the mutual flattery of love letters, creating a world that could scarcely exist when they were actually together—all the themes that later became pathologically exaggerated are here already.

When Jack was able to come, it was partly because he had work that could be done away from England; Martin Secker had commissioned a book on Dostoevsky, which would pay off the final debts from the *Blue Review*. Katherine rediscovered the manuscript of "The Aloe," and wrote in her *Journal*:

> *The Aloe* is right. *The Aloe* is lovely. It simply fascinates me. . . . Oh, Bogey—I must hurry. All of them must have this book. It is good, my treasure! My little brother, it is good, and it is what we really meant.[16]

At this time she conceived what was to be the final scene of "The Aloe"—the birth of the little boy who is to "mean the world to Linda." In the event, she did not write this scene until "At the Bay"; but it is clear that the death of her brother had touched off something very profound in her, more profound than she was ever able to explain.

> Oh, I want for one moment to make our undiscovered country leap into the eyes of the Old World. It must be mysterious, as though floating. . . . But all must be told with a sense of mystery, a radiance, an after-glow, because you, my little sun of it, are set. You have dropped over the dazzling brim of the world.[17]

The "undiscovered country" was not only New Zealand, but the childhood they shared; the "afterglow" had something to do with the poignant quality of life lived with a sense of the imminence of death. This is the quality that Katherine was later to say she had discovered through her own fatal illness—but here it is already. She is already haunted by the idea of death, early death. Her brother's death seems partly to represent the war, whose devastation was already engulfing their friends; but it also seems a strange harbinger of her own death.

She began calling Jack "Bogey"; she had named LM, too, after her brother. She was often, in her letters, to see herself and Jack as brother and sister. In her New Zealand stories, she appears as the child Kezia, who is still uncommitted by any acquaintance with corrupting sexuality and the choices it entails. The idea of her childhood self seemed to haunt her; but she was even more haunted by the idea of her brother, and it had something to do with his being, in the eyes of Katherine, the only one of the children that her mother had really loved. She identified with them both—

often with the mother, who learns to love with the birth of her baby boy—often with the favored child himself. It is for this kind of reason—complex, unclear, difficult to express completely—that the death of Chummie had such resonance for her.

With his death, she was able to transfer to Jack some of the nostalgic tenderness that the idea of her childhood with her brother evoked. He replaced Chummie in her emotions, and for the first time she could love him in a full and permanent way. Her restlessness left her.

Jack responded to her renewed love by entering into the full use of his creative talents. Finally the inhibitions that had crippled him were lifted, and he began the prolific writing life that was not to cease until his death. *Dostoevsky: A Critical Study*, published in 1916, was his first of many attempts to discover in the artist a sort of hero, a "striving soul" of the sort he was always to learn from and in a way to become. It is a pioneer effort not only because of its subject—for Dostoevsky was only then appearing in English, in the Constance Garnett translations—but because Murry treats him as a moral exemplar rather than simply as a writer, in the manner now the province of the "psychohistorians."

With both of them working at full capacity, the three months at the Villa Pauline, as Murry said, were "to be a memory of beatitude between us forever." They wrote at opposite sides of the kitchen table (and Katherine surreptitiously put the clock forward to hasten lunch). They walked the hills and the beach, and watched the luxurious, early southern spring arrive. In the evenings, by their own small fireside, they composed alternate stanzas of verses:

> Our shutters are shut, the fire is low,
> The tap is dripping peacefully;
> The saucepan shadows on the wall
> Are black and round and plain to see.

In April, their books were almost finished, and they were receiving importunate letters from Lawrence, who wanted them to join him at Tregerthen in Cornwall. In a manner reminiscent of Katherine's letters to Jack, he tempted them with a house.

Really, you must have the other place. I keep looking at it. I call it already Katherine's house, Katherine's tower. There is something *very* attractive about it. It is very old, native to the earth, like rock, yet dry and all in the light of the hills and the sea.

We count you two as our only two *tried* friends, real and permanent and truly blood kin. I know we shall be happy this summer; *so* happy.[18]

Katherine and Jack obeyed the summons, unwillingly. They felt that their southern haven might be swept away in any case by the war; and winter in England was over. It was not long after their arrival that they knew they had been wrong to come. Lawrence and Frieda were engaged in a battle that horrified onlookers as much as it engrossed the participants. Toward the end of her life, Frieda reminisced about this period, almost fondly, in a letter to Jack:

Once, I remember he had worked himself up and his hands were on my throat and he was pressing me against the wall and ground out: "I am the master, I am the master." I said: "Is that all? You can be master as much as you like, I don't care." His hands dropped away, he looked at me in astonishment and was all right.[19]

Lawrence was furious at the censorship of *The Rainbow*, and at the eclipse of his reputation after the success of *Sons and Lovers*. He was working on *Women in Love*, and searching for the ideal relation to another man to complement his "ideal" marriage. But he was being frustrated in both quests. He was jealous of Jack and Katherine's attachment to each other, jealous of Frieda's longing for her children, at war with England and with himself. Although he had commanded Murry to come, now he turned on him and said, "You're an obscene bug, sucking my life away."

Murry was later to unravel the tortured history of Lawrence's frustration in his quest for love and for a role as a leader of men. At the time, he did not know that he and Katherine were being cast as the villains of *Women in Love*; nor did he understand Lawrence's furious rages and his violent alternations of love and hate. All he knew was that Lawrence was demanding the loyalty he had to give to Katherine; that Katherine was miserable in consequence; and that both of them were sick of sheltering a terrified Frieda and putting up with the black humors of her husband.

Gerald and Gudrun in *Women in Love* are sufficiently unlike Murry and Mansfield for it to be obvious that Lawrence's imagination had outdistanced reality. But the argument of the book—that Birkin subdues his woman, and that Gerald is destroyed by his because he refuses Birkin's offer of blood-brothership—is the kind of Lawrentian fantasy that Katherine, for one, saw through. In a perception that was later to be elaborated by Murry into a full-scale thesis, she wrote to Koteliansky, "The sight of his humiliating dependence makes me too furious." His overbearingness, as she saw it, was merely a cloak for the fact that it was Frieda who was the stronger.

Jack and Katherine soon left Tregerthen. Lawrence wrote to Lady Ottoline Morrell,

> Unfortunately the Murrys do not like the country—it is too rocky and bleak for them. They should have a soft valley, with leaves and the ring-dove cooing. And this is a hillside of rocks and magpies and foxes.

Katherine corroborated this at first, when she wrote to Koteliansky,

> This is not really a nice place; it is so full of huge stones. . . .

But later, when Virginia Woolf bought the house, Katherine wrote:

> Perhaps the house itself is very imperfect in many ways but there is a . . . something . . . which makes one long for it. . . . the house is like a ship. I mustn't talk about it. It bewitched me.

They moved first to the south coast of Cornwall; then to London. Murry was conscripted for war work, and with the help of the Morrells, got a post as a translator at the War Office. Soon he was editing a daily review of the foreign press, which was circulated to heads of government departments. It became indispensable reading in Whitehall, and he was awarded the OBE for his work on it in 1920. At the same time, he continued his reviews of French books for the *TLS*, and began writing political articles for the *Nation*.

He and Katherine had found separate flats—partly because they were still unmarried, and landladies were strict, but also because Katherine's writing and Murry's absorption in his new job were incompatible. Murry overworked and underate; depression preyed on them both; and in November 1917 he was ordered two months' sick leave, which he spent at Garsington. Tuberculosis was again suspected. But when Katherine arrived one weekend, she was stricken with her recurrent pleurisy—and it was she who was diagnosed as consumptive, and ordered to the South.

> . . . there is a spot in my right lung which "confirms him in his opinion that it is absolutely imperative that I go out of this country and keep out of it all through the future winters" . . . you see I feel that life has changed so, and it has all happened so quickly—all my plans are altered, all my future is touched by this. . . . What is so difficult to realize is that this has happened to *me* and not to *you*. . . .[20]

It was difficult for Murry to realize that too. Both of them felt doomed by the war, along with European civilization; both felt identified with the Romantic poets who symbolized England for them. Murry was working on a verse play, *Cinnamon and Angelica*, in which he is the one who dies suddenly. Katherine had been the dominant one in their relationship, and he the one who had needed looking after. Suddenly their situations were reversed.

Cinnamon and Angelica captures their feeling of isolation, of seeking shelter in each other from the destruction and brutality that surrounded them, and of the imminence of early death.

> Ah, love, if you and I were ever old
> We should be lovers still; your arms would fold
> Me to your heart, and my dim eyes would light
> With the unfading spark of the dear smile
> That wrestled with the tears within your eyes.
> We should be children, children, children ever;
> Each give to each immortal love as now
> That age cannot diminish: we shall die
> As we were being born into our love

> Like sleeping beauties locked in each other's arms,
> Babes in the wood whom only babes shall wake,
> The babes that are our children, when they love
> And loving bring us into life again. . . .
> So died my prince, and so the bleeding heart
> Of his sweet princess into stone was turned . . .
> While Caraway gazed silent in the flame
> Of the palace fire and watched it leap from blue
> To red, to white, to gold, then sink to embers grey
> And woke listening to the words dream-children say.[21]

Their feeling of doom was well founded. After a nightmare journey, Katherine arrived in a Bandol completely changed by war. The Hotel Beau Rivage was cold, unfriendly, desolate, and expensive. The elation and despair characteristic of her disease began to appear in her letters to Jack; and when she finally got down to work, it was to write "Je ne parle pas français" (her first words to Carco when she arrived in Paris with Murry so long ago)—the story of Mouse, abandoned in Paris by her lover, and facing the corruptions of a brutal and unfeeling world represented by an epicene Frenchman.

When she sent the story to Murry, he was struck "dumb and numb with pain," though he sent a telegram which arrived as "STHRY RECEIVID MAFNIFIIENT MURLY." If "Prelude" was the expression of love and peace, "Je ne parle pas français" was her "cry against corruption." Carco and Murry were the originals of the two men in the story, and the Mouse is abandoned by both. Murry, however, proved himself her most perceptive critic by being wounded: the impervious Carco speaks of

cette magique nouvelle . . . où je me reconnais avec elle et son futur mari, John-Middleton Murry. Ces pages ont une fantaisie, une verve, une couleur délicieuses.[22]

(this magical story . . . in which I recognize myself with her and her future husband, John Middleton Murry. These pages have a delicious imagination, verve, color.)

Murry's war work kept him irrevocably in London; but LM eventually received permission to travel, arriving on February 12. Katherine was ungrateful. As she wrote to Murry:

"If there wasn't Jack"—that is what she says,—and that I really CANNOT STAND from anybody. . . . What she can't stand is you and I—*us*. You've taken away her prey—which is me. I'm not exaggerating. Well, you have. So there, and now she knows it.[23]

Partly, this was a rebellion against being dependent, against needing anyone. But it was also, as LM understood, a way of coping with her disappointment that Murry had not in fact "taken away" LM's prey—that it was LM and not Jack who was there. It began her pattern of complaining to each about the other, a pattern that was a necessary safety valve at times, though it led to misinterpretations. LM explains,

. . . at other times Katherine's complaints were deliberately made, and I knew it, to give Murry just the kind of self-support that his character needed, an assurance that he was the first, the all-important. . . .

This was as true of her complaints to LM about Murry as it was the other way around, though it was harder for LM to recognize that.

Katherine did need LM in Bandol, because by this time she was seriously ill. Her *Journal* records, for February 19,

I woke up early this morning and when I opened the shutters the full round sun was just risen. I began to repeat that verse of Shakespeare's: "Lo, here the gentle lark weary of rest," and bounded back into bed. The bound made me cough—I spat—it tasted strange— it was bright red blood.

She cannot help but have connected this with Keats at the same fateful moment in his illness, when he said to Brown, "I know that colour—it is arterial blood. That blood is my death warrant—I must die!" From this time forward, she seems to have associated herself ever more strongly with the Romantic poets, for whom consumption was a kind of family illness. Her letters filled with nostalgia for the English countryside, and desire for the kind of conjugal peace she had only experienced at the Villa Pauline. She and Jack planned the Heron, the farm they were to have some day, and which was reminiscent of the Wordsworths' lake country idyll. Named, of course, for Leslie Heron Beauchamp, the Heron grew to include the flowers Katherine particularly loved, the children they were never to have, the peace and work and comradeship that both she and Jack longed for. As Katherine's own faith in her recovery waned, her insistence on the faith of others grew. Her new fear of death turned her passionately to her work, to Jack, to the kind of life she wanted to attain and knew she might not have time for. The company of the English Poets sustained her through these difficult months, and she identified with them:

> Our house must be honest and solid like our work—everything we buy must be the same—everything we wear even. Everything must ring like Elizabethan English and like those gentlemen I always seem to be mentioning: "the Poets." There is a light on them, especially upon the Elizabethans and our "special" set—Keats, W.W., Coleridge, Shelley, De Quincey and Co., which I feel is the bright shining star which must hang in the sky above the Heron as we drive home.[24]

In March, she finally obtained permission to start for home. But she arrived in Paris just as the long-range bombardment with Big Bertha began, and all communications were suspended for three weeks. Staying in hotels, without news from Jack, making the rounds of consulates and ticket offices in the frantic attempt to secure a place on a boat—she finally arrived in England on April 11, but as Murry writes, "The hardships she had suffered had given phthisis a secure hold upon her."

On May 3, the Murrys were finally married. Katherine's long-delayed divorce from Bowden had come through. Frieda Lawrence gave Katherine her wedding ring, and the marriage was to have been a new beginning in their lives, one that would erase the memory of separation. But Katherine could not stay in Murry's cold, damp rooms in Fulham, with no one to look after her while he was at the War Office. Against her will, she went to Looe, in Cornwall, where her old Paris friend Anne Estelle Rice, sunny, blue-eyed, and cheerful, had found her a room in a luxurious hotel. Looe was peaceful and healthy, but the alternations in Katherine's mood, following the vagaries of her fever, made her accuse Jack of wanting to be rid of her; of not believing in the Heron.

At long last, a house was found in Hampstead—the house that now bears the blue plaque with their names on it. Katherine was determined to try a home cure rather than enter a sanatorium—which in any case was not a proven method of treatment at the time. She came under the care of Dr. Sorapure, who appears in her letters as a mysterious and Chekhovian figure. Consumptive himself, he understood her terror of isolation and her need for work, and advised her philosophically that while staying at home might not cure her, the frustrations of sanatorium life would kill her far faster.

The Murrys ran out of decorating money just after the painters had finished the pale gray undercoat, and they were so pleased with the effect that they left it, and named the house "the Elephant." Decorated with lemon yellow, cherry red, and black, it was dramatic, charming, and original. For the first time, Katherine was the mistress of a real ménage, complete with housekeeper (LM), cook, and occasional seamstress.

Katherine was reaching a more varied public with her work by now. "Prelude," bound as a single slim volume, was one of the first books published by the Hogarth Press, and "Bliss," which she had written in France, appeared in the *English Review*. Murry and his younger brother Richard, an art student, began printing "Je ne parle pas français" on their hand-press in the basement. And in January 1919, Murry was offered the editorship of the *Athenaeum*, an old-established but moribund literary magazine that was about to be revived by injections of Rowntree money.

Though the *Athenaeum* made both Murry and Katherine work too hard, and tied Murry to London while Katherine was spending the winters in France, it was a major event in both their professional lives. Katherine had a market for her stories, and she began regularly reviewing novels. To be living at the center of the literary establishment, and to have Murry there as a constant and reliable sounding board, increased her confidence as a writer. Murry entered into one of his most productive periods, and made his reputation as both editor and critic. His list of contributors is dazzling: Virginia and Leonard Woolf, E. M. Forster, Aldous Huxley, Bertrand Russell, T. S. Eliot—the last of whom called the period of Murry's editorship "the high summer of literary journalism in London in my lifetime."

Murry's own criticism, too, had established itself. His articles on French books in the *TLS* were well ahead of their time, bringing Proust and Valéry to the attention of English readers. *The Evolution of an Intellectual* appeared in 1919, *Aspects of Literature* in 1920—both collections of essays; from then on, not a year passed until the end of his life when he did not publish a book. Eliot spoke of his "solitary eminence" in his generation as the kind of critic whose criticism is itself a creative act.

He continued to publish novels and poetry in the early 1920s, but criticism was his real métier, and this fact became increasingly obvious to him and to those around him. Bringing the work of Lawrence and Katherine Mansfield before the public had established his own aesthetic, and convinced him that he could never rival it himself. But he was very far from being a "frustrated artist." Beginning with his Dostoevsky book, he had discovered that exploring the mind of a creative artist was for him a far more exciting and fruitful adventure than trying to be one himself. He was capable of losing himself in dialogue with another, of following the other's argument and restating it in accessible terms; but there had to be an "other" for the dialogue to take place at all. Few critics have had the ability to submerge themselves so joyously in the works they study; this ability is proof enough that he did not feel in any sense the competitor of the creative writer. The most serious emotional commitments of his life, particularly of course to Katherine, paralleled this professional orientation.

The excitements of the *Athenaeum* were professionally stimulating; but they did not improve Katherine's health, and by the end of the summer of 1919, she was unwilling to face another winter in England. Her descriptions of the Hampstead "cure" and of England itself became gradually more critical.

Light refreshments, bouillon, raw eggs and orange juice were served on
the journey. M. came in, fell over the screen, went out again, came
back, dropped a candle, groaned, and went again, and the Faithful One
changed the hot water bottles so marvellously often that you never had a
hot water bottle at all. It was always being taken or brought back.[25]

The Faithful One was LM, who had been summoned to the Elephant to help Katherine with her cure. She had been doing war
work in a south London factory, and her "heart sank" at the summons. Indeed, this was in a sense her final choice between Katherine and any possibility of another life. She was making friends,
and even saw the possibility of marrying a young officer she had
met on the boat from Rhodesia. But when the call came, she made
her decision unhesitatingly, though it was not easy for her to be the
third side of a triangle with Katherine and Jack, or to cope with
Katherine's jealous possessiveness about her house. Of this possessiveness Katherine herself was well aware; she wrote LM:

. . . untrue to my first talk about Hampstead, I have never made you
feel part of it, and every time you say "our" I give you a vile look. This
is wrong in me, but at present I can't control it.[26]

If the house was Katherine's last attempt at a home for herself and
Jack, excluding the rest of the world, LM was an interloper. But
LM was also the kind of nurse, servant, confidante, and travel
companion that she needed. Even if Jack had been suited to this
role, he still had to earn the living on which they both depended,
and could not accompany Katherine to the south. And, at times,
Katherine was as possessive toward LM as she was toward the Elephant or even Jack. She wrote LM, "Yes, I only love you when
you're blind to everybody but us. That's the truth." [27]

Why was Katherine so anxious to leave England, after she had
sworn never to "love and live apart"? Some of it was genuine longing for the sun, the life, of France.

It would be much happier if one could feel—like M.—mankind is born
to suffer. But I do feel that is so wrong—so wrong. It is like saying:

> mankind is born to walk about in goloshes under an umbrella. Oh
> dear—I should like to put a great notice over England, *closed* during the
> winter months.[28]

It was also the fact that when she was with Jack, her fear of separation was replaced by a longing for independence and freedom. Her
old impulse to break the bonds, no matter how eagerly she had
chosen them, came to the fore. As she wrote to Koteliansky, always
the recipient of her most disloyal letters,

> These last days are hideous. It is not being ill that matters, it is the abuse
> of one's privacy—one's independence—it is having to let people serve
> you and fighting *every moment* against their desire to "share." Why are
> human beings so indecent? But soon it will be over, and I shall be at
> work.[29]

In September, Jack escorted her and LM to the Italian Riviera,
where he installed them in the Casetta Deerholm at Ospedaletti.
The tiny, charming Casetta, "in the sun's eye and the sea's eye," at
first enchanted Katherine. But her black moods began to sweep her
with unprecedented violence, until the memory of the Casetta became a nightmare that haunted her for the rest of her life.

First she turned on LM, accusing her of a predatory delight in
her weakness, and of clumsiness that seemed almost deliberate:

> The worst of it is I always feel she thinks it "so nice and homey" to oc-
> casionally smash a thing or two.[30]

Her rage grew until LM became the Albatross, her "worst enemy,"
and she had fantasies of shooting her and seeing her lying at the
bottom of the stairs. Being closeted in isolation with one person was
even less private than the comings and goings of the Elephant, and
LM's desire to "share" just as unbearable as that of anyone else—
more so, perhaps, because with Jack, the rage of dependence was
tempered by love and cooperation in work.

Her letters to Jack grew black with despair and rage. The climax
came in early December:

Last night under the inspiration of a fever attack I wrote these verses:

> . . . Who's your man to leave you be
> Ill and cold in a far country?
> Who's the husband—who's the stone
> Could leave a child like you alone?

Murry writes,

> The effect of these verses upon me was shattering. At that time I did not
> fully understand how uncontrollable is the mood of despair which
> engulfs the tubercular patient. . . . They struck me as a terrible accusa-
> tion of myself—the harder to bear because it was unfair: for it was not of
> my own free choice that I stayed in England at my job. My livelihood
> and Katherine's depended on it, at the time.[31]

Jack's daily letters were numbered in decreasing order with the
number of days to her return in the spring; but there was nothing
he or LM could do to alleviate the crisis that Katherine was facing.
Her accusations and despairing moods were the symptoms of a
crisis that she had to undergo alone, and that ultimately no one
could help her with: she was facing the imminence of her own
death. In a sense, her charges against them are not personal
charges, but part of a generalized resistance to the fate that was
engulfing her. In her rational moments, she knew that she was not
being abandoned by Jack or persecuted by LM; her record of her
dreams indicates her struggle to accept the finality of the sentence
she was under, to give up her tenacious hold on life and her hopes
for the future. She says in late November,

> Once the defences are fallen between you and Death they are not built
> up again. It needs such a little push, hardly that, just a false step, just
> not looking, and you are over.[32]

Her nightmares return again and again to the feeling that she has
died already:

I said, "Doctor Sorapure, I can see you'd rather not attend me any more." We shook hands and he walked out—and I saw the greenish fog in the window . . . and knew I was caught. To wake up and hear the sea and know I had not done the dreadful thing—that was joy.[33]

Katherine was intermittently aware that it was her fear of death that haunted her even more than her longing for Jack; the movement of her thought is there to see in a long and fascinating *Journal* entry.

As I grew depressed, he grew depressed, but not for me. He began to write (1) about the suffering I caused him; *his* suffering, *his* nerves, *he* wasn't made of whipcord or steel, the fruit was bitter for *him*. (2) a constant cry about money. . . . The letters—ended all of it. *Was* it the letters? I must not forget something else.

All these two years I have been obsessed by the fear of death. This grew and grew *gigantic*, and this it was that made me cling so, I think. Ten days ago it went, I care no more. . . . I am become—Mother. I don't care a *rap* for people. I shall always love Jack and be his wife but I couldn't get back to that anguish—joy—sweet madness of love of the other years. Such love has gone for me. And life either stays or goes.

I must put down here a dream. The first night I was in bed here, i.e. after my first day in bed, I went to sleep. And suddenly I felt my whole body *breaking up*. It broke up with a violent shock—an earthquake—and it broke like glass. A long terrible shiver, you understand—and the spinal cord and the bones and every bit and particle quaking. It sounded in my ears—a low, confused din, and there was a sense of flashing greenish brilliance, like broken glass. When I woke up I thought there had been a violent earthquake. But all was still. It slowly dawned upon me—the conviction that in that dream I died. . . . I am (December 15, 1919) a dead woman, and *I don't care*.

This was the central moment of her crisis. Her fury with LM seems to have abated after that, and she set about trying to rethink all her relationships on a new basis.

The new basis with Jack involved abandoning their "man-to-man" kind of equality. Financially, he contributed what he could to augment Katherine's allowance from her father, but the expenses of her illness meant that it was never enough. The horror of debt drilled into him by his father, exacerbated by his own bankruptcy, meant that he was cautious, even mean; and Katherine had, up to this point, been unwilling to feel dependent on him. Emotionally, the situations were even harder to reverse: his dependence on Katherine had made her illness a devastating blow to him, as she realized so well.

> How clear it all is! Immediately I, as a tragic figure, outfaced or threatened to outface him (yes, that's exactly the truth) the truth was revealed. He was the one who really wanted *all* the tragedy.[34]

The other half of the truth is that Katherine, too, wanted it all, and yet furiously resisted the fact that it was she who had been chosen to bear it. Jack had been sure that he would be the one to get tuberculosis, the one to die young. The reversal in their fortunes was something they both had to learn to accept.

One effect of the new regime was to turn Katherine back to her family. "I am become—Mother." Therefore the kind of man she needed was not the dependent Jack, but someone much more nearly approaching her father. Indeed it was her family who came to the rescue, but only after the horrifying dreams had spent themselves, giving way to an unearthly calm. LM records,

> One evening she was lying in bed, strangely still for a very long time, so long that I feared she was skipping away across the thin border-line between life and death. But she came back, and in quite a full voice said, "I have had a most wonderful dream. I dreamt I was dead and was walking in a garden. The flowers were so beautiful, with glowing colours, more lovely than I have ever seen or imagined." That night she seemed very peaceful.

Her father, on a long visit to Europe, came to visit her one day at the Casetta, bringing with him his cousin Connie Beauchamp and her friend Jinnie Fullerton, two rich Catholic ladies who lived in great luxury at Menton. Before they left, they decided to try and get Katherine to come to them for her cure—and, although this was not revealed at first, to try to convert her to Catholicism.

Katherine was suspicious of luxury, more suspicious of her

family—and she gently ridiculed Connie and Jinnie, who were not intellectuals.

> By the way, my dear, I gave Connie the Oxford Book of English Verse to look at yesterday . . . she said a moment after, "There are some quite pretty things here, dear. Who are they by?" [35]

But when Murry came for a Christmas visit, after receiving the "verses," the lift to her spirits was only temporary. The weather had turned cold and stormy; and the series of strikes had begun that were to herald the rise of Fascism in Italy. Foreigners were suspect, and to the fear of loneliness and disease was added the fear of violent marauders. Katherine and LM escaped in a taxi to Menton, and gratefully lapsed into luxury. Katherine's mood changed:

> My hate is quite lifted—quite gone; it is like a curse removed. Lesley has been through the storm with us . . .
> I confess that now I do lean on her. She looks after me. . . . It was only when I refused to acknowledge this—to acknowledge her importance to me—that I hated her. . . . I think my hatred must have been connected with my illness in some way. [36]

Her illness also continued to change her attitude toward Jack, and to make her into the kind of person she had, earlier in her life, sworn she would never be. The most pathetic aspect of the change was that she had to abandon her favorite persona, that of the classless artist, the free comrade, the independent spirit who met her husband, her lover, on equal ground. She reverted to being the demanding, fussy bourgeoise that she had hated in the other women in her family. This spiritual malaise was compounded by the fact that her slow convalescence from the rigors of life at the Casetta prevented her from doing more than desultory work.

Even her most valued friends from earlier days seemed determined to push her into this new role, and to insist that she abandon them:

> I want to mention something else. Lawrence sent me a letter today. He spat in my face and threw filth at me and said: "I loathe you. You revolt me stewing in your consumption. . . ." [37]

She allowed a neurotic triviality to creep into her letters: she up-braided Jack for not "knowing" that she needed an extra £10; for giving a picture of her that he "knew she hated" to her publishers; she brooded over why he didn't understand her feelings the time she asked him to stop scraping his porridge saucer. She decided that she must always spend her winters in the south, and that the Heron must be postponed—a far cry from the days when she accused Jack of "not believing in the Heron."

Going shopping and sightseeing in the car, being given presents, playing with the baby Pekingese—she was being corrupted by the money lavished on her by Connie and Jinnie, and she was perfectly aware of the fact. At times, she defended herself:

> . . . this time next year I *ought* to be as well as I ever shall be i.e. as well as Mother was. She and I seem to be exactly the same: my heart trouble, I mean, is exactly like hers. I have written Father about this because I must have my £300 a year for life certain. [38]

At other moments, she had flashes of her detached, artist's vision of the life around her, as when she described Monte Carlo as "*real Hell.* . . . There at those tables sit the damned. . . ." Only on the question of religion did she resist the blandishments of Connie and Jinnie. They were offended by the portrait of Raoul Duquette in "Je ne parle pas français":

> "But how could you say that about the Blessed Virgin!" said she. "It must have hurt Our Lady so terribly."
> And I saw the B.V. throwing away her copy of *Je ne parle pas français* and saying: "Really, this K.M. is all that her friends say of her to me." [39]

Finally spring came and she was free to go back to England. But it was not a permanent return and she knew it, even made provisions for it. Before she left Connie's house, the Villa Flora, Katherine had been promised a small adjacent house, the Villa Isola Bella, for herself the next winter.

The summer in Hampstead meant more reviewing, little story-writing, and further deterioration in health. She was diverted by the literary characters who came to see Murry: Aldous Huxley rolling on the sofa groaning over Smollett's *vulgarity*; Max Bodenheim, "a new American just fresh from New York," saying "Say, Mr. Murry, I've got the goods to hand over if you've got the window space for them." [40] She was also glad to have the chance to see Virginia Woolf, whom she had first met in 1917, and to whom she wrote, "You are the only woman with whom I long to talk *work*. There will never be another." [41]

But Katherine was anxious to return to Menton, and the new villa, equipped with a splendid cook named Marie, was all she had hoped. LM was with her; *Bliss*, her second book, was published in December and received good reviews. Jack was expected for Christmas, and the idea was that in the spring he would give up the *Athenaeum* (which was rapidly losing money in any case) and they would be able to live together permanently outside England.

The plan worked well until early December, but then the letters filled again with jealousy and unreasonable accusations. Katherine was by now too ill to defer her needs; her need for Jack was paralleled by her need to get as many stories as possible onto paper, to outrun death in this way; and Jack arrived to find that she had had a serious relapse brought about by overwork. For the rest of her life, desperate bouts of work were to alternate with physical collapse. Jack returned to England only long enough to resign the paper and wind up his life there; he returned to Menton with the idea that in the spring, he and Katherine would go to Switzerland.

The stories in *Bliss* had been a collection of her best work since the *German Pension*, dominated by the great opposing pair of "Prelude" and "Je ne parle pas français"—which represented, as Katherine said, the poles of love and despair which were her two "kickoffs" as a writer. In a sense, it is a Jamesian pair of themes—provincial authenticity contrasted with European corruption. It also contrasts the innocence of childhood with the horror of sexuality—a theme that derived some of its power from Katherine's own searing bouts of "experience."

The new stories, written at the Villa Isola Bella, were clustered around a new theme: women alone, on the edges of life. "The Daughters of the Late Colonel," the story from this period that Katherine herself was most satisfied with, used LM (Ida Constantia

Baker) and her cousin Sylvia Payne ("Jug") as models. She shows them as fussy, aging spinsters, so terrorized by their father that even after his death, they are afraid to touch his belongings. But the portrait is gentle, loving, without malice—and perhaps reflects some of her own concern for what will happen to LM after her death. "The Lady's Maid" is a variant on the same theme; and "Miss Brill," one of her most unbearably poignant stories, shows a life in which the tiny, almost imperceptible pleasures left to the old woman are spoiled by the unthinking callousness of youth. "Bliss," the title story, shows the spoiling of a young woman's happiness by discovery of her husband's sexual infidelity—one of the charges that Katherine was flinging at Murry at the time. He appears in these stories only as the remote and shadowy "literary gentleman" for whom Ma Parker cleans house—and who does not notice Ma Parker's despairing grief at the death of her only remaining grandchild. Clearly, Murry was out of sight and out of mind except as a focus for reproach and accusation. Even in the stories written after his arrival at the villa, she seemed to be drawing on the material stored up during her months in the spinsterhood.

In May, Katherine and LM made the journey to Switzerland together, while Murry returned to Oxford to give a series of lectures—later to become one of his best books, *The Problem of Style*. He joined them at Montana-sur-Sierre in June, according to their plan, although LM has a more uncharitable view of his movements:

> In June Murry finished his Oxford lectures, and, as he had left the *Athenaeum* and had no home in England, he decided to join Katherine in Switzerland. . . .

LM was, as she herself confesses, unhappy to find that their reunion at Montana seemed to the Murrys a continuation of the idyll at the Villa Pauline.

> The difficulty was that when she and Jack were happy together I always felt that I must try and be independent too and make my own plans, though it was bitter pain for me to do this.

Nonetheless, the Chalet des Sapins was good for Katherine in almost every way. Her tuberculosis came closer to being arrested than it had for several years, and she was working well. Significantly, it was there that she wrote "At the Bay," the continuation of "Prelude" in exactly the way that her happiness was now a continuation of the period at the Villa Pauline. If "Prelude," plotless though it is, concerned the Beauchamp family's move to the earthly paradise of Karori, "At the Bay" dealt with their summer paradise on the New Zealand shore. A long meditation on the shadow of death that heightens the beauty of life, the story moves from the group of children, including the observant Kezia, who witness the killing of a duck for the family to eat; to Aunt Beryl, longing for romance but disillusioned by the cynicism of a married friend; to the grandmother, gently and wisely schooling Kezia in the acceptance of death; to Linda, finally touched and made able to love by her newborn son. This story has the "radiance, the afterglow," that Katherine had promised Chummie she would achieve.

From July to December, Katherine was peacefully at work, to the limits of her strength—"I have felt exhausted with all these stories lately and yet—couldn't stop." [42] The Swiss appealed to her no more than the Bavarians had done years ago, but the difference in her sensibility can be seen by the fact that now the satire is light and amused, the tearing bitterness quite gone.

> To me, though, the symbol of Switzerland is that large middle-class female *behind*. It is the most respectable thing in the world. It is Matchless. Everyone has one in this hotel; some of the elderly ladies have two. [43]

One of the most mysterious things about her life story has always been why she left her Swiss haven in search of a miracle cure that she must have suspected would not succeed. It was becoming increasingly intolerable to her to be on the periphery of life, and she felt that she had almost come to the end of such material as her incomplete, invalid's life presented. The old restlessness was not entirely dead, and a few months with Jack served, as usual, to erase the memory of her vow never to leave him again.

Ever since her time with Connie and Jinnie, she had vaguely thought that though she could not accept a dogmatic religion, her illness was in some way connected with a lack of faith, that if she could only penetrate the mysterious workings of the mind's influence on the body, she would know how to get well. Indeed she seems almost to have accepted the idea that her disease was psychosomatic: in her most famous and beautiful letter to Murry, she wrote:

> I believe the greatest failing of all is *to be frightened.* Perfect Love casteth out Fear. When I look back on my life all my mistakes have been because I was afraid. . . . Was that why I had to look on death? Would nothing less cure me? You know, one can't help wondering, sometimes. . . . No, not a personal God or any such nonsense. Much more likely—the soul's desperate choice. . . .[44]

When she attempted to apply these insights to the business of actually getting well, though, Katherine was clutching at straws. She was reading a book called *Cosmic Anatomy,* which had attracted a cult following in England among her old Orage group. It put forward the doctrine that the mind could influence the body—and since physical regimes did not seem to be reversing her disease, this seemed like the only hope.

By December, she was writing to Koteliansky asking for information about Manoukhin, a Russian doctor who had begun treating tuberculosis with X rays. The treatment was seemingly scientific, but its adherents spoke of it with mystical awe, and its effects were not medically documented. Katherine was anxious to go to Paris and begin the new treatment; Murry was just as anxious that she should stay quiet in Switzerland. He was in despair at her new line of thought. He knew that she had turned to varieties of faith-healing because she despaired of other methods—ironically, just as the other methods seemed to be having some success. Katherine accused him of not believing that she could yet recover—perhaps he did not, but he did believe that she would live longer in the peace of Sierre than in exhausting searches for new treatments. Katherine herself confessed to a friend, "Manoukhin is not only a doctor. He is a whole new stage on the journey. I hardly know why." [45] Murry knew why, all too well—it was a plunge into unreason, where he refused to follow her. Angered at his refusal, Katherine left for Paris with LM. Covering her tracks by misleading letters, Katherine went on to London, where she met, through her old friend Orage, the disciples of the Russian mystic Gurdjieff. Gurdjieff, in the words of Edmund Wilson, was a "Russo-Greek charlatan" who

> . . . undertook to renovate the personalities of discontented well-to-do persons. He combined making his clients uncomfortable in various gratuitous ways—such as waking them up in the middle of the night and training them to perform grotesque dances—with reducing them to a condition of complete docility, in which they would hold, at a signal, any position, however awkward, that they happened to be in at the moment. They were promised, if they proved themselves worthy of it, an ultimate initiation into the mysteries of an esoteric doctrine. . . . Gurdjieff . . . had apparently a rogue's sense of humor. A young man in the office, a bishop's son who had lost his faith and was groping for something to take its place, told me of the banquets of roast sheep or goat, served in great pots in the Caucasian style and eaten with the fingers, to which Gurdjieff would invite his disciples and at which he would have read aloud to them a book he had written called *A Criticism of the Life of Man: Beëlzebub's Tale to His Grandson.* "It sounds as if it had been written," said this neophyte, "just on purpose to bore you to death. Everybody listens in silence, but every now and then Gurdjieff will suddenly burst out laughing—just roaring—nobody knows about what." [46]

The Manoukhin treatment had made Katherine slightly stronger, but once she was embarked on this spiritual journey, she had to follow it to its conclusion—and the Gurdjieff circle was one kind of conclusion, one road to a kind of spiritual regeneration.

Murry eventually followed Katherine to London, but they lived in adjacent houses in Bloomsbury, and Katherine's new doctrines were an impassable barrier between them. She saw his disapproval as a reflection of his lack of hope for a cure; and he saw her abandonment of him as a sign that she felt his love had failed her. He was deeply opposed to what he now saw as her intention—to enter Gurdjieff's

Institute for the Harmonious Development of Man, at Fontaine-bleau.

Katherine was never completely convinced by Gurdjieff's doctrines, which were in any case vague enough to admit many interpretations. But he, like Manoukhin and Koteliansky and Chekhov, was a Russian; as an added lure, the widow of Chekhov was expected to visit the Institute. In October, Katherine went there herself. The Russian atmosphere reached right back to her adolescent notions of the bohemian life of the artist—ideas drawn from Marie Bashkirtseff, Kuprin, Dostoevsky, Chekhov, and the other Russian masters who were first being translated as she came of age. Gurdjieff did everything he could to encourage this romantic exoticism—the communal meals, the dividing up of the farm and house tasks, the spartan simplicity of dress and diet were all rather stagy copies of life in a Russian peasant village.

As usual, the moment she had made a decision, entered a new life, she began to turn back to those she had left behind. In November she wrote to LM, "I am not dead though you persist in pretending I am. And of course I shall not be here all my life." [47] At first, she had a large, comfortable, warm room in the château, which had been a luxurious house. Soon she was assigned a bare cell like most of the other inhabitants. A platform was built for her in the cowshed, as Gurdjieff believed in the nineteenth-century remedy for consumption: the exhalations of cows. She gave LM detailed instructions about which clothes to send, what kind of skirt she needed for the evening folk dancing, and so on—showing that her new "simplicity" was as carefully considered an image as any other she had adopted.

In part, she was rebelling against the "bourgeois" self she had adopted at the Villa Flora, her preoccupation with hotels and maids and money, the things for which she had so mercilessly criticized the neurasthenic, spoiled women in so many of her stories. Now she wrote to Koteliansky,

. . . I mean to change my whole way of life entirely. I mean to learn to work in every possible way with my hands, looking after animals and doing all kinds of manual labour. I do not want to write any stories until I am a less terribly poor human being.[48]

And to her cousin "Elizabeth,"

> I want much more material; I am tired of my little stories like birds bred in cages. [49]

In all this, there was not so much a turning away from Jack as an attempt to purify herself again, to make herself strong and whole, to earn her life with him at the Heron. Did she still believe that this was possible, that she would win through after all? All we know is that Jack finally accepted her effort at self-renewal as genuine, and that she turned back to him again. But even now, there were flaws in her loyalty, or perhaps she did not believe strongly enough in the future to overcome the doubts and the bitterness. At the end of the summer, in London, she had written to Koteliansky,

> . . . I am arranging a splendid scheme by which Murry shares a country house with a man called Locke Ellis, who will live with him for ever and ever, I hope. This is a truly magnificent idea. I shall have to go there later on with Ida Baker to wind up the works and start the toy going. But then I do not think it will ever run down again.
> . . . Will you come in the evenings then? It is the time I like best of all. . . . [50]

Perhaps this tone cloaks real concern for Jack's future, and the bitterness is that she has to accept the fact that his future will not include her. By the time she invited Jack to visit her at the Institute, for the opening of their new theater early in January of 1923, acceptance had once again triumphed over tormented doubt. When he arrived on January 9, Katherine seemed to him "a being transfigured by love," and "there was a blend of simplicity and seriousness in most of the people I met there, and in the company as a whole, which impressed me deeply." [51]

They talked quietly, and helped with the painting of colored designs in the large hall. As Katherine climbed the stairs to her room that evening, she was seized by a fit of coughing that became a violent hemorrhage. Within half an hour, she was dead. She was buried at Fontainebleau, and on her gravestone was carved her motto from Shakespeare: "But I tell you, my lord fool, out of this nettle, danger, we pluck this flower, safety."

Jack returned, alone, to a cottage in the English countryside. LM took up agricultural work on a farm near Lisieux. Months later, they met to go through Katherine's papers and to decipher the minute handwriting of her remaining manuscripts. LM writes,

> I saw her face, radiant with light, as she smiled and passed through the room, telling me that all was well. Murry, looking up when she was gone, said quietly and simply: "You have just seen Katherine." [52]

CHAPTER 3

Murry Post Mortem

With an host of furious fancies,
Whereof I am commander,
With a burning spear, and a horse of air,
To the wilderness I wander.
By a knight of ghosts and shadows
I summoned am to tourney,
Ten leagues beyond the wide world's end.
Me thinks it is no journey.

—Tom o'Bedlam's Song

Katherine Mansfield was the most extraordinary event in the life of John Middleton Murry. He spent the rest of his life in living out the themes established with her, and to trace the course of his career is to discover in a fuller way what those themes were. To see the kind of women he loved, the kind of cause, political and literary, that engaged his attention, is to see what kind of intellectual universe he and Katherine began to create together. It provides some keys to the baffling vagaries of their love for each other, and to the extraordinary loyalty that held them together during all the disastrous history of their marriage.

After Katherine's death it seemed to Jack that there was nothing left in the world, that he would somehow have to learn to exist in an empty universe. He was offered the loan of an isolated cottage in Ashdown Forest, and went there to face his solitude. Then he experienced "the one entirely revolutionary happening" of his life.

. . . a moment came when the darkness of that ocean changed to light, the cold to warmth; when it swept in one great wave over the shores and frontiers of my self; when it bathed me and I was renewed; when the room was filled with a presence, and I knew I was not alone—that I never could be alone any more, that the universe beyond held no menace, for I was part of it. . . .[1]

He had sought with Katherine a way of making contact with life, of overcoming his intellectual isolation. Now it seemed that, in dying, and in the kind of spiritual struggle she had undergone in the months before her death, she had given him another clue to follow. The kind of contact with life he had been seeking was opening up to him just as he had despaired of ever reaching it. He was to spend the second half of his life following this clue, after spending his first thirty-three years trying to find it.

For months, his estrangement from Katherine over Gurdjieff had left him miserable and unable to write. The block suddenly disappeared—but now, it seemed to him that all writing was irrelevant that was not directly concerned with the question: "What must I do to be saved?" The apocalyptic, Dostoevskian style that had attracted him as a beginning writer returned with a vengeance; but this time, it was combined with the romantic theory of art that he and Katherine had shared.

Within a few weeks, he had decided to found a new journal, the *Adelphi*, "in which subjects of vital interest to modern readers are treated with honesty and conviction." A sale of about 4,000 was optimistically expected: instead, the first issue sold over 15,000.

To read Murry's *Adelphi* essays now is to have some idea why. They have a vitality, a sense of joyous release. The long, dragging weight of Katherine's illness, her "gravitational pull" as a writer and a personality, and the past year of disagreement, are all gone. Murry bounds into life again. He restates his "religion of art" with evangelistic fervor.

> Shall I say then, read *Antony and Cleopatra* till the bugle-call of that unearthly challenge to human loyalty echoes in the remotest chamber of the soul? Or, Listen to the last piano sonatas of Beethoven, till you feel that in the high B of op. 109 all that human desire can imagine of the crystalline perfection of the ideal is cracked and shattered, *must* be cracked and shattered, with a faint, far-away sound of breaking that stabs the very quick of being; till you know that Beethoven faced this disaster, pressed its inevitability home against his heart, and saw what lay beyond

and triumphed and was free? Or shall I say, Read Tchehov's *The Cherry Orchard*. Read and listen, till you know what secret harmony and high design lies within all human discomfiture, to be discovered only by those who feel, and feeling, do not turn their faces away?

These men, and other men like these, knew the secret of life. They fought for it and conquered. Listen to them. Learn to listen to them. Learn to wait for the silence which descends when the importunate mind grows weary of asking its unanswerable questions, and to discern what echoes are awakened in that stillness by the notes which these men plucked out of their souls. Learn to live by that music, earthly and divine, or even learn only to desire to live by it, and you also will triumph and be free.[2]

This passage not only confirms Katherine's suspicion that her illness was causing Jack almost as much suffering as it was causing her, and that her death would be a liberation for him. Most important, it also shows how closely he identified his religion of art with Katherine herself, who, in her letters to him, seemed to have touched and revealed the "secret of life." If his own search for this kind of revelation gave a kind of impulsion to her insight, she in turn expressed it in a way that touched off this response in him. Thus theirs is a story of mutual creativity, and the subsequent history of what Middleton Murry gave to English letters is an essential part of the story of Katherine Mansfield; his contribution was, in a very real sense, another product of her genius.

The success of the *Adelphi* led Murry to believe that England was waiting for his message—that the time was ripe for the kind of "change of heart" that World War I, and the prospect of another war, made imperative—that in fact the world could be won for love and humanity through the medium of great art. This is why he harps on the theme of the utility of art in the everyday lives of ordinary people. Whether he really believed in the revolutionary power of art, which the evidence of his century so thoroughly denied, he wrote as if he believed something very like it.

His capacity for ideological fresh starts was only equaled by his capacity for renewed faith in love every time he fell in love with a new woman. He seemed, in fact, to be searching for that nearly perfect unity he had found with Katherine, and each time he thought he had attained it. Within a few months of Katherine's death, he was in love with Violet le Maistre—a lovely girl of twenty-three, who wrote stories in what she believed to be the Mansfield manner and who assumed Katherine's hair style, gestures, and phrases. Murry himself could scarcely tell the difference between them, so bemused was he by the power the past still had over his mind. He was amazed to learn that Violet did not welcome her pregnancies—he had attributed to her Katherine's own longing for children. He was even more astounded when she greeted the news that she was consumptive with

> "O I'm so *glad!* . . . I wanted this to happen."
> I stared into her shining eyes. "You wanted this to happen," I repeated, slowly and dully, while my world turned upside down.
> "You see, Golly!" she explained. "I wanted you to love me as much as you loved Katherine—and how could you, without this?" [3]

Violet had two children, Katherine (called Weg) and Colin, before succumbing to tuberculosis. Murry, who had sworn that this time he would not fail, that she would not die as Katherine had died, was shattered by this second blow of fate.

But he was still the falling-in-love type, and looked for comfort, as usual, in the form of another woman. Nearest to hand was Betty Cockbayne, the woman who had nursed Violet. Warned by Betty's father about her terrible temper, he persisted in believing that she was the spontaneous, natural woman of the people who would at last bring him into a real relation with life, and introduce him to a kind of love that would not prove deathly.

His early illusions about Betty are couched in Lawrentian language, and it seems to have been a long-deferred affair with Frieda (Lawrence had died, also of tuberculosis, a year before Violet) that started him looking for a new kind of woman. But if it was the belated influence of Lawrence that sent Murry into the arms of Betty, it was certainly a case of Lawrence having the last laugh. For Frieda was an intellectual as well as a spontaneous animal; her loyalty to Lawrence had been based on full understanding of his work. Betty, however, was stupid, vicious, and jealous of the mental life in which she could not participate. She was a really epic shrew, terrorizing the children (she and Murry had two, Mary and David, whom she systematically preferred to Weg and Col) and beating and abusing her husband, to whom she habitually referred as "the old bugger."

This was Murry's "political" period—the 1930s were everyone's political period, but certainly Murry seems to have looked for activities that would keep him out of the house. The *Adelphi* spawned the Adelphi Summer School, then the Adelphi Centre in East Anglia, where Murry eventually moved when he left Betty in 1939. Pacifism, socialism, the religion of love—these were the themes of Murry's preaching during the thirties, when he managed to alienate both the left and the right.

He never abandoned literary criticism, though his method at this time had some limitations that show how necessary a sympathetic emotional environment was for him to do his best work. *Shakespeare*, for example, was written while he lived with Betty, and it has some curious omissions, the most glaring of which is any mention of Shakespeare in love. The Dark Lady, the period of jealousy and sensual disgust—all of which most critics interpret as indictating that an unhappy love affair was the most searing experience of Shakespeare's early maturity—are all but passed over by Murry. He talks of the Sonnets in terms of Shakespeare's disillusion with his patron; he suggests that Shakespeare must have had a nagging wife; and he concentrates on the heroines of the final period—Miranda, Imogen, Perdita—making them Shakespeare's hypothetical love-objects the way his young daughters Weg and Mary were currently his own.

During this time he also reedited Katherine's books; she was still providing a refuge for him, but this time one that turned him away from the unhappy life around him, back to the past that they had shared. His guilt over her death, his feeling that he had failed her, were intimately connected to his endurance of the punishment he received at the hands of Betty. This almost masochistic streak showed itself in his political opinions, too—he discovered the beauties of Shinto just as England declared war on Japan, and, later, decided on the necessity for a holy war against the Soviet Union just at the time that the ban-the-bomb movement was getting off the ground.

His spiritual home, however, turned out to be the vein of British socialism that ran from the early days of the Fabian Society to the Aldermaston marches. His followers came from this group, and he met one of them just as life with Betty was becoming intolerable. Mary Gamble was a fortyish spinster, a plain, earnest, and thoroughly nice woman. Her account of their first meal together reveals them both:

> There was cold chicken to start with and he served me with some of that, but, utterly absorbed in what he was saying, forgot to offer me anything else. He helped himself liberally to apple tart, followed by cheese and biscuits and coffee and I, far too nervous to draw attention to my plight, sat and listened hungry but enthralled. [4]

Murry's recurrent dream of founding a cooperative farm—a dream compounded of socialism and the Heron—reasserted itself, and he and Mary found a possible site in Norfolk, where some of the personnel from the Adelphi Centre joined them. Putting the farm in order and mediating among the combative group of pacifists who were trying to farm it was Murry's war work. He was happy, in spite of postcards from Betty (in large capitals to startle the postman): "ARE YOU STILL LIVING WITH THAT OLD WHORE?" His enthusiastic happiness with Mary induced some to feel that he had committed the error of which he accused Lawrence, and confused the calm after the storm with the peace which passeth understanding.

Murry's belief in the power of love was reinstated as his only religion, and Katherine was still its high priestess. As he wrote to Mary,

> Never—and I do know something about this passion of love—has any woman given me such total and entire happiness as you have done. I can see Katherine and Violet lifting their eyebrows at one another when I write this: but they do it in a laughing, gay kind of way; and they quite agree. They say to one another: "But *we* taught him how to love." [5]

The sensible Mary had a further insight, which she expressed in a postscript to his book *Adam and Eve.*

> Perhaps I am a naturally happy woman, and should have been happy whether I had fallen in love or not.[6]

This was the kind of simple truth never visible to Murry himself, who still inhabited an intellectual dreamland where metaphysical explanations had more validity than psychological ones. Though his criticism is full of insight, his perception of the people around him was utterly lacking. His biographer says,

> His misjudgments of character were so numerous, naive and notorious that one of his assistant editors confessed that he would have had the gravest doubts as to his own integrity, had Murry appointed him to the post.[7]

This kind of thing tells us a great deal about what Katherine found so baffling, so maddening, in his personality—but his critical method, when contrasted with that of his contemporaries, shows what there was about him that she needed and valued. His witty combativeness is as marked as Katherine's own, and they shared an insistence that the routing of the enemy, to make way for the valuable, was the indispensable task of modern criticism. The Georgians and the Bloomsburies were their main enemies. Murry called David Garnett's *Lady into Fox* "about as classical as a carved cocoanut"; and his attack on the anthology *Georgian Poetry* made his reputation as a polemicist.

> All that remains to be said is that Mr. Monro is fond of dogs ("Can you smell the rose?" he says to Dog: "ah, no!") and inclined to fish—both of which are Georgian inclinations.[8]

But the Leavis-Grigson school of uncompromising critical battle was producing a narrowness, a technical preoccupation, that Murry felt to be insufficient in explaining the moral value of good writing, the basic reasons for its importance. He said much later that he and Katherine and Lawrence were alone in their time in not being "phonies" in the *Catcher in the Rye* sense (indeed, the similarity of Katherine and Salinger is unexpected and striking); they had a concept of seriousness that included political and social morality, a notion that the new critics looked on as inimical to the pure attention to the text they demanded.

"In Defence of Fielding" is the essay where Murry took Leavis to task. Murry states his own point of view:

> I admire Fielding the writer; and I admire Fielding the man. . . . Generosity of soul, he seems to say, is rare in either [class]; but where it exists, it reveals class-distinction as the accident he asserted it to be.[9]

This is why Fielding's contemporaries called him "low," and why Fielding satirized Richardson's "rather fulsome picture of the upper classes." But this kind of moral stance, which seems to Murry both admirable and important, does not interest Leavis. Leavis says of Fielding,

> He is important not because he leads to Mr JB Priestley but because he leads to Jane Austen, to appreciate whose distinction is to feel that life is not long enough to permit of one's giving much time to Fielding or any to Mr Priestley.

Murry dismisses the reference to Priestley as "bad manners," and asks whether Leavis's appreciation of those he terms "major" writers has spoiled his ability to delight in Fielding.

> If so, it is a lamentable end to a lifetime meritoriously spent in literary scrutiny.

This was written in the early 1950s, when the Georgians were long since routed and the Moderns, including Lawrence, enshrined— partly because of the efforts of both Leavis and Murry. But Leavis is still fighting old battles, and Murry is able to enlarge the scope of his pantheon and, as always, to relate literature to life itself.

As far back as *The Problem of Style*, the book derived from his 1920 Oxford lectures, he is pointing out that stylistic perfection is conspicuously missing from most of the works that have been felt to be "great"; and his own canon is established for quite other reasons.

I, personally, find it impossible to regard this problem of style for long without being compelled to relate it to the practice and possibilities of the present time; and inevitably I find myself more or less out of sympathy, or rather out of living contact, with styles that seem to me remote from our present necessities.[10]

Murry loved the kind of artist who could perform the miracle for him, who could put him in touch with life by the intensity and communicability of the artist's own experience. This is what Keats did for him, what Lawrence did, what Katherine did. He would not have loved these people so much if he had not felt that he himself had lost the faculty for life, and that they gave it back to him. But he could not have responded to them so fully had he not been halfway there already. He felt, indeed, that he was different from them, but that if all had gone well with him in early life, he would have been of their company. There are signs of his connectedness with life—his excellence at practical labor on the land; his successes with women. Frieda Lawrence wrote to him, interestingly reversing the received notion about him and Katherine: "You weren't a pure intellectual as your farm shows, but she was. . . . you never wanted to be a highbrow." [11]

He was by no means, in fact, the desiccated intellectual portrayed in the many parodies of him that Lawrence and Lawrence's other disciple, Aldous Huxley, engaged in. If he had been, he could never have offered Katherine the loving support, the passionate involvement with life, that were necessary to her art. Nevertheless, Huxley insisted on satirizing him as Burlap in *Point Counter Point*—a straight copy of the attacks of Lawrence, whom Huxley (like Murry) admired as the "natural man" who was everything that he himself was not. Huxley's attacks, and Murry's counterattacks, present us with the curious picture of two of England's most topheavy intellectuals skirmishing for position as true acolyte and blood brother of the sexy and charismatic Lawrence, each accusing his rival of bloodless intellectualism.

The general unpopularity of Murry during the 1930s and '40s had other causes. The English in general did not care whether he was intellectual or emotional; but they were offended by his adherence to such unpopular causes as pacifism and socialism. Moreover, he was a petit-bourgeois with the education of a gentleman; he was an incessant autobiographer, revealing not only his thoughts and the outward events of his life, but the emotional and sexual complexities of it; he went "too far" in both religion and politics. Further, he had the temerity to put forward the claims of foreign or otherwise unacceptable writers—Lawrence, Dostoevsky, Joyce, Proust—and to relate their achievements to those of Shakespeare and Keats. To the conventional mentality of his time, all these things were enough to get him accused of the American vice of "earnestness."

The attacks of the Bloomsbury set took a contradictory line. The attitude represented by Virginia Woolf is repeated, without qualification or criticism, by her biographer Quentin Bell, when he describes how, for her, Murry came to represent what she called "the Underworld."

> She used this term with malicious intent and certainly with a kind of snobbery, sometimes with a purely social meaning, but also to classify those who were not so much creative artists as critics and commentators—people who could write a clever essay or a smart review; people who were more interested in reputations than in talents. . . . Grub Street, I suppose, has always been like this. . . . But for her the perpetual president and oracle of the Underworld was John Middleton Murry, for he added another ingredient—a high moral tone, a pretentious philosophy borrowed in part from his friend D. H. Lawrence—which allowed the game to be played under the cover of deep, manly, visceral feelings and virtuous protestations. I think that most of Virginia's generalisations about the Underworld are really based upon Murry; he was so very much "the coming man." She and Lytton agreed that he would probably end as Professor of English Literature at Oxford or Cambridge. [12]

Virginia's inaccurate prediction is an index of the extent to which snobbery had warped her judgment, and made her see intellectual opportunism and charlatanry where the rest of the English reading public saw an embarrassment of sincerity and awkward conviction.

She and Katherine considered each other their only female colleague; but before examining their relation to each other as writers, it is worth mentioning that Virginia's first impression of Katherine (and, incidentally, of the hapless LM) was as wildly askew as her condemnation of Murry. She wrote in her diary for October 11, 1917,

> We could both wish that our first impression of K.M. was not that she stinks like a—well, civet cat that had taken to street walking. In truth, I'm a little shocked by her commonness at first sight; lines so hard and cheap. However, when this diminishes, she is so intelligent and inscrutable that she repays friendship. . . . A munition worker called Leslie Moor came to fetch her—another of these females on the border land of propriety and naturally inhabiting the underworld—rather vivacious, sallow skinned, without any attachment to one place rather than another.

Lawrence's attacks on Murry, though even more vicious, were more to the point. There is even something furiously loving about them. Gerald in *Women in Love* is not really Murry; but the hero of the story "Jimmy and the Desperate Woman" indisputably is. It is an imaginative sending of Murry the Oxford intellectual into Lawrence's own mining country, with comic results. The hero falls in love with the wife of a miner and brings her back to London, but he finds that she is still irrevocably the property of her very masculine husband. It is yet another excursion into the tedious Lawrentian question—who will get the woman to submit. Murry's precipitate quality with women is well described, as is the search that culminated in his marriage to Betty:

> He imagined to himself some really *womanly* woman, to whom he should be *only* "fine and strong," and not for one moment "the poor little man." Why not some simple uneducated girl, some Tess of the D'Urbervilles, some wistful Gretchen, some humble Ruth gleaning an aftermath? Why not? Surely the world was full of such! [13]

Lawrence hated the Murry who had refused him—whatever it was that Murry did refuse him. He was jealous of Murry's ability to earn money at journalism, and jealous of Katherine. He wrote to Murry, who had sent him her posthumous book,

> I got *Dove's Nest* here. Thank you very much. Poor Katherine, she is delicate and touching—but not *great!* Why say great? [14]

The next year, he wrote,

> Your articles in the *Adelphi* always annoy me. Why care so much about your own fishiness or fleshiness? Why make it so important? Can't you focus yourself outside yourself? Not for ever focused on yourself, *ad nauseam?* [15]

There is an inescapable feeling that Lawrence, in letters like these, was partly addressing himself. The man who had so signally failed to get other men to join with him in some enterprise that would "transcend the personal," and who explored the world—as Murry did—through the medium of his own psyche, was maddened by his failure, and by the limitations of his own technique. Just as he attacked Katherine for her weakness in succumbing to tuberculosis partly because he knew he had it himself, so he attacks Murry for qualities he is trying to root out of his own personality.

What irked him was that Murry had suffered when he, Lawrence, should have had the monopoly of suffering; that Murry then made money, when he, Lawrence the genius, should have made more. In fact, Murry had gotten out from under his thumb. "Submission" is his theme. He wanted submission, and he didn't get it. Murry moved away from the house Lawrence had chosen for him; he wouldn't print many of the articles Lawrence sent him. He reiterated his accusations that Murry was a worm, a Judas, just because he was enraged that Murry was independent of him at last.

The attacks that writers made on each other throughout this period have baffled many chroniclers. Murry's brother Richard has recently suggested that this "two-faced" quality, friendliness in public and character assassination in private or in print, has to do with the fact that writers in the 1920s, at least those who were trying to break with literary convention, needed each other's moral support and yet were fighting fiercely for their own independence. Just as Katherine struggled for emotional and creative independence, and at the same time desperately needed love and support, she and Lawrence and Virginia Woolf needed artistic allies, yet jealously guarded their own uniqueness.

The sexual struggle was bound up with the artistic one. To bring Freudian discoveries about sexuality in literature was one of their aims; and sexual liberation was as important to Bloomsbury as it was to Lawrence. But these innovations set up tension and guilt in the innovators, and some of their fury and inconsistency has to be seen in this light.

The extent to which the imperatives of the modern movement had distorted Murry's literary personality can be seen when we compare his sufferings with Katherine and Lawrence, the most profound and intense emotional experiences of his life, with the serenity he eventually achieved.

Murry's last years were spent peacefully at the community farm he founded. His erratic ideas on farming dated from 1920, "when a complete stranger said to me on top of a London bus: 'No civilization can be secure that wastes its sewage as ours does.' " Though his own role was closer to that of a country squire than to anything we would now associate with the leader of a commune, he had found one way of perpetuating the English village idea, which remained the focus of his nostalgia.

By the time of his death in 1957, the strands of his early life had been woven together. Weg and Col married; he played with his grandchildren; with the death of Betty (from "malignant hypertension"), all four of his children were, as he had hoped, reunited with him and Mary. To him, Lodge Farm was in some sense the Heron, and his children were in some sense the children he had dreamed of with Katherine. His friend Max Plowman said,

> JMM is one of those people who don't miss any of the steps of experience; they follow in inevitable sequence and are followed with a fidelity unique in my experience. (It is for that fidelity that I love him as Jonathan loved David.) [16]

Katherine would have recognized him in this description.

CHAPTER 4

The Art of
Katherine Mansfield

Death is the mother of beauty, mystical,
Within whose burning bosom we devise
Our earthly mothers waiting, sleeplessly.

—*Wallace Stevens*

It has always been hard for critics to describe what it was that
Katherine Mansfield did—the particular kind of magic that she exerted on all who came close to her, and still exerts on all who read
her attentively enough. She was not a very self-conscious artist;
Murry has described how fleeting her inspirations were, and how
she had to write more and more rapidly, until her hand became all
but indecipherable, in order to put down a story before it vanished.
She never knew where or how she would find the conditions to
write, and her travels often seem aimless and impulsive because
they are in search of something so elusive and nebulous.

All the same, she has described in some detail her attention to
technique, and the relation she was aiming for with her material.
In her self-discovery as an artist, she also discovered herself as a
person—the perfection of her technique was never an empty perfection of style or construction, but a perfection of attitude. Thus to
analyze what she did in terms of point of view, construction, vo-
cabulary, and the rest of the critic's arsenal is of limited use; much
more relevant is the Murry style of criticism, of thinking and feeling oneself into the mind of the creator.

The moribund short story was revived by her, and she absorbed the lessons of Chekhov and made them accessible to her successors in English. Her unique achievement was to capture in prose some of the qualities of English lyric poetry—and why in prose? Middleton Murry spoke slightingly of the audience for poetry in his day, saying that the novel had had, since the middle of the nineteenth century, the mass audience that the Elizabethan dramatists once had. He also observed pertinently that writers wrote not only what they were inspired to write, but what they could sell—and in his day, that meant novels.

He might well have gone on to say that without an allowance from her father, and intermittent support from her husband, Katherine Mansfield might have found herself writing novels—or at least not waiting so long and patiently for inspiration to visit her. Indigence might have provided the kind of spur to her talent that imminent death eventually proved to be. As it was, she knew that prose was her only guarantee of any audience at all, and she embarked on her search for "a kind of special prose" in which to embody her New Zealand vision.

Prose was a medium she felt to be unexplored; its possibilities had never been realized. The modern poets of her time were also, in a sense, moving toward "special prose" in their rejection of the "iambic straitjacket" and the rules of rhyme. Free verse and rhythmic prose were capable of subtler effects than the kind of verse the Georgians, say, were still writing. Eliot represented, from this point of view, one reaction against poetry—Mansfield a reaction against prose. He was making poetry more prosaic; she was making prose realize the possibilities of poetry. She recognized this when she wrote to Virginia Woolf, about Eliot, "I don't think he is a poet— Prufrock is after all a short story." [1]

Katherine Mansfield and Virginia Woolf were together in the development of "special prose," because the feminine sensibility as it existed in them was uniquely equipped to fill the void left by the demise of the traditional Victorian novel. The artificialities of both prose and poetry, as previously categorized, were giving way to a looser, freer kind of thing, which allowed their delicately nuanced perceptions to be expressed. What they had in common explains a great deal about the peculiar strengths of women's art at this period; the differences between them reveal the dangers, the complexities, of the task they set themselves. They both felt themselves to be part of a movement that encompassed all the arts, especially painting, as well as writing; the contact with painters that Virginia got through her sister, the painter Vanessa Bell, was very like the kind of conversation that Katherine had during Murry's days as an art critic, and later from his brother Richard.

Music as well as painting helped Katherine to find the images she sought. She wrote in her *Journal*, after a visit to Fergusson's rooms,

> Very beautiful, O God! is a blue tea-pot with two white cups attending: a red apple among oranges addeth fire to flame—in the white book-cases the books fly up and down in scales of colour, with pink and lilac notes recurring, until nothing remains but them, sounding over and over. [2]

This early passage is straining for its effects of music and color, but it does have something of the effect of a Matisse. And it was to the Fauvist painters that she turned for her first examples of the kind of "direct contact with life" that she wanted to capture in her writing. Toward the end of her life, she wrote to the painter Dorothy Brett about the Post-Impressionist exhibition of ten years earlier, in particular about Van Gogh's sunflowers, "They taught me something about writing, which was queer, a kind of freedom—or rather, a shaking free." [3] When she went to Cornwall, it refreshed her vision in the way it was to do for the English painters who absorbed the lessons of the Fauves:

> I am going to *Looe* which is full of pigs and bluebells, cabbages and butterflies and fishermen's orange shirts flung out to dry on pink apricot trees. [4]

If her color came from the Post-Impressionists, her sense of sound and rhythm came from the years she had spent playing the cello. Her playing and singing were much admired by Murry; early in her life, she had been undecided whether music or writing was to be her career. She wrote to Richard Murry about what this had done for her craft:

In *Miss Brill* I chose not only the length of every sentence, but even the sound of every sentence. I chose the rise and fall of every paragraph to fit her, and to fit her on that day at that very moment. After I'd written it I read it aloud—numbers of times—just as one would *play over* a musical composition—trying to get it nearer and nearer to the expression of Miss Brill—until it fitted her.[5]

Precision of effect was the ruling passion of both Katherine Mansfield and Virginia Woolf, and it was part of their lesson from poetry. As early as 1915, Katherine was writing to Koteliansky,

. . . the very dampness of the salt at supper that night and the way it came out on your plate the exact shape of the salt spoon . . .

Do you, too, feel an infinite delight and value in *detail*—not for the sake of detail but for the life *in* the life of it.[6]

To Richard Murry she wrote some of her best letters about technique; he was then experimenting with printmaking and drawing, and they shared a common concern with craft.

People have hardly begun to write yet . . . —now I mean prose. Take the very best of it. Aren't they still cutting up sections rather than tackling the whole of a mind? [7]

One could only "tackle the whole of a mind" through the choice of significant detail—and finding that detail meant, for Katherine, being in touch with real life—with living people and things—so that a fresh, uncluttered vision could happen without the intermediaries of tradition and convention. Virginia Woolf's journey was inward rather than outward, so to speak—a movement that produced effects richer and more delicate than anything Katherine was to achieve, but that eventually took its toll of her life.

Nevertheless, both Katherine and Virginia Woolf started out with the same preoccupations. Katherine wrote in 1917,

We have got the same job, Virginia, and it is really very curious and thrilling that we should both, quite apart from each other, be after so very nearly the same thing. We are, you know; there's no denying it.[8]

Katherine's malicious wit was sometimes startlingly reminiscent of the kind of thing that is so familiar from the letters and diaries of Virginia herself. Katherine wrote to her,

> Here is Murry. "I want to read you a note on Perception. Do you mind?" "Not at all. Pray proceed." And now an enormous blue Government Note Book is opening . . .[9]

But Katherine's effort was always to overcome this impulse in herself, to achieve the vision of love rather than of distance. Although she could admire Virginia Woolf's perfect technique, which in the subtlety of its music and haunting atmosphere surpasses Katherine's more earthbound quality, she could not stand the use to which it was put. She and Murry were close to the Bloomsburies, who worked on the *Athenaeum* and befriended them both up to a point; but they felt irrevocably divided from them—and this division expressed itself in views about the moral function of art. They felt that Bloomsbury had made an empty, snobbish game of both life and art; and that as the war had made a new organization of society necessary, so it also demanded a relevant, urgent search for a new art. Murry expressed this urgency in his criticism, in his attacks on Bloomsbury elitism and his elevation of Lawrence. Katherine preached by example, Murry by precept—but Katherine expressed her feelings directly in her letters.

> Inwardly I despise them all for a set of *cowards*. We have to face our war. They won't. . . . What *has* been, stands. But Jane Austen could not write *Northanger Abbey* now—or if she did, I'd have none of her. . . . *utter coldness* and indifference . . .[10]

She reviewed Virginia Woolf's *Night and Day* for the *Athenaeum*, and made the perceptive and damning observation that

> With Miss Austen, it is first her feeling for life, and then her feeling for writing; but with Mrs. Woolf these feelings are continually giving way the one to the other, so that the urgency of either is impaired.[11]

In her letters to Jack, she went further.

> Talk about intellectual snobbery—her book *reeks* of it. . . . The war
> never has been: that is what its message is.[12]

She would have undoubtedly had kinder words for the later novels,
beginning with *Mrs. Dalloway*; but she could never have got over
the basic difference between herself and Virginia Woolf—the perfection of technique, divorced from life because the writer herself
was not fully engaged in it; and Katherine's subordination of technique to emotion. Virginia Woolf's coldness and Katherine Mansfield's warmth are not arbitrary choices, or mere artistic prefer-
ences—they are the basic characters underneath the style—the
"soul's desperate choice."

Mrs. Dalloway was not published until after Katherine's death.
But its similarity to some of Mansfield's later work is striking, and
the development of Virginia Woolf's style in her subsequent novels
leads one to wonder what new directions Katherine would have
found had she lived. The resemblance between the two writers at
this time can be seen in a passage from *Mrs. Dalloway*. Lucrezia
takes the arm of her mad husband to cross the street—

> She had a right to his arm, though it was without feeling. He would give
> her, who was so simple, so impulsive, only twenty-four, without friends
> in England, who had left Italy for his sake, a piece of bone.

That is a Katherine Mansfield effect—being plunged into Lucrezia's thoughts in mid-action and knowing that that is where we are,
without explanation. Both writers insisted that the "scaffolding" of a
story be dismantled, that the artificialities of plot be done away
with. Most of Virginia Woolf's criticisms of the Mansfield technique are aimed at those stories that retain a closely organized plot
line. But Katherine Mansfield uses dramatic irony in a more skill-
ful way: the Woolf novels often seem like long meditations on the
characters' feelings, while Katherine Mansfield's dramatic construction gives you the emotions themselves. The wrenching effect of
such stories as "Ma Parker" and "The Doll's House" is partly the
result of their being seen through the eyes of naive characters—in
the first story, Ma Parker herself describes the death of her little
grandson, last in a series of tragedies that has left her no one to love

and not even a place to cry about it. In "The Doll's House," the cold, unsentimental child's-eye view of the despised Kelvey sisters, who are shooed from the garden after one glimpse of the elaborate new doll's house, contrasts painfully with the reader's emotions. Dorothy Parker was also to use this technique, and with similar effect—playing off wit against poignancy. And Katherine Mansfield, though she is not usually thought of as a comic writer, used her irony for comic as well as tragic effects. The widowed mother in "The Doves' Nest" plucks up her courage and invites the nice, well-dressed Englishman to lunch:

> "I think a leg of lamb would be nice, don't you, dear?" said Mother. "The lamb is so very small and delicate just now. And men like nothing so much as plain roast meat. Yvonne prepares it so nicely, too, with that little frill of paper lace round the top of the leg. It always reminds me of something—I can't think what. But it certainly makes it look very attractive indeed."

The inadmissibility of the idea that she is offering the man a leg with a lacy frill round it is precisely, vividly witty, in itself and not because of the author's attitude toward it, in a way that few things in Virginia Woolf are simple enough to be.

Virginia Woolf's more formal use of imagery, and Katherine Mansfield's liveliness with it, are illustrated by the flower imagery in *Mrs. Dalloway* and in "The Garden Party," which is in a sense Mansfield's variation on the same theme. Mrs. Dalloway, the society woman preparing for a party, receiving a visit from an old lover, at the center of her carefully arranged London world, is contrasted with the mad, shell-shocked Septimus and his Italian wife, who wander through the same London in a vain attempt to stave off his suicide. The two movements of the story converge, until a guest at Mrs. Dalloway's party tells her of the death of Septimus. Mr. Dalloway gives his wife roses instead of telling her he loves her; the flowers are a substitute for emotion, a symbol of the distance between them. Mrs. Dalloway goes to a flower shop to buy flowers for her party; she suddenly feels that the flowers are the embodiment of all her love of luxury and the London season; but although the effect is rich and sustained, it is curiously disembodied.

And then, opening her eyes, how fresh, like frilled linen clean from a laundry laid in wicker trays, the roses looked; and dark and prim the red carnations, holding their heads up; and all the sweet peas spreading in their bowls, tinged violet, snow white, pale—as if it were the evening and girls in muslin frocks came out to pick sweet peas and roses after the superb summer's day, with its almost blue-black sky, its delphiniums, its carnations, its arum lilies, was over;

"The Garden Party," too, deals with the contrast between preparations for a party and the death of a workingman in the nearby cottages; Laura, the daughter, at first feels that the party should be called off, but after a visit to the cottages, accepts the idea of mortality lying just under the surface of life. Unlike Virginia Woolf's flowers, which are often substitutes for emotion or for people, the flowers in this story embody emotion. Even the roses have feelings:

As for the roses, you could not help feeling they understood that roses are the only flowers that impress people at garden-parties;

The flowering karaka trees ("like trees you imagined growing on a desert island") must be hidden by the marquee. Symbol of New Zealand, they are out of place on this day when conventionality means Englishness. Mrs. Sheridan is the one who brings the florist into things, with her insistence that "for once in my life I shall have enough canna lilies." The bought flowers, now changed to arum lilies, are considered as a gift for the wife of the dead man— "people of that class are so impressed by arum lilies"—but Laura does not take them because "the stems would ruin her lace frock." The inappropriate gesture does not take place; the death makes such class-conscious things irrelevant.

Mrs. Dalloway has two main characters: Clarissa Dalloway herself, and mad, suicidal Septimus. Neither one loves other people as other people love them, and they are constantly being reminded of this failing. Peter Walsh, the rejected lover, says to himself,

But women, he thought, shutting his pocket-knife, don't know what passion is. They don't know the meaning of it to men. Clarissa was as cold as an icicle. There she would sit on the sofa by his side, let him take her hand, give him one kiss on the cheek—

And Clarissa replies in her mind to Peter, who she imagines has said to her in his mind, "what's the sense of your parties?"—

> What's your love? she might say to him. And she knew his answer; how it is the most important thing in the world and no woman possibly understood it.

Men have love; Clarissa has parties—balancing-acts of groups of people, the creation of patterns, a way to keep a distance between herself and emotion.

> Love and religion! thought Clarissa. . . . How detestable, how detestable they are! . . . —love and religion would destroy that whatever it was, the privacy of the soul.

At the heart of Virginia Woolf's books is a cold, fearful shrinking, an idealization of madness and death. Her alienation chills as much as her technique enthralls. And one clue to why this is can be found in *To the Lighthouse*, the most emotional of her novels because it is the story of her parents' marriage, her sadness over the early death of her idealized mother, and her long struggle with her father. It is a desperately sad book. James, the child, is at first denied a boat trip to the lighthouse during a summer holiday in Scotland; years later, the trip is finally made, and James receives a coveted word of praise from his father—but it is too late, and the moment has none of the sense of epiphany, of celebration, that Katherine Mansfield brought to such climaxes. The father has a habit of shouting at people, unexpectedly, "we perish, each alone"—and this is the sense of distance and alienation that Virginia Woolf's novels so perfectly express.

Early in the book, there is a key to the source of these feelings. James's mother is reading him a story, and the moment is interrupted by a demand from the father:

into this delicious fecundity, this fountain and spray of life, the fatal ste-
rility of the male plunged itself, like a beak of brass, barren and bare. He
wanted sympathy. . . . So boasting of her capacity to surround and pro-
tect, there was scarcely a shell of herself left for her to know herself by;
all was so lavished and spent; and James, as he stood stiff between her
knees, felt her rise in a rosy-flowered fruit tree laid with leaves and
dancing boughs into which the beak of brass, the arid scimitar of his father, the egotistical man, plunged and smote, demanding sympathy.

Virginia Woolf identifies with the son in this Oedipal struggle; and
the imagery recalls nothing so much as D. H. Lawrence's view of
the war between the sexes, seen from the other side. To him, the
"beak of brass" is what the unfeminine woman develops, in place
of her submissive softness, and what tears at the man who is attempting to subdue her. The two writers are playing the same
game; the ultimate aridity of their technique is related to this failure
to transcend the sex war in their own lives, and therefore in their
works. Not for them the moments when love triumphs over inability to love.

Lawrence and Mansfield had, as we have seen, many similarities, temperamental as well as strictly technical. His physical immediacy was close to what she was trying to do: "When he bites
into an apple," she said of his writing, "it is a sharp, sweet, fresh
apple from the growing tree." [13] For both, psychological reality
started with a search for the hidden sources of emotion: the work-
ing-out in life of the conflicts of childhood. In this they were both
harbingers of modernism. But the difference in their ways of presenting this reality shows something of why the early Lawrence is so
much more vital and immediate than the later one; and why Katherine Mansfield was able to transcend and resolve her own conflicts, while Lawrence spent years fighting the same fruitless battles.

In *Fantasia of the Unconscious*, Lawrence sets out the basic
source of his own conflict:

The unhappy woman beats about for her insatiable satisfaction, seeking
whom she may devour. And usually, she turns to her child. Here she
provokes what she wants. Here, in her own son who belongs to her, she
seems to find the last perfect response for which she is craving. He is a

medium to her, she provokes from him her own answer. So she throws herself into a last great love for her son, a final and fatal devotion, that which would have been the richness and strength of her husband and is poison to her boy. . . .[14]

Lawrence was to work out the psychological consequences of this love in all his works and in his life. In the view of Murry, it is the crippling effect of this love that prevented Lawrence from fulfilling himself in adult love, and turned him to empty sexuality. The love of his mother was a love that no other woman could compete with.

Katherine, too, felt that the relation with her parents had inhibited her capacity for emotional development. She felt rejected by her mother, attracted and repelled by her father, and jealous of her brother. The death of her brother released her creative energies in the same way that the death of his mother released those of Lawrence. But instead of suffering these wounds over and over, she was left with enough psychological strength to attempt to work them out—in work, in love with Jack, in a new relation to her family. In a long letter about "blaming" parents, she talks of what she has tried to do:

One is NEVER free until one has done blaming somebody or praising somebody for what is bad and good in one. . . . Life is relationship— it's giving and taking—but that's not quite the same thing as making others *responsible*—is it? But like everything else in life—I mean all suffering, however great—we have to get over it—to cease from harking back to it—to grin and bear it and to hide the wounds. More than that, and far more true is we have to find the *gift* in it. We can't afford to waste such an expenditure of feeling; we have to learn from it—and we *do*, I most deeply believe, come to be thankful for it. By saying we can't afford to . . . waste . . . feeling! I sound odious and cynical. I don't feel it. What I mean is. *Everything must be accepted.*[15]

She has entered the world of Chekhov's phrase—"where all is forgiven, and it would be strange not to forgive." That world Lawrence was never to reach.

Look, for example, at a scene that appears in both of their works—the birth of a baby boy who melts his mother's heart with unexpected love. In *Sons and Lovers,* it is a description of Lawrence's own birth.

> In her arms lay the delicate baby. Its deep blue eyes, always looking up at her unblinking, seemed to draw her innermost thoughts out of her. She . . . had not wanted this child to come, and there it lay in her arms and pulled at her heart. . . . A wave of hot love went over her to the infant.

In "At the Bay," the baby is Chummie.

> The boy had turned over. He lay facing her, and he was no longer asleep. His dark-blue, baby eyes were open; he looked as though he was peeping at his mother. And suddenly his face dimpled; it broke into a wide, toothless smile, a perfect beam, no less.
> "I'm here!" that happy smile seemed to say. "Why don't you like me?" . . .
> Linda was so astonished at the confidence of this little creature. . . . Ah no, be sincere. That was not what she felt; it was something far different, it was something so new, so . . . The tears danced in her eyes; she breathed in a small whisper to the boy, "Hallo, my funny!"

Lawrence's description has in it the implication that the mother's love contains the sinister seed of the boy's crippled manhood. In "At the Bay," love is the sudden coming of grace, the release of the mother's heart from her own crippling inability to love. It is wholly benign in its effect, and marks Katherine's own forgiveness of her mother for failing to love her daughters, of her brother for being the favored child. Love and religion—there is something in the way the baby provokes a response from the world around him that is like the baby Jesus drawing worship from stars, Magi, and the very animals in the stable in the Christmas carols. To Katherine Mansfield, love may be difficult to achieve, but it is wholly good and wholly necessary; to Lawrence, it is devouring and destructive.

Mansfield never grappled with the mature sex-relation as Lawrence did; it is her great limitation and his great strength. But she saw how his frantic imaginings of the ideal relationship had carried him far from the intuitive perception of life that she had valued in him. His sexual dogmatism had weakened his art and led him into fruitless abstraction. He was a living reproach to the aridities of Bloomsbury; but he developed his own peculiar aridity as an artist. She put her finger on it in her criticism of his story "The Lost Girl."

> Oh, don't forget where Alvina feels *a trill in her bowels*, and discovers herself with child. A TRILL. What does that mean? And why is it so peculiarly offensive from a man? Because it is *not on this plane* that the emotions of others are conveyed to the imagination. It's a kind of sinning against art.[16]

What was the matter with Lawrence, that he committed this sin? His relations with both the Murrys provide some clues—clues that Jack was to follow up when he wrote *Son of Woman*, his presentation of Lawrence as the symbolic man of his age. The sexual wounds of his childhood had left Lawrence with an inability to achieve the complete relation with a woman that he continually sought. Because he was conscious of himself as an emotional and sexual cripple, his insistence on the woman's submission became an obsession. To Murry, this was the central problem of alienated modern man: his powerlessness had given him power fantasies that could never be satisfied, and his lovelessness had led him into a sexual search that was doomed to failure. Both these tendencies were embodied in Lawrence; and indeed, though Murry does not say so, the power fantasies in his novels have much of the fascist in them—he is the jack-booted male tyrant, in imagination at least, that Sylvia Plath tried to exorcise in her poetry.

A long letter Lawrence wrote to Katherine in 1918 explains some of the springs of these ideas, and shows why they led to the explosions that drove the Murrys away from Cornwall.

> The man . . . casts himself as it were into her womb, and she, the Magna Mater, receives him with gratification. This is a kind of incest. It seems to me it is what Jack does to you, and what repels and fascinates you. I have done it, and now struggle all my might to get out. In a way, Frieda is the devouring mother. It is awfully hard, once the sex relation has gone this way, to recover. If we don't recover, we die. But Frieda

says I am antediluvian in my positive attitude. I do think a woman must yield some sort of precedence to a man, and he must take this precedence. I do think men must go ahead absolutely in front of their women, without turning round to ask for permission or approval from their women. Consequently the women must follow as it were unquestioningly. I can't help it, I believe this. Frieda doesn't. Hence our fight.

Secondly, I do believe in friendship. I believe tremendously in friendship between man and man, a pledging of men to each other inviolably. But I have not ever met or formed such friendship. Also I believe in the same way in friendship between men and women, and between women and women, sworn, pledged, eternal, as eternal as the marriage bond, and as deep. But I have not ever met or formed such friendship.[17]

Katherine was to realize both these forms of friendship. She got the loyalty that Lawrence wanted from Murry; and she and LM formed the bond that Lawrence and Murry failed to achieve. She wrote to LM, "The truth is friendship is to me every bit as sacred and eternal as marriage."[18] Why was she able to get the kind of relation with other people that Lawrence wanted? Why was her art to remain valid instead of turning to exhortation and abstraction? There is something pathetic in his frantic insistence on friendship, love, which is denied him and so spontaneously given to her. She did not insist on her own primacy, on a rigid definition of roles; a loving person herself, she received love. When she and LM saw a blackened, withered fig tree, with a dark stem and black leaves,

> L.M. who was with me said "Of course the *explanation* is that one must never cease from giving." The fig tree had no figs—so Christ cursed it. *Did you ever!* There's such a story buried under the whole thing—isn't there—if only one could dig it out.[19]

Looking backward, it is clear how deeply conventional were Lawrence's views about women, and how unconventional it was of Murry not to accept them, when he accepted so much else that Lawrence had to say. To Lawrence, it was intolerable that a woman should demand the rights of the artist. This is why the existence of Murry was so crucially important to Katherine: here was a man who could let her have her genius, her primacy, and still give the love she needed.

Katherine, too, was concerned with the question of the submissive woman. She was not sure in her own mind whether that was what women should be. Her Grandmother is praised and revered in the stories for her perfect self-abnegation; the Mother is criticized for her selfishness. But ultimately, it was impossible to accept the notion that the submissive woman was the greater; it is the demand for submission that alienates Linda from her husband, as autonomy would have given her happiness.

Lawrence related his own treatment of this question to his opinion of Katherine. In *The Plumed Serpent*, Kate Leslie (named, perhaps, after Katherine and LM, but modeled on Frieda) is contrasted with the submissive Teresa. To the man it seems that

> Teresa, with her silence and infinitely soft administering, . . . would heal him far better than Kate, with her expostulation and her opposition.
>
> Kate was accustomed to looking on other women as inferiors. . . . suddenly she had to question herself whether Teresa was not a greater woman than she.
>
> Teresa! A greater woman than Kate? What a blow! Surely it was impossible.
>
> Yet there it was.

Lawrence's refusal to recognize Katherine as an artist, to allow a woman any value other than ministering to the male, has here carried him into territory where few will follow him—the view that LM's service is worth more than Katherine's genius.

The healthiness of Katherine Mansfield's art, her ability to use her imagery in an emotion-laden way, to express a sense of transcendent love, has to do with her psychological strength as a person in comparison with Virginia Woolf and Lawrence. This is why she could achieve a full love-relationship with Murry, and use it to gain the sustenance she needed for her work.

But her love for him was not without its hesitations, denials, and failings. He scarcely ever appears as the hero in her stories; more often he is the villain. Her failure to portray adult love fully is related to these flaws in her own relation with him, and shows what a difficult time she had in trying to move beyond the youthful phase of the life cycle. The struggle between hesitation and acceptance, between love and refusal, is spelt out most fully in her imagery. If flowers represent the gratuitous joy of life, the loving impulse, the imagery of food that permeates her stories carries the message of the attractions and repulsions of sexuality.

Katherine herself notices the pervasiveness of this image: "I always seem to be talking of emotion in terms of food." [20] Not that, as George Henry Lewes once suggested, food imagery is natural to the woman writer because she spends her life dealing with food—Katherine could cook, though probably not as well as Lawrence; but the food in her stories is treated from the point of view of the consumer, and could have been written by anyone as familiar with food as three meals a day could make them. It is brought by caterers or servants, or served in hotel dining rooms, or simply exists on the plate before the scene opens.

In Mrs. Poyser's kitchen in *Adam Bede*, we get a full sense of the labor that goes into providing beer and meat for the farm workers every day of the year—how many gallons have to be brewed, the vats of milk for the cheese, the essential discipline that surrounds these crucial tasks. Food is part of the economics of a whole society. For Katherine Mansfield, it is part of the individual relations among human beings—a revelation of character.

The contrast between gluttonousness and fastidiousness is basic to Katherine's sense of herself, and her sense of what she was doing as a writer. She abhors the thought of writing being produced in bulk, as fodder for the masses, in contrast to her own delicate mouthfuls; her reviews are full of strictures on the glut of the novel market:

> "Are they fresh?"
> "Yes, baked to-day, Madame . . ."
> Melancholy, melancholy thought of all those people steadily munching, asking for another, and carrying perhaps a third one home with them in case they should wake up in the night and feel—not hungry, exactly,—but "just a little empty." [21]

In her letters, her gradual alienation from each new place is continually expressed in terms of food. The gluttonous Germans in the Pension are as horrifying as the experiences Katherine was going through there. The cynical, materialistic French earn her contempt because "not a leaf grows in their gardens that is not 'bon pour la cuisine.' " [22] When she is longing to escape from bourgeois England, she writes,

> Now and again a handful of rain is dashed against the window. The church bells have stopped ringing and I know that there is a leg of something with "nice" spring greens, rhubarb tart and custard in every house in Hampstead but mine. [23]

The ideal world she and Jack inhabit together is contrasted with this adult gluttony; but the only place where food is really delicious is the childhood world of her New Zealand stories. It is nursery food—the cream puffs in "The Garden Party," the ice-cream house in "Sun and Moon," Kezia's porridge—it has more in common with the mud pies and leaves of her children's pretend tea parties than with the food served in the German Pension. The brown, glazed roast ducks that appear at the end of "At the Bay" are admissible only because Kezia has witnessed their decapitation, and her acceptance of the whole of life, including its horror, is symbolized by her acceptance of the ducks, adult food though they are.

But food not only reveals character in the people who eat it. It can embody emotion itself—" 'Very Old Pale Cognac'—one can't help pitying it." And the famous passage in which she uses food to reveal her complex emotions about LM:

> "Does nobody want that piece of bread and butter?" says L.M. You would really think from her tone that she was saving the poor little darling from the river or worse, willing to adopt it as her own child and bring it up so that it should never know it was once unwanted. She cannot bear to see solitary little pieces of bread and butter or a lonely little cake—or even a lump of sugar that someone has cruelly, heartlessly left in his saucer. And when you offer her the big cake, she says resignedly: "Oh, well, my dear, I'll just try a slice," as though she knew how sensi-

tive and easily hurt the poor old chap's feelings were, if he's passed by. After all, it can't hurt her.

L.M. is also exceedingly fond of bananas. But she eats them so slowly, so terribly slowly. And they know it—somehow; they realise what is in store for them when she reaches out her hand. I have seen bananas turn absolutely livid with terror on her plate—or pale as ashes. [24]

The loving sympathy of LM, her soft heart, are there—but so is Katherine's touch of horror—the consumptive's horror at the healthy appetite of her caretaker, and the feeling that she herself is LM's prey.

The "ideal" meals in her letters are always those she can imagine sharing with her mother—"unexpected cups of tea brought out of the air, by ravens"—or the tea, brown bread, and cherry jam of her youthful Russophile bohemia. The snacks, the childhood meals— these are to the "whole rich banquet," as she describes it in her reviews, just as her small stories are to the "whole rich banquet" of literature. This is what came to torment her at the end of her life: by keeping herself undevoured, undiminished, by resisting gluttony and sexuality, she had in some way limited her work. At the end of her life, she was trying to reach out to a fuller relation with life, and a fuller acceptance of her love for Murry, which she needed if her work was to expand and become more inclusive.

Her stories deal, very often, with women alone, or with their difficulty in relating to men, or with the solitariness of a human being in the face of the failure of human relationships. There is a sense that her characters are peripheral to life, pushed aside out of the mainstream. But just as she coped with her childhood wounds in a way that Lawrence could not, and made her characters open to love in a way that the women of Virginia Woolf could not, she was, at the end of her life, facing the problem (partly caused by her long illness) of achieving adult emotional relationships in her stories. While she was ill, she could not face and solve this artistic problem—and this is why she so desperately sought a cure.

The central events in her stories, she feels, are often "scamped" —she concentrates on what comes before and after the Garden Party, for example, rather than on the party itself; and the same

thing happens to the lunch party in the Doves' Nest. She regretfully says,

> What I chiefly admire in Jane Austen is that what she promises, she per-
> forms, i.e. if Sir T. is to arrive, we have his arrival at length, and it's ex-
> cellent and excels our expectations. This is rare; it is also my very
> weakest point. Easy to see why. . . .[25]

Does the last sentence indicate that she felt herself pushed to the
edges of life, that because she is not in the center of the stream, her
work cannot be either? Her own expectations from her work are not
fulfilled—nor are her expectations from life—and the two failings
are inescapably connected.

Her *Journal* entry for July 23, 1922, from Montana, shows that
she is trying to break through this very thing. She is dissatisfied with
the stories she is writing:

> NO. Once I have written two more, I shall tackle something different—
> a long story; *At the Bay, with more difficult relationships. That's the
> whole problem.*

This, I believe, is the clue to her abandoning work and looking for
a healing miracle. The Swiss regime had been good for her health,
and she had written "At the Bay," but after that there was no kind
of progress to be made. She had reached the end of her story of the
family group, with herself as the child. Now she needed to move
back toward the center of life, even at risk of life itself.

She had reached the midpoint of life, which seemed to her the
age when people either gave up or turned the corner into the real
serious business of their work. She was ready to abandon the freedom of youth, to commit herself. She says of her first conversation
with Orage, when she was considering entering the Gurdjieff Institute,

> On that occasion I began by telling him how dissatisfied I was with the
> idea that Life must be a lesser thing than we were capable of "imagin-

ing" it to be. I had the feeling that the same thing happened to nearly everybody whom I knew and whom I did not know. No sooner was their youth, with the little force and impetus characteristic of youth, done, than they stopped growing. At the very moment that one felt that now was the time to gather oneself together, to use one's whole strength, to take control, to be an adult, in fact, they seemed content to swop the darling wish of their hearts for innumerable little wishes. Or the image that suggested itself to me was that of a river flowing away in countless little trickles over a dark swamp. . . . sooner or later, in literature at any rate, there sounded an undertone of deep regret. There was an uneasiness, a sense of frustration. One heard, one thought one heard, the cry that began to echo in one's own being: "I have missed it. I have given up. This is not what I want. If this is all, then Life is not worth living." [26]

Katherine felt she had her real task still to accomplish—that all that had gone before had simply cleared the way for real achievement. To Murry, however, she had already accomplished the primary task of the romantic artist: the acceptance, the forgiveness, the perception of beauty in the whole of life. In a sense, he was right: she had passed through Keats's "Vale of soul-making"; she had accepted her coming death, and with it the love of both Murry and LM. She had stopped her furious resistance of the need to be dependent. She had grown up. Her adult vision was not yet fully embodied in her stories, but the letters contained the deepened perception of life that lead her readers to feel that, like Keats, she was capable of a more perfect art than life gave her time to achieve.

And then suffering, bodily suffering such as I've known for three years. It has changed for ever everything—even the *appearance* of the world is not the same—there is something added. *Everything has its shadow.* Is it right to resist such suffering? Do you know I feel it has been an immense privilege. Yes, in spite of all. How blind we little creatures are! . . . We resist, we are terribly frightened. The little boat enters the dark fearful gulf and our only cry is to escape—"put me on land again." But it's useless. Nobody listens. The shadowy figure rows on. One ought to sit still and uncover one's eyes. [27]

This is the passage that made Murry, her most perceptive critic, feel that she had achieved real greatness—that even if she had never written another word, it would place her in his particular pantheon:

> an experiencing nature which obeys the compulsion of experience, which accepts experience truly for what it is, which does not turn the head away or avert the eyes, becomes ultimately the vehicle of a final wisdom. [28]

PART II

George Eliot
&
George Henry Lewes

CHAPTER 1

Each Alone

. . . birds build—but not I build; no, but strain,
Time's eunuch, and not breed one work that wakes.
Mine, O thou lord of life, send my roots rain.

—Gerard Manley Hopkins

The mystery of George Eliot is that for the first thirty-seven years of her life she was Marian Evans, a formidably intellectual spinster, whose strict country upbringing and interest in evangelical Christianity had given way, after the death of her father, to an arduous career as a literary journalist and translator of German theologians. Yet two years after her elopement in 1854 with George Henry Lewes, whose wife's adultery had freed him in fact though not in law from marital obligations, she became one of the most instinctive and psychologically penetrating novelists ever to write in English. It is as if she were waiting, throughout the painful emotional struggles of her young womanhood, for the moment when she was mature and confident enough to accept the love that awakened her creativity; and as if Lewes, brilliant, witty, and amorous in his youth, had achieved enough depth of character to discover the passionate woman behind the forbidding mask. Though the heroines of her books are all searching for a fulfilling role, and several of the heroes are examples of selflessness and humility, she never wrote a story that is as triumphantly satisfying as the story of her life.

George Eliot was born in 1819, the same year as Queen Victoria, near Coventry in the English Midlands. Her father, Robert

Evans, managed the estates of several large landowners in the district, principally that of the Newdigate family—his employer was the founder of the Newdigate prize at Oxford. The parish of Chilvers Coton was still a country district, but its landscape of quiet hedgerows and streams and plowed fields was beginning to undergo the transformation of the Industrial Revolution. The work of Robert Evans had ceased to be purely agricultural, and he supervised canal-building, coal mining, and the cutting and selling of timber. Today, the "George Eliot country" is completely covered by the works of the automobile industry; and it was the early phase of this rapid change to industrial prosperity that formed her imagination. The new manufacturing interests were beginning to challenge the supremacy of the landed families with whom Robert Evans identified himself—evangelicalism, rationalism, and interest in science were the cultural manifestations of this social change.

Robert Evans's first wife had died, leaving him with two children, Robert and Fanny. His second wife was Christiana Pearson, of a prosperous farming family. They had three children—Isaac, Chrissey, and Mary Ann (who was to call herself Marian, Polly, and Pollian, as well as Mrs. Lewes, Mrs. Cross, and George Eliot). The birth of the third child weakened Mrs. Evans's health, and she was a remote, ailing figure throughout Mary Ann's childhood.

It is tempting to see the members of George Eliot's immediate family as they appeared in her early novels—to identify Robert Evans with Adam Bede; the Pearson aunts with the aunts in *The Mill on the Floss*; Isaac with Tom Tulliver; Chrissey with Lucy Deane and (later) Celia Brooke. Though the novelist herself claimed that her books contained no portraits of real people, she would hardly have denied that her own experience went into the emotional relationships she portrayed. Though so few family documents have survived that we can only speculate, everything George Eliot herself said about her early life indicates that it was centered around her father and brother, and that the women in her family represented pressures toward conventionality. She is practically silent on the subject of her mother—but Mrs. Tulliver in the *Mill* is a nagging, complaining woman, constantly comparing the untidy Maggie to her neat, pretty cousin Lucy. But George Eliot's strongest criticism of her is that she fails to take responsibility for her own life—she bewails the loss of her linen and china when the family goes bankrupt and its effects are sold, but she shows no initiative in either preventing or coping with disaster. Why is the apparently growing prosperity of the Evans family transformed, in the *Mill*, into financial failure? A plausible speculation might be that George Eliot was portraying the reality of her mother's fears and accusations, rather than a more literal "reality," just as the deaths of Maggie and Tom, who drown in each other's arms, are a way of representing the fatal differences between them that inevitably ended their childhood companionship.

George Eliot's sonnet sequence "Brother and Sister" is an idealized account of this relation; the two children escape the pursuing, correcting glance of their mother in a way that leads George Eliot's latest biographer, Ruby Redinger, to speak of "the overprotectiveness of an essentially rejecting mother." [1] By the time she was five years old, Mary Ann (like the other children) was away at boarding school; and this early maternal rejection, complicated by guilt at being the immediate cause of her mother's poor health, was augmented when her playmate Isaac developed boyish interests that left his little sister behind. Like Katherine Mansfield's mother, Mrs. Evans used her illness to barricade herself from children to whom she did not feel close—and again like Mrs. Beauchamp, her son was an exception to this blanket disapproval. The mythical Isaac is, like the mythical Chummie, the representative of a childhood paradise that may never have really existed, and the focus of his sister's longing to be the favored son herself.

In 1828, Mary Ann was sent to Mrs. Wallington's Boarding School in Nuneaton. Here she came under the influence of an evangelical teacher, Maria Lewis, who was to be her closest confidante for many years. She seems to have made of Miss Lewis a kind of mother figure—a mother more sympathetic than her own, for Miss Lewis in later years remembered Mary Ann as

> very loveable, but unhappy, given to great bursts of weeping; finding it impossible to care for childish games and occupations. [2]

Inevitably, Miss Lewis's opinions were eagerly adopted by the grateful Mary Ann, who became seriously religious and earnestly studi-

ous. The Miss Franklins' School in Coventry was her introduction
to a wider intellectual world; she excelled in English composition
and music, and her letters had a pompous, Johnsonian turn of
phrase. She developed a passion for the Romantic poets and the
novels of Scott.

In 1836, Mrs. Evans died, and the seventeen-year-old Mary Ann
returned home to keep house for her father. Her evangelical
seriousness had increased if anything, apparently augmented by her
isolation from friends of her own age and by her immersion in intellectual tasks. She worried about the propriety of reading novels
or listening to music, and she began to compile a Chart of Ecclesi-
astical History, which she only abandoned when a rival chart was
published. She studied Italian and German, alone and with occasional tutors, and had the run of the Newdigates' library. She
also had the supervision of kitchen, dairy, preserving, and the rest
of the running of a large household.

The fussy curls and elaborately constructed dresses of this period
did not suit Mary Ann's large, austere features, nor did cosy domesticity suit her temperament. Harvest festivals and village entertain-
ments made her desperately unhappy, and her disapproval made
life uncomfortable for those around her. She was happiest when
immersed in her solitary studies, and she seems to have established
her right to these hours in much the same way that Katherine
Mansfield earned her flight to London—by making life miserable
for anyone who attempted to stand in her way.

In 1841, Robert Evans left his business in the hands of his eldest
son, and he and Mary Ann moved to a large, pleasant house less
than a mile from Coventry. Here her intellectual life began in earnest when she met Charles Bray, his wife Cara, and his sister-in-
law Sara Sophia Hennell. Bray was a prosperous ribbon manufacturer, and his house, Rosehill, was the center of whatever was
lively and progressive in the intellectual life of Coventry. Unlike
their more conventional neighbors, they were not put off by Mary
Ann's plainness, earnestness, and lack of interest in social trivia.

Sara Hennell inherited Miss Lewis's role as confidante and companion of Mary Ann's flights of intellectual argumentation. But the
quiet, affectionate Cara aroused deeper feelings, and began her admiration of "womanliness" which was always to provide a correc-

tive to a purely cerebral life. But perhaps it was Charles Bray himself who was at this time the most attractive of the trio, and his own
analysis of her character indicates the reason why. He had swal-
lowed wholesale the quackery of phrenology and went about making casts of his friends' heads; his description of Mary Ann con-
cludes:

> In her brain-development the Intellect greatly predominates; . . . In the
> Feelings, the Animal and Moral regions are about equal; the moral
> being quite sufficient to keep the animal in order and in due subservi-
> ence, but would not be spontaneously active. The social feelings were
> very active, particularly the adhesiveness. She was of a most affectionate
> disposition, always requiring some one to lean upon, preferring what has
> hitherto been considered the stronger sex, to the other and more im-
> pressible. She was not fitted to stand alone.[3]

Since the days when she adored Isaac and was her father's "little
wench," she had felt a need for male affection even stronger than
her need for a female mentor and companion, and Charles Bray
was one of the first to fill this need. A visitor to Rosehill described
her as "hanging on his arm like a lover"; and Cara, who had already indicated that her husband's infidelities did not bother her,
was undisturbed by malicious suggestions that a close relationship
was growing with the new visitor. There is, in any case, no evidence that Charles Bray was more to her than a kindly, sympathetic
adviser.

At about this time, Mary Ann's circle was enlarged by her introduction to Charles Hennell, the brother of Sara and Cara, who
had just married Rufa Brabant, the daughter of a retired doctor and
amateur pedant who lived at Devizes. Mary Ann was invited to visit
Rufa's parents, the Brabants, and she soon became an uncritical
worshipper of the vain old man, who called her "Deutera." But his
wife was not as tolerant as Cara, and Mary Ann was sent home to
Coventry in disgrace. After this episode, her need for affection was
tempered with caution; and her tendency to intellectual idolatry
steadily diminished until the time when Dr. Brabant formed one of
the models for Casaubon.

Her family was not happy about her new acquaintances, especially when Mary Ann refused to attend church with her father, a heresy that he attributed entirely to the influence of the Brays. Robert Evans's religion was quiet and conventional, more a matter of outward propriety than of intense feeling. The Church represented for him part of the established social order, which was being challenged by new wealth, new thought, new industries. The self-reliance of the new entrepreneurs was reflected in their search for a personal relation with God, for salvation and revelation with no earthly intermediary. Evangelicalism was the name given to this movement, though it was a vague term for a broad current of thought that touched the lives of people as disparate as the conventional Maria Lewis, whose influence the Evanses had wholly approved of, and the more heretical group at Rosehill. Freethinking of all varieties was discussed there, and Mary Ann was startled to find that doubts she had scarcely formulated to herself were already the small change of conversation.

Mary Ann's evangelical sincerity had changed by this time to a generalized horror of hypocrisy, mingled with defiance of her father; and it was probably as a result of both feelings that she rebelled against conformist churchgoing. Her family took steps to quash the revolt: her period of doubt lasted a mere three months before she was brought around to outward observance of convention, though with the implicit liberty of thinking what she liked in the meantime. But her brother Isaac had more practical reasons for wishing to remove her from the malign influence of the independent minded Brays: as Cara wrote to Sara,

> It seems that brother Isaac with real fraternal kindness thinks that his sister has no chance of getting the one thing needful—i.e. a husband and a settlement—unless she mixes more in society, and complains that since she has known us she has hardly been anywhere else; that Mr. Bray, being only a leader of mobs, can only introduce her to Chartists and Radicals, and that such only will ever fall in love with her if she does not belong to the Church.[4]

Soon, however, Mary Ann had other preoccupations besides matrimony, which in any case she was inclined to regard as a prison. A recent example of such imprisonment was the marriage of Rufa Brabant, who was, as a new bride, forced to give up the task of translating David Friedrich Strauss's *Das Leben Jesu,* a work of rational theological criticism that was the book of the moment in Germany. Joseph Parkes, the Radical politician, had arranged for the translation to be subsidized by several rich Reformers; and Mary Ann's suspicion that there were compensations for spinsterhood was confirmed when the task was offered to her. For two years she worked on this monumental book, refreshed by occasional holidays with the Brays, and suffering the first bout of the headaches that were always to accompany her work.

Strauss described his point of view as "mythical"—that is, he did not believe, with the orthodox, that the Gospels contained a supernatural history; nor, with the rationalists, that they were merely factual history. The mythical interpretation, he asserted, was not subversive of faith; it merely put Christianity among the other mythical expressions of natural religion. This was to be George Eliot's view, and she could have said, with Strauss, that she was enabled to hold these opinions by virtue of

the internal liberation of the feelings and intellect from certain religious and dogmatical presuppositions; and this the author early attained by means of philosophical studies. [5]

But at this time, Mary Ann's "internal liberation" was not complete; she would still have described herself as a Christian, though one with many disagreements from the established Church. The translation caused her considerable suffering as she saw the religion to which she was still sentimentally attached "dismembered"; she was only sustained, she said, by the crucifix and religious picture over her desk.

Mary Ann had matured greatly during this time; she had lost much of her painful shyness, and could now play the piano in company and help to entertain the Brays' varied guests. The work on Strauss had matured her command of English and her powers of thought; she had also begun writing reviews and articles for the Coventry *Herald,* which Charles Bray bought in 1846. She had seen enough of life to suspect that conventional matrimony would be inimical to her other interests, and Rufa Brabant was not the only example to point to. Her sister Chrissey had married in 1837; she was to bear nine children, only four of whom outlived her. Redinger suggests that

> Chrissey may well be the progenitor of the long line of "prolific" women in George Eliot's fiction who are loving but debilitated mothers, ranging from Milly Barton in the first of the *Clerical Scenes* to Gwendolen's mother in the last novel, *Daniel Deronda*. [6]

The production of books, with all the attendant pains, was in some ways safer than the production of real children. Mary Ann hinted to her friends that her ambitions were not confined to translating, but she had somehow to relate these ambitions to the business of supporting herself.

Decision was postponed, then made more urgent, by the necessity of nursing her father through his last illness. He died in May 1849, and Mary Ann, confused and exhausted, was taken to Geneva by the Brays. Here they installed her in a comfortable pension, where she could live for a while on the money left her by her father—£100 in cash and the interest on £2,000 in trust. Soon she moved to lodgings kept by M. and Mme. François D'Albert Durade, a painter and his competent wife, who looked after her as kindly as the Brays had done.

Certainly the thirty-year-old Marian, as she now called herself, needed looking after. She had no matrimonial prospects, very little money, and no prospect of work. She began a translation of Spinoza, indicating that she had moved beyond Strauss in the matter of religious unorthodoxy, but the difficult work progressed slowly. The next spring, she returned to Coventry and began a round of family visits. But her family were anxious to wash their hands of her— Isaac feared having to contribute to her support, Chrissey was overburdened with her large family and impecunious husband, and Fanny did not even bother to answer her letters. Soon she was making inquiries about lodgings in London, where at least she could hope to get occasional work reviewing and translating.

At Rosehill, Marian had met the publisher John Chapman, who was then engaged in publishing and selling the works of many of the most advanced thinkers of the day. He had commissioned an article from the "Translator of Strauss" (as Marian had, in her diffidence, signed herself), which he placed in the *Westminster Review*. In the period before her sojourn abroad, Marian stayed once or twice at the Chapman house at 142 Strand, where his wife Susannah (an heiress fourteen years older than her husband) and his housekeeper/mistress Elisabeth Tilley kept a boardinghouse. Visiting Americans such as Horace Greeley and Emerson stayed there, as did a varied and constantly changing assortment of writers and journalists who worked for Chapman. By 1851, Marian herself took up residence with the Chapmans, following the pattern of her previous relationships with couples like the Brays and the Brabants.

Nicknamed Byron by his friends, Chapman was an attractive and vigorous figure, a year younger than Marian. He was an affectionate father to his two young children, and was constantly getting entangled with women who—to his great regret—had a tendency to be jealous of each other. His diary records in hilarious detail his moral struggles with himself—struggles that usually involved balancing the claims of the various women who felt themselves emotionally dependent on him. How could he placate them all at once?

At the same time, Chapman was a serious intellectual, committed to publishing unpopular but important books. He was considered a man of principle and high ideals. As a young man, he had turned from authorship to publishing as a surer means of supporting himself, but he never managed to make the business pay. He was attempting to rescue it by buying and relaunching the *Westminster Review*, but he was much too preoccupied with publishing and bookselling to look after the editorial side of things himself. Nor could he afford to hire an editor.

This is where Marian came in. She had written several articles for him already, and translated Feuerbach as well as Strauss and Spinoza. She was well up in the intellectual controversies with which the *Westminster* concerned itself. Her capacities were beyond doubt, and soon, too, was her growing devotion to Chapman. Here she had found "someone to lean upon" who was, from the point of view of charm and intelligence, far superior to Dr. Brabant or Charles Bray. Soon she was being exploited by Chapman both emotionally and intellectually.

Marian's need to lean, to find both father and mother figures, diminished as she grew older. When she met Chapman, it was already being replaced by a need to be needed, to feel that she was an important and useful figure in someone else's life. She admired Chapman, but she also mothered him as all his women did, and they were closer to being colleagues than to having the kind of unequal relationship she had experienced before.

At first, Marian's presence was resented by both Mrs. Chapman and Miss Tilley, who were used to each other but not prepared to countenance another competitor. They held secret meetings and presented ultimatums, and Marian was sent back to Coventry as she had been by the female inhabitants of Dr. Brabant's house. But Chapman's need of her was too great, and he exerted all his formidable charm to persuade the other women to accept Marian as part of the household.

Marian had long been prepared to serve others anonymously— she had not signed her name to the translation of Strauss, and she did not object to editing the *Westminster* in fact but not in name. Chapman paid her for her occasional articles, but she received no salary as assistant editor. However, it was soon well known that she was the moving spirit behind the new *Westminster*, and her closer acquaintance with intellectual London was assured. Though many articles in the *Westminster* of those years have been attributed to her, she generally confined herself to linking together the notices by other contributors, rewriting, assigning books for review. It was said that the *Review* had not been so brilliant since the days of James Mill's editorship—Froude outlined his fresh interpretation of Tudor England, Herbert Spencer wrote a remarkable series on evolution, James Martineau wrote on religion, George Henry Lewes on Shelley, John Stuart Mill on philosophy, and the notices of American books were more complete than in any other London review. The city was full of refugees from the European revolutions of 1848, and Pierre Leroux, Louis Blanc, and Mazzini found a sympathetic mouthpiece in the *Westminster*. Karl Marx also visited 142 Strand, though there is no evidence that Marian met him.

This busy, competitive intellectual life helped to demystify for Marian the business of making a living by writing. Her recognition in this world of literary and social ferment made her more confident, and the growing realization that she was being exploited by Chapman gave her the courage to ask for fair payment for her work. Intellectual women like Harriet Martineau and Bessie Rayner Parkes came to be numbered among her close friends, and the successes of literary entrepreneurs like Eliza Lynn Linton convinced her that she, too, could support herself by her pen. Bessie, the daughter of the Radical reformer who had arranged for the translation of Strauss, brought with her to the Strand Barbara Leigh Smith, daughter of another Radical politician and granddaughter of the abolitionist William Smith. Because her father had never married her working-class mother, though they formed a most devoted family, Barbara and her brothers and sisters were "tabooed" from polite society. But by this time, Marian was not deterred by such considerations—she could see many advantages in being tabooed, from what she knew of polite society—and Barbara became perhaps her closest friend. Katherine Mansfield had had to leave New Zealand in pursuit of social freedom; the death of her parents, and rejection by the rest of her family, had gone far toward freeing Marian.

Among the men who visited the Strand and contributed to the *Westminster* was the young Herbert Spencer, just Marian's age and at work on his first book. Spencer's interests were scientific and evolutionary; his views have in this century been traduced as "social Darwinism," but he was a pioneer in his time in applying the scientific method to the study of society. He was a lifelong bachelor, but his interest in Marian was such that, for a while, their friends expected them to marry. Marian was less headstrong by this time, and she was able to profit intellectually from Spencer's friendship without disgracing herself emotionally as she had done with Dr. Brabant and John Chapman. On his side, any possible romantic interest was cooled by a terror of sexuality that persisted until his death at eighty-seven, and that he rationalized by saying that he found Marian physically unattractive, which may also have been part of the truth.

Spencer's influence on the novelist George Eliot is easier to assess when we note that he considered her spiritual heir to be Beatrice Potter Webb, one of his later protégées, and—with her husband Sidney Webb—founder of the Fabian Society and the English welfare state. What the novelists were to the mid-nineteenth century, the social scientists were to be to the twentieth—and Herbert Spencer was a prophet of the change. The families of the young Beatrice Potter and of George Henry Lewes were tenuously linked—Lewes's son Charles married a sister of Octavia Hill, who trained Beatrice in social investigation. But Spencer provided an even stronger link: his brief flirtation with Marian Evans was succeeded by a lifelong friendship with the Potter family, one or another of whose many daughters was often expected to marry him.

Beatrice's father, who might almost have served as a model for Mr. Brooke in *Middlemarch*, used to say to her, "Poor Spencer, he lacks instinct, my dear, he lacks instinct—you will discover that instinct is as important as intellect." When George Eliot died, the newspapers implied that Spencer had been one of her suitors; and when Spencer wondered whether he should correct the published accounts, and assert that it had been she who was in love with him, Mr. Potter replied, "My dear Spencer, you will be eternally damned if you do it."

Though Spencer's ungallant attitude must have increased Marian's sensitivity about her appearance, it was high praise from a man of his powers to be classed as "the most admirable woman, mentally, I ever met." And his hesitations about marriage were expressed in terms that she would have found congenial: "no woman of truly noble mind will submit to be dictated to," as attractive a proposition as that with which he delighted the Potter children: "submission not desirable."

Their potential affair waned gently; Marian soon came to see his transparent vanities and his capacity for self-deception, and, as Gordon Haight remarks, "studied in him a human trait of which she was to be one of the greatest delineators—egoism." However, Spencer's defection, by the time it occurred, was all but irrelevant, for Marian had already met George Henry Lewes.

Lewes, like Marian, was making his way in the world of London intellectual journalism; like her, he had no money and heavy family responsibilities—in his case an estranged wife and four sons. So he could readily understand the burdens Marian increasingly had to shoulder: among them Chrissey Evans Clarke and her six surviving children. Chrissey's husband Edward died in December of 1852, and Marian went to stay with her sister for a week, which was filled with the wailing of babies and the bad temper of Isaac. Despite Chrissey's evident need of sisterly support, Marian decided that ultimately her best chance of helping the family would be to earn more money in London. Her work for Chapman was increasingly onerous, and though he had been bailed out at least once by Samuel Courtauld, the silk manufacturer, his whole publishing empire was perilously near to bankruptcy. Naturally he met Marian's requests for payment with evasion.

Soon Lewes was taking Spencer's place in escorting Marian to theaters and opera and concerts, to all of which he had reviewer's tickets; she wrote to Cara,

> Mr. Lewes especially is kind and attentive and has quite won my regard after having a good deal of my vituperation. Like a few other people in the world, he is much better than he seems—a man of heart and conscience wearing a mask of flippancy. [7]

Lewes's marriage had been broken up by his wife's adultery with Thornton Hunt, co-founder with him of the *Leader*, where he wrote weekly articles and reviews over a variety of pseudonyms. After his wife had borne Hunt a second child, Lewes considered himself morally free of obligation to her; though, since he had registered her first adulterous child as his own, he was legally precluded from seeking a divorce—a ruinously expensive procedure in any case.

To support this varied ménage, and himself separately from them, Lewes worked tirelessly at journalism; adapted plays for the Lyceum under the name Slingsby Lawrence; and wrote books, the most recent of which was *Comte's Philosophy of the Sciences*. When ill health put him behind with his work, the self-sacrificing Marian, with whom he was now on terms of greatest friendship, took on some of it herself—and as it had done with Chapman, the feeling of being needed was the prelude to falling in love.

What drew them together was not only their present isolation, but a whole history of alienation from conventional roles and a conventional place in the world. Lewes's opinions were, at this time, even more radical than Marian's, and they derived from a far more unusual background.

Less is known about Lewes's childhood than about Marian's. His father, John Lee ("Dandy") Lewes, was a sometime writer and theatrical manager. His grandfather was a much better-known figure; Charles Lee Lewes was one of the leading comic actors of the eighteenth century, and his grandson seems to have inherited some of his wit and high spirits, as well as his sense of democracy and his taste for low life. The older Lewes's memoirs are full of thumbnail sketches of the Kemble and Kean tribes, of the *louche* behind-the-scenes life of the theater, which still had more in common with the troupes of traveling players in Shakespeare's day than with the modern profession.

George Henry Lewes was born in London, but his childhood and early schooling took place in Boulogne, Jersey, and Brittany as well as in England. At thirteen he was sent to Dr. Burney's academy at Greenwich, where he studied the classics and learned to write admirable English. His command of French was already perfect, and in adulthood his "Frenchness" was to seem slightly alien to his London colleagues. At seventeen he left school, and for the next few years his literary ambitions were pursued in the intervals of a variety of jobs—he worked for a notary, for a Russia leather merchant, studied medicine, and taught. At eighteen he went to Germany for at least a year, where he mastered the language, tried to write books, and sent articles to the London papers.

In a sense, his lack of formal education was to be his strength: instead of being narrowly confined to one course of study, he had dabbled in everything that took his interest. His knowledge of Continental literature was wider than that of most of his contemporaries; he felt no artificial barrier between science and the arts; and his knowledge of the great world, and of how a living was to be got in it, was built into an understanding of economics and politics usually missing (even today) from the genteel world of literary journalism.

Living at home with his widowed mother and his brother, Lewes was the protégé of several eminent and successful men: Leigh Hunt, whose son Thornton became his closest friend and his wife's lover; William Bell Scott, the friend of the Romantic poets; and John Stuart Mill, who published some of his articles, praised others, and gave him kind but rigorous criticism that moved him in the direction of greater seriousness.

Lewes's ideals were Romantic, democratic, and freethinking. He wrote the first English biography of Robespierre, which he claims, in Murry-esque terms, to be

> the Life of him, who in his heart believed the Gospel proclaimed by the Revolution to be the real gospel of Christianity . . .

George Eliot was to describe him, early in their acquaintance, as "a sort of miniature Mirabeau in appearance," and it is evident from his *Robespierre* that he identified with Mirabeau, the ugly, wizened man who was the soul of the French Revolution.

His sensitivity about his appearance seems to have been almost as great as that of Marian, and his two early novels are interesting in what they have to say about this as well as about the early vicissitudes of the man of letters. *Ranthorpe* is an early example of the "grub street" novel (the most famous of the genre is probably *Pendennis*); Lewes makes his hero, Percy Ranthorpe, Shelleyan in appearance and Lewesean in ambition—he has gone to Germany, tried to write a verse tragedy, and suffered from the condescension of polite society. He grows out of egotism in a way that strikingly foreshadows the emotional pattern of George Eliot's novels—and the heroine, Isola, has a grave Italianate beauty that George Eliot gave to Romola. In its combination of autobiography and idealism, *Ranthorpe* is altogether comparable to Murry's *Still Life*—both are early works by young men who were decidedly not to become novelists. Both show the early patrons, the femmes fatales, the chances of work and money and love, that formed the classic first experiences of the budding man of letters.

Rose, Blanche, and Violet is a potboiler considerably longer than *Ranthorpe*—it is in the three-decker form beloved of the popular circulating libraries. In the interstices of the tedious marrying off of three sisters, Lewes delivers himself of some heartfelt speeches on two of his most preoccupying subjects: the chances of success in a literary career, and the possibility of an ugly man winning the love of a beauty. He again mentions "Mirabeau, and other hideous men celebrated for their successes with women"; and he makes his ugly hero triumph in the end. At the same time, he has some strictures on ugly, intellectual, and strong-minded women that are interesting in view of his later history:

> poor faded creatures, who toiled in the British Museum, over antiquated rubbish which they extracted and incorporated with worse rubbish of their own—women who wrote about the regeneration of their sex—who drivelled in religious tales—compiled inaccurate histories—wrote moral stories for the young, or unreadable verses for the old—translated from French and German (with the assistance of a dictionary, a dashing contempt for English idiom),—learned women, strong-minded women, religious women, historical women, and poetical women; there were types of each class, and by no means attractive types. [8]

He goes on,

> It is one of the most amusing scenes in the comedy of society to witness the grateful attentions of a woman who is not "received," to those of her female acquaintance who shut their eyes to her real position. . . . with what untiring perseverance do women in equivocal positions manoeuvre to obtain the presence of virtuous women at their houses!

One wonders whether George Eliot read this book before the days when Lewes was the cause of her not being "received," and how he excused himself for writing it.

His personal credo of hard work and the demystification of genius is also contained in the novel, and it sums up his own experiences in a way that he would undoubtedly have stood by to the end of his career:

> . . . would Beethoven and Mozart have poured out their souls into such abundant melodies? would Göthe have written the sixty volumes of his works,—had they not often, very often, sat down like drudges to an unwilling task, and found themselves speedily engrossed with that to which they were so averse?
>
> "Use the pen," says a thoughtful and subtle author, "there is no magic in it; *but it keeps the mind from staggering about.*" This is an

aphorism which should be printed in letters of gold over the studio door of every artist. Use the pen or the brush; do not pause, do not trifle, have no misgivings; but keep your mind from staggering about by fixing it resolutely on the matter before you, and then all that you *can* do you *will* do: inspiration will not enable you to do more.

Lewes had already put his own precepts to the test in both these areas of life. His lack of hesitation was such that by 1850, in addition to his journalism, the life of Robespierre, the two novels, and a tragedy in blank verse (a hymn to women's infidelity, in contrast to the eternal love delineated in *Cinnamon and Angelica*), he had written one of his most enduringly popular books, the *Biographical History of Philosophy*. Even today, it is hard to find second-hand copies of the book in Charing Cross Road: they are snapped up by London University students, who, like the Cambridge students in Lewes's day, make of the book "a private textbook" because of its clarity and approachability and air of intellectual excitement.

The assiduous author had also won the love of a beauty. One of his early jobs had been as tutor in the family of Swynfen Jervis, a Staffordshire lawyer and Member of Parliament. He fell in love with the eldest daughter, Agnes, and married her in 1841. The nineteen-year-old bride was, according to William Bell Scott, "one of the loveliest creatures in the world," with blond curls and pink cheeks. She was accomplished enough to help Lewes in his work by translating from the French and Spanish; they had four sons, one of whom died in early childhood. The vagaries of a literary career must have placed a strain on the marriage, and Lewes was often absent from home collecting Continental material for his books and articles, reviewing plays in Manchester and Liverpool, and leaving Agnes alone with the four babies and not much money. Jane Carlyle, in a letter to a cousin, was one of the first to observe signs of trouble:

> In fact his wife seems rather *contemptuous* of his raptures about all the women he has fallen in love with on this journey, which is the best way of taking the thing—when one can.
> I used to think these Leweses a perfect pair of love-birds always cuddling together on the same perch—to speak figuratively—but the female

love-bird appears to have hopped off to some distance and to be now taking a somewhat critical view of her little shaggy mate.

In the most honey-marriage one has only to *wait*—it is all a question
of time—sooner or later "reason resumes its empire" as the phrase is.[9]

The disillusioned Agnes, like her husband, was a liberal thinker
who saw no virtue in clinging to outworn marriage bonds. And
when she began an affair with Thornton Hunt, Lewes seems to
have raised no objections.

Hunt and his wife and their large family (ultimately to number
ten children) lived with various cousins and sisters-in-law in a "Phalanstery," founded on the Fourierist model, in Bayswater. The
household practised a sort of practical communism that extended,
theoretically at least, to sexual relations. The philosophy of all of
them on these matters was derived quite explicitly from Godwin
and Shelley—only love could sanctify a relationship, and legal permanence where the emotional bond did not exist was simply slavery.

The Leweses never actually lived in the Phalanstery. But their
involvement with its members became clear when Agnes bore a
child fathered by Thornton. It was reported that Lewes encouraged
the situation so that Agnes would give him a free rein to pursue
other women; what is clear in any case is that he registered Thornton's child as his own, and that this recognition of his wife's adultery prevented him from later seeking a divorce. Thornton, however, had not left his own wife for Agnes: twice the two women
bore his children within weeks of each other.

Relations between Hunt and Lewes continued to be amiable. In
1850 they had jointly founded the *Leader*, a radical weekly intended to fill the gap between the dailies and the quarterlies. Their
business manager was Holyoake, an old radical; and from the first,
the new magazine was outspoken, lively, and unconventional. The
1848 revolutionaries found a warm welcome in its pages; it began
the first "letters to the editor" column; and many of the subjects it
tackled seem radical even today: the outlawing of unemployment,
the necessity of socialism, the right of men to claim sustenance
from the soil. Hunt, in his founding manifesto, said that the *Leader*

stood for free discussion of all subjects, alliance of peoples against allied oppressors, Anglo-American alliance, and socialism. Lewes attacked the English economic system, the conventional educational system, and the established church.

Darwinism and science in general seemed to the *Leader* to be one aspect of democratic progress; and Lewes was aggressive in his attacks on pseudo-science—phrenology, séances, spontaneous combustion. To prove that nothing was sacred, he even attacked the profession of letters:

> For the most part literary men have no *raison d'être*, have no justification in their talents for the career they stumble through. . . . How few men of letters *think* at all: How few think with originality and success! How few do the thing they pretend to do! Literary talent is, strictly speaking, the talent of *expression*; it is frequently the whole budget of an author. Without for a moment ignoring or undervaluing the pleasures and the uses of such a talent, we cannot in sober seriousness declare that its possession implies greater *intellectual calibre* than is implied in the successful exercise of the other professions. [10]

There are clues in this to his ability to value George Eliot at her real worth: his strictures on scribbling women were matched by his disgust with dilettantes of his own sex, and she herself considered that her novels were only justified by their content of ideas.

But it was the liveliness of its style that made the *Leader* a success, and this quality was mainly due to Lewes. Under the pseudonym "Vivian" he wrote a man-about-town column, mainly theatrical criticism but full of digressions and anecdotes. As Professor Kitchel puts it,

> Vivian was always raving over some beauteous lady or other, narrating his heart-adventures with "the stately Harriet" or the lovely Lucy, and then turning from this frivolous discussion to remark on his fondness for the church fathers, on the depth and passion of his love of learning. [11]

His articles for the *Leader* formed the basis of Lewes's income, but when he met Marian he was already at work on a book which he hoped would put him into quite another position in the eyes of the educated public: the life of Goethe. As early as 1842, John Stuart Mill had written to him,

> I think your article on Goethe decidedly your highest flight as yet. Without being the *dernier mot* on such a man, it recommends itself to my knowledge of him as *truer* than any other writing on the subject which I have met with. [12]

Work on the biography was going slowly, however—Lewes was plagued by illness, including psychosomatic headaches like the ones that had tormented Marian while she was engaged on the Strauss translation. He was as much in need as she of a settled relationship, giving the emotional sustenance necessary for solid and productive work.

No one knows what was Lewes's attitude toward the breakup of his marriage; he carefully destroyed all letters and diaries relating to the years before his liaison with Marian. Certainly he was unhappy, lonely, overburdened with work; but did he really feel betrayed? He had written in his mediocre verse tragedy, *The Noble Heart*,

> *Garcia:* Well, here's to woman,
>   May she deceive us, so that she will love us;
>   Give me the love to-day, and I will bear
>   The pain of her deceit to-morrow.
> *Antonio:* That's philosophy!
> *Garcia:* It is, for I am certain of the joy
>   Her lips will give to-day—and her deceit
>   I am not sure 'twill spoil a moment's rest.

After the criticism of a dependent wife who felt that he was not all she would have liked in the way of affluence and success, he was undoubtedly ready to appreciate the charms of an independent woman, who feared the conventional wifely role above all things, and would not expect to live through her husband.

How much he and Marian had in common is already evident.

Both were autodidacts, whose ideas of genius, intellectualism, and philosophy were taken from the German idealists. Both had edited and contributed to literary periodicals; the search for contributors, the struggle to make ends meet, and the constant pressure of deadlines were the stuff of both their lives. Lewes was the more experienced in bludgeoning editors and publishers for payment, driving a satisfactory bargain, and appealing to a varied public. He had much to learn from Marian's thoroughness and seriousness, as she had much to learn from his lively style and clarity of thought.

Contemporary descriptions of Lewes all emphasize his charm, his quickness, his mercurial quality. His thin face was deeply pitted with smallpox and surrounded by bushy whiskers; Carlyle called him the Ape, and Douglas Jerrold said he was "the ugliest man in London." Others saw him as "witty, French, flippant," and Eliza Lynn Linton said that wherever he went, there was a patch of intellectual sunshine in the room. His Frenchness offended many of his more stolid English acquaintances, who were apt to refer to him as a barber, a dancing-master, a monkey. George Eliot was to ridicule this habit of thought in *Daniel Deronda*, where she describes a bishop's wife "of strict propriety, who objects to having a French person in the house."

For all her large-featured plainness, which some called masculine, Marian was both attractive to and attracted by philanderers—that is, to men who made her feel charming. Her tenacity once she had initially attracted them seems to have had something of emotional blackmail in it—tears and scenes and the ability to arouse feelings of guilt. For the first five years of their union, she and Lewes spent scarcely a night apart, and unkind observers attributed this to her vigilance over possible infidelities. But each seems to have been so exactly what the other was looking for at this time that their relation had little trouble in surmounting initial crises of adaptation.

The first sign of their growing closeness was that Marian finally weaned herself from the Chapman ménage, and in 1853 moved into lodgings in Hyde Park Square. It was here, according to their friend Oscar Browning, that her affair with Lewes began. In spite of the massive amounts of work she got through for Lewes as well as for herself, she was in radiant health: the headaches that had plagued her during the equivocal, emotional years at the Strand disappeared.

Chapman had commissioned Marian to translate Feuerbach's *Das Wesen der Christenthums*, a bold humanist document which contained passages on love that must have been close to her credo at this time. It could almost have served as an apologia for her decision to live with Lewes:

> But marriage—we mean, of course, marriage as the free bond of love—is sacred in itself, by the very nature of the union which is therein effected. That alone is a religious marriage which is a true marriage, which corresponds to the essence of marriage—of love. . . . Yes, only as the free bond of love; for a marriage the bond of which is merely an external restriction, not the voluntary, contented self-restriction of love, in short, a marriage which is not spontaneously concluded, spontaneously willed, self-sufficing, is not a true marriage, and therefore not a truly moral marriage. [13]

In the five years since her father's death, Marian had served an arduous apprenticeship. She had passed well beyond the interests and capabilities of the trio of amateurs at Rosehill, and beyond the feckless worldliness of Chapman and the egotistical theorizing of Spencer. She knew the classics and the important modern languages. She had edited what was for a while the most serious and brilliant of the quarterlies. She had published translations of two of the most important works of "advanced" theology of her day—and the last, at Lewes's insistence, she had had the courage to sign "Marian Evans."

At the same time, she showed a remarkable intellectual stability: her basic conservatism had not left her, and she had in no case rebelled violently against the beliefs and influences of her early life. She was prepared to judge any point of view rigorously, though as her friend Bessie Parkes observed, rigorous judgment was, in her, uniquely combined with sympathy. She had also learned a great deal about the mastery of her own unruly emotions: she was not snatching at the chance of a liaison with Lewes simply out of a need for "someone to lean upon"; they had worked together and all but lived together for many months before they took the irrevocable step.

It was in the criticism of marriage that her intellectual audacity had perhaps gone furthest. The hypocrisy of the sexual double standard, and the injustice of a married woman becoming a legal nonentity, not even entitled to her own earnings, aroused all her indignation. She had won her emotional and financial independence through struggle, and even if there had been a possibility of renouncing it in matrimony, the prospect would scarcely have attracted her.

Was her interest in Lewes, then, partly based on the fact that it was not marriage she was being offered? Certainly she was ambivalent about marriage long before she met him; and she could see no clear way to reconcile this reluctance with her need for a total and loving relationship.

It is still not completely clear why Marian and Lewes decided at this point to make the dramatic gesture of going off together, when they could have discreetly carried on their affair in London. They confided in no one, though Marian did apparently discuss the plan of flight with Chapman and Charles Bray, both precluded by their own practice from arguing against such a decision on strictly moral grounds. They may have advanced the consideration that she would have been cut off from society—which was not strictly moral so much as strictly hypocritical. But Marian considered that she held no place in society in any case, and that as she lived so much apart from her family, no odium would attach to them. They may also have considered Lewes a bad bet as a reliable lover; but whatever his early reputation as a philanderer, he had been considerably sobered by his recent domestic experiences.

One clue to Marian's action is provided by a letter to Maria Lewis, during the "Holy War" when she was refusing to attend church with her father. She writes,

> Beautiful ego-ism! to quote one's own. But where is not this same ego? The martyr at the stake seeks its gratification as much as the court sycophant, the difference lying in the comparative dignity and beauty of the two egos. People absurdly talk of self-denial—why there is none in Virtue to a being of moral excellence—the greatest torture to such a soul

would be to run counter to the dictates of conscience, to wallow in the slough of meanness, deception, revenge or sensuality. [14]

This is exactly what Erikson means when he refers to

. . . the simple and yet so fateful proposition that nothing is more unbearable than the vague tension of guiltiness. [15]

Marian was already too unconventional to allow anything, even her own conscience, to dictate to her: the Holy War had ended when she decided that loving humility was more valuable than religious principle, whatever the evangelical conscience might say. She was ready to pursue her own course of action and to take the consequences. Like the Holy War, her affair with Lewes led to a course of action that was more deeply moral than conventional morality. Her courage and honesty would not permit her to live as Chapman did; to, as she later put it, "have what she wanted and still be invited to dinner."

It was probably at Lewes's suggestion that they departed for Germany in July 1854. He needed to go in any case, to finish his Goethe researches, and the opportunity for a clean break with the past presented itself. Marian sent a note to the trio at Coventry:

Dear Friends—all three
I have only time to say good bye and God bless you. Poste Restante, Weimar for the next six weeks, and afterwards Berlin.
Ever your loving and grateful
Marian. [16]

Whether or not the escapade was intended to be permanent, at least on Lewes's side, is open to doubt: Marian wrote from Germany to Charles Bray,

Circumstances, with which I am not concerned, and which have arisen since he left England, have led him to determine on a separation from Mrs. Lewes. [17]

Did Agnes, hearing the news of his flight, tell him that he need not trouble to return?

In any case, after they had been a few weeks in Germany, Marian began calling herself Mrs. Lewes and considering herself to be married, morally and socially if not legally.

From this time forward, it becomes difficult to say with certainty what were the ways in which Lewes and his Polly influenced each other. But some deductions can be drawn from observation of what they were before and what they became afterward. The serious, intellectual woman with the pedantic style became the most popular novelist of her day; and the lightweight journalist became an eminent biographer and man of science. They wrote no letters to each other, at least none that have survived, for they were hardly ever apart; but from the glimpses given in their diaries, as well as from the internal evidence of their books, the growing identity of their intellectual interests can be traced.

C H A P T E R   2

Partnership

O Love! they wrong thee much
That say thy sweet is bitter,
When thy rich fruit is such
As nothing can be sweeter.
Fair house of joy and bliss,
Where truest pleasure is,
  I do adore thee:
I know thee what thou art,
I serve thee with my heart,
  And fall before thee.

—*Anonymous*

From the first, Marian seems to have been willing to jettison every other relationship in favor of that with Lewes. She left Charles Bray to tell the news to Cara and Sara, which understandably wounded them. She informed Isaac of her whereabouts—necessary since it was he who sent her half-yearly income—but not of her new situation. She kept on with Chapman, because she needed him to commission work from her, but she was entirely ready to break with him, and did so when the success of *Adam Bede* assured her independence.

Public reaction to their departure was swift and hostile. Harriet Martineau convened a group of intellectual women to discuss the matter; the majority agreed that it was to be condemned as a bad precedent. One confirmation of this theory, had the ladies but known it, was that Chapman was using the argument of Marian's example to try and induce Barbara Leigh Smith to live with him—her father, on hearing the news, put a speedy end to things by packing Barbara off to Algiers, where she married the romantic and mysterious Dr. Eugene Bodichon.

Carlyle wrote that Lewes had gone off with a "strong-minded woman"; another hostile witness called Lewes and Hunt "hideous satyrs and smirking moralists . . . stink-pots of humanity." However, intellectual society in Germany seemed quite ready to receive them—they met Strauss at Antwerp, while the most impressive of their acquaintances at Weimar were Liszt, now living openly with the Princess Caroline Sayn-Wittgenstein, and Clara Schumann.

Chapman abetted their dwindling bank account by commissioning from Marian what turned out to be one of her best articles: "Woman in France: Madame de Sablé." She argued that only in France have women had "a vital influence on the development of literature"; and that one reason for this is "probably the laxity of opinion and practice with regard to the marriage tie." She concluded,

> Madame de Sablé was not a genius, not a heroine, but a woman whom men could more than love—whom they could make their friend, confidante, and counsellor; the sharer not of their joys and sorrows only, but of their ideas and aims. [1]

Marian was sharing Lewes's ideas and aims by translating the passages from Goethe's works that he wished to include in the biography, while he interviewed Goethe's friends and acquaintances; she herself was not a genius nor a heroine as yet, but she showed every wish to be a friend, confidante, and counselor. She wrote to Charles Bray, "I have had a month of exquisite enjoyment, and seem to have begun life afresh." The rural setting of Weimar, the old-fashioned simplicity of life there, refreshed her as much as did absence from the complex difficulties of her life in London. Love and literary industry were both easier abroad, as Mansfield and Murry had found at the Villa Pauline.

When the Leweses, as they now called themselves, reached home by way of Berlin and Brussels, after eight months away, there was a sense of facing the music. The first problem was the strict propriety of English landladies, and Marian waited in Dover while George tested the ground in London. Chapman was praying "against hope" that he would prove to be faithful; and even Marian herself may have been assailed by some doubts.

However, all was well again when George found a small villa at East Sheen, still in the country then and only a few minutes from

Kew Gardens. The regime of hard work and reading aloud in the evenings, which had begun at Weimar, was continued; Marian was translating Spinoza's *Ethics* as well as doing the "Belles Lettres" section of miscellaneous reviews for the *Westminster*. Both there and at their next home, in nearby Richmond, Marian was continually uneasy lest their few callers should ask for, or post letters to, "Miss Evans." Lewes, always the more sociable of the two, continued to dine out; but solitude held no terrors for Marian, and she was grateful to be left to her studies, with a simple meal provided by the landlady, after the demanding years spent with her father and then with the Chapmans. Freedom from distracting social demands was her idea of pleasure, for she was still intellectually rather than socially ambitious. As Haight notes,

> This genuine knowledge of the classics—more solid than that Thackeray got at Charterhouse and Cambridge, probably wider than that Trollope got at Harrow and Winchester—was acquired during the long period of social ostracism when, because of her honest avowal of the union with Lewes, she was not invited to dinner.[2]

Her astonishing emergence as one of England's best-equipped novelists, whose acute observation of London and provincial life was given depth and significance by the classical, philosophical themes she drew out of her stories, was less surprising to those who had known her during this period.

She and George made occasional expeditions to the south coast and to the Scilly Isles, where Lewes had begun to pursue his "seaside studies" of marine biology. In July 1856, Barbara Leigh Smith came with them to Tenby, where she spent long hours in conversation with Marian. She wrote to their mutual friend Bessie Parkes that the Leweses were practising birth control and had decided against having children (though she does not go into detail about the method; the fact that it was discussed at all is surprising). In spite of Lewes's reputation as a sensualist, Marian reported that in their intimate life he was "extremely considerate."

It is interesting that Marian's only known discussion of her sexual relationship with Lewes took place at Tenby; for it was on this visit that he first urged her to try her hand at fiction. And her description of the genesis of her first story indicates that there was a close connection between sexual happiness and the release of creativity. She wrote in her journal,

> One morning as I was lying in bed, thinking what should be the subject of my first story, my thoughts merged themselves into a dreamy doze, and I imagined myself writing a story of which the title was—"The Sad Fortunes of the Reverend Amos Barton." I was soon wide awake again, and told G. He said, "O what a capital title!" and from that time I had settled in my mind that this should be my first story.[3]

Many have wondered that such an intellectual and serious woman was able to write with such ease and spontaneity—that far from using her characters as the mouthpieces for her well-developed ideas, she was a truly "daemonic" novelist in full touch with what we would now call her unconscious. Keats's phrase for this was "negative capability"—it had, in his description, a somnolent genesis, when the "irritable reaching after certainty" of the conscious mind was in abeyance. In Keats himself, it was closely connected to sexuality; and the same deduction can be made about Marian.

"Amos Barton" was from the first intended to form one of a series of "Scenes of Clerical Life," depicting what Marian called "the real drama of Evangelicalism." Lewes was soon convinced of her ability to write a story of sufficient interest for publication, and he sent the first installment off to his own publisher of the moment, John Blackwood.

Blackwood, the inheritor of a family firm in Edinburgh, was a sympathetic and charming man, of the highest business scruples and the most respected intellectual integrity. *Blackwood's Magazine*, "Maga" as it was called, published the most eminent writers and was read in the most respectable houses. It was the new writer's good fortune that Blackwood was immediately struck by her talent. Not that he knew the sex of the author of "Amos Barton"—it was signed "George Eliot," a name chosen by Marian because Lewes was called George and Eliot sounded a nice, rounded word. Lewes explained that his "clerical" friend was diffident, and Blackwood accepted the story and paid £50 for it without insisting on penetrating the incognito.

This seemed relatively easy money to Marian, who was in despair about her slavery to Chapman and their inability to keep Agnes from running up debts that Lewes was obliged to pay. Remonstrating with Agnes had no effect: Lewes noted in his journal, "I fear she is quite hardened." Thornton Hunt and Swynfen Jervis were helping to support the brood, but even so, the life of the Leweses was often too austere for comfort.

As the "Scenes" continued, Blackwood was occasionally disturbed by their realism, and George Eliot toned down several passages to meet his objections—realizing, whatever her own views, that the book had to be kept acceptable to a family magazine and to the circulating libraries. Serialized in *Maga* and then published as a volume, the "Scenes" brought her over £400 in 1857. It looked as if the years of poverty were ending, especially when the book was favorably and lengthily reviewed in *The Times*.

The obvious next step was a three-decker novel, the bread and butter of novelists and publishers throughout the Victorian Age. Marian had an idea for one that Lewes thoroughly approved: she told him a story she had heard from her Methodist aunt Mrs. Samuel Evans, about visiting in prison a young girl condemned to death for child murder, bringing her to confess, and riding with her to the scaffold. Blackwood was delighted to hear, after the moderate but gratifying success of the "Clerical Scenes," that George Eliot was at work on a three-decker; and the story as it unfolded exceeded his expectations—its verisimilitude, humor, and nostalgia were, as he predicted, to be its most popular qualities. He wisely considered his own reaction an index to that of the general public, and he offered £800 for four years' copyright.

Still, even Blackwood was unprepared for the runaway success of *Adam Bede*. The reviewers raved, the public talked, the circulating libraries bought. And with its reputation grew unbelief that such a thoroughly professional book could have been written by a new and unknown author. Surely this was the work of a practised hand— and if so, why was he hiding under a pseudonym?

George Eliot herself said, after the fact, that she had wanted to be judged as a writer—a privilege never extended to women. But the Brontës and Mrs. Gaskell received serious critical attention, so this account is not wholly believable. In fact, she feared the effect on sales and reviews of her marital status—and later events were to justify her caution. Barbara Bodichon said that if the authorship of *Adam Bede* had been known, not a single critic would have praised it, though having once done so, they could not take back their words.

Various members of her family, and residents of the Coventry district, recognized characters in the book, as indeed they had done with the "Clerical Scenes." Only Dickens declared, on internal evidence, that the author was a woman—though Lewes said that anyone should have been able to make that deduction because of the "virtual absence of references to field sports."

By this time, Blackwood was in on the secret. Herbert Spencer and John Chapman were suspicious—especially Chapman, who inexplicably could not get Marian to do any more work for him—but their insistent questions enraged the Leweses, who used this "indelicacy" as an excuse to break off friendships that reminded them of less happy times.

Then the Rev. Liggins, a retired Midlands clergyman, modestly admitted to questioners that he was the author of both the mysterious books. An explanation of the mystery was arrived at that satisfied the Victorian romantic sensibility. Liggins was a true Wordsworthian "natural"—he did his own housework and cooking, lived a solitary country life, and even claimed that he had received no money for his work—a claim necessitated by his unchanged and spartan way of life. Odium began to fall on Blackwood, who at the time was in fact paying his new star £400 more than he had agreed to in view of the runaway sales.

The Liggins hoax aroused all George Eliot's *amour-propre*; when it came to it, she valued her anonymity less than her pride of authorship. Eventually she stopped denying the rumors and questions, and the truth gradually became common knowledge. But *Adam Bede* had given her a start that could not be undone by revelation of her irregular marital status, and she was already in the forefront of the novelistic ranks.

George Eliot herself later claimed that her terror of publicity, her jealousy of her reputation, and her distrust of critics all stemmed from the treatment she received after the publication of *Adam Bede*. However that may have been, the publishing history of this book was certainly remarkable and unlike anything else in her career.

Whatever the torments of the authorship question, they were eased by the fact that Marian was now a financial success, and that working conditions for both her and Lewes were easier as a result. They moved to a larger house, Holly Lodge at Wandsworth, and engaged a servant. Far from increasing her diffidence, the revelation of her authorship seems to have increased Marian's self-confidence, or at least to have allayed her fear of exposure—for she was now at work on the most autobiographical of her novels, *The Mill on the Floss*. Blackwood, after negotiations complicated by other bidders, offered her £2,000 for a first edition of 4,000 copies. She wrote to him,

> I don't know which of those two things I care for most—that people should act nobly towards me, or that I should get honest money. I certainly care a great deal for the money, as I suppose all anxious minds do that love independence and have been brought up to think debt and begging the two deepest dishonours short of crime.[4]

George Eliot certainly reveled in the deep pleasure, not often granted to a woman of her time, of feeling herself independent by virtue of her own earnings. It has often been said that Lewes shielded her from business negotiations, and that his rapacity led the magnanimous George Eliot into unbecoming hardness with the generous Blackwood. It is true that after the Liggins affair, which exacerbated Marian's extreme sensitivity to reviews or comments on her work, Lewes began to vet the post and the newspapers in order to shield her from adverse opinion, especially while she was at work on a book. But he never took financial matters out of her hands; she was at least as astute a negotiator as he. His real part in her work at this time is difficult to assess, because it took place in conversations between them rather than in letters. Her many acknowledgments of the importance of his encouragement are sincere but vague, and though he may have given her technical advice while she was working on the "Clerical Scenes," by the time she wrote *Adam Bede* she had far outstripped him as a novelist.

One significant clue is that while her books from the first dealt with the theme of humility, she herself needed a great deal of ego bolstering in order to produce them. Her feelings of unworthiness alternated wildly with feelings of isolated importance, and her unwillingness to read reviews was not due so much to mistrust of her own powers as to extreme pride in them—pride that was violated by being treated as just another novelist. She repeated Mrs. Gaskell's praise to Barbara, because her words about *Adam Bede* "do her honour, and will incline you to think more highly of her"; she wrote to D'Albert Durade, apropos of a French review,

> But the most ignorant journalist in England would hardly think of calling me a rival of Miss Mulock—a writer who is read only by novel readers, pure and simple, never by people of high culture. A very excellent woman she is, I believe—but we belong to an entirely different order of writers. [5]

Her own egotism, the trait she so ruthlessly dissected in her characters, shows through these statements; and so, perhaps, does a kind of defensiveness that her life with Lewes had increased. From the days when she was an untidy and unlovable child, she was anxious to prove her worth to the people who had slighted her—feelings that must have been revived by the social ostracism she was now experiencing. The emotional support of Lewes was all-important, because it was her only defensive armor against the world. Alone, she had managed to build a life for herself and to control the "ardent nature" that her early acquaintances remarked on. But to reveal herself as much as she did in her novels, she needed a foundation of security; this is what Lewes provided.

Just as if they were producing actual children during this "procreative" phase of the life cycle, the Leweses withdrew into the "dual solitude" they grew to prize so highly. Far from cutting them off from life, they both felt that social engagements tended to be inimical to really living, and that they had more valuable friendships and a deeper conjugal love because these emotions were not diluted by meaningless socializing.

Thus Marian was uncomplaining about her life as a pariah, and even asserted that she found her sympathy for women increased by not actually having to converse with them. But the impulse to *show* them can only have been increased by the treatment she received at the hands of the sanctimonious. Lewes traditionally spent Christmas at the home of his close friend Arthur Helps, for example—but it was out of the question that Marian should accompany him. Isaac refused to communicate with her, and managed to pass the embargo on to Chrissey. Male friends who came to dinner habitually left their wives behind. Barbara had written her when the authorship was still a secret, that she had tried to induce Mrs. Owen Jones, the wife of the famous art critic who later decorated George Eliot's home, to call.

> I tried to make Mrs. OJ say she would like to know you (not that you would like to know her) but she seemed to feel fear! I do not think she would call even if she knew you were George Eliot. I said a great deal about my pleasant visits. I was trying experiments on her for my own satisfaction not on your account at all. Oh Marian, Marian, what cowards people are! [6]

However, the effects of this kind of thing were not all on one side. Marian's self-mistrust may have been increased, but she also began to feel that she was altogether out of the ordinary—that her proud stand in life added stature to her books. Along with all her sympathy for common humanity, there was also a current of contempt for the mass opinion that had first condemned her, then forgiven her because she became rich and famous. Late in her career, she wrote to Frederic Harrison,

> . . . all the miseries one's obstinate egoism endures from the fact of being a writer of novels—books which the dullest and silliest reader thinks himself competent to deliver an opinion on. [7]

As she had hinted in her early views on the ego satisfactions of martyrdom, her sense of her own mission was bound up with the feeling of doing the unconventional, unpopular thing—though she needed the approval of Lewes and of her reading public in order to be able to do it. Her sense of being a man among men, at those dinners to which wives never came, was as gratifying to her as was her sense of being an exception among novelists.

Though *Adam Bede* deals with the countryside of Marian's childhood, and to some extent with her feelings about her father, it manages to bathe these memories in a nostalgic glow; its effect on her, and on the reader, is one of greater happiness than any of her other books. But once her ability to recapture past emotion was released in this way, it continued to deeper and more painful levels. *The Mill on the Floss* was painful to write and is painful to read, because here George Eliot is talking about her own young self—her feeling of rejection by her mother, her thwarted love for her brother, her search for happiness. She spoke of the book as of her own child—Lewes wrote to Blackwood, after a Continental holiday, "Mrs. Lewes feels greatly benefited by the trip, and will rock the cradle of the new 'little stranger' with fresh maternal vigour." As the conclusion drew near, he reported "she is crying her eyes out over the death of her children." The death of one of Chrissey's small daughters at the same time heightened the poignancy of the moment.

After this bout of self-revelation, Marian's anxiety over reviews and public opinion was greater than ever, and the Leweses left for their first trip to Italy in time to avoid the first newspaper notices. The book sold well, but readers who had taken *Adam Bede* to their hearts were somewhat dismayed by the less pleasurable, more intense experience they were now subjected to. George Eliot herself needed a respite from agonizing personal memory, and she was already contemplating an historical novel set in Florence. Lewes, in one of the few concrete pieces of literary advice he gave her, suggested that the time of Savonarola would make a picturesque background. But during the long labor that was to become *Romola*, George Eliot was distracted by the last of her English "country" novels, *Silas Marner*. The story came to her as a memory of an old linen weaver, with a pack on his back, whom she had seen as a child; and she put everything aside to follow it.

. . . I should not have believed that any one would have been interested in it but myself (since William Wordsworth is dead) if Mr. Lewes had not been strongly arrested by it. . . . I have felt all through as if the story would have lent itself best to metrical rather than prose fiction, especially in all that relates to the psychology of Silas; except that, under that treatment, there could not be an equal play of humour.[8]

Again we see that the approval of Lewes was necessary for her to continue with an idea once she had begun; and that his approval was, in her mind, bound up with humor, approachability, and appeal to the public. He was the only critic she trusted, partly because his taste and judgment were such sure guides to the market. His critical ideology had always been anti-elitist, considering popular appeal, continued over the years, as the surest guide to literary excellence; and George Eliot's self-esteem required a wide readership and financial success. And she was right to consider herself, in this way, the successor of Wordsworth: Browning and Tennyson, the two poets of her own time who had a success comparable to the novelists, were less central to the popular imagination than Wordsworth had been, or than George Eliot wished to be. Like Katherine Mansfield, she had turned to prose to find her audience, though her inclinations might have been poetic in another time.

With the perfect and spontaneous *Silas Marner*, George Eliot reached the close of the first phase in her career. She was at the point, in fact, that Virginia Woolf reached after *The Waves*—she had gone as far as she could along a certain path, and she was casting about for a new direction. But whereas her first great creative period exhausted Virginia Woolf, and left her without the resources to subdue her mental illness and strike out afresh, George Eliot undertook a long discipline of study and training—and though the immediate results are not among her best work, the ultimate effect was to revitalize her creativity and to give her resources that no novelist had had before. Her learning, her studious, isolated life, her happiness with Lewes—all these elements were put to use. She had first subdued and then exorcised the demons of her youth, and though they lingered on in the form of headaches and bilious attacks while she was at work, and pathological sensitivity to criticism, the strength that flowed from her success as a novelist and as a woman was more than sufficient to organize and direct her creative energy. She was experiencing the happiness of genius, as Lewes described it:

> Genius is the happiest, as it is the greatest, of human faculties. It has no immunity from the common sorrows of humanity; but it has one glorious privilege, which it alone possesses; the privilege of turning its sorrows into beauty, and brooding delighted over them! [9]

Following the publication of *Silas Marner*, and after a second journey to Italy in search of material, the Leweses moved into London—to Blandford Square, a few doors away from Barbara Bodichon—in order to make a home for Lewes's eldest son Charles while he got settled in a career. All three of the surviving boys had been at school in Switzerland, though for some years their home had been, theoretically at least, with their father and Marian, who referred to them as "our three boys" and herself as "Mutter." Anthony Trollope helped Charles to find a niche in the Post Office, and the two younger boys emigrated to begin farming in South Africa.

Marian enjoyed the presence of the boys (particularly of Charles, who adored her), and the unfamiliar sensation of having a rising generation to provide for gave her deep pleasure. But she confessed in letters that she missed the "dual solitude" and the possibility of country life, and it was with some relief that she saw Charlie eventually married off.

This busy period was also one of hard and unrewarding literary effort: the laborious writing of *Romola* caused George Eliot much torment, and she felt a sense of release when she handed it over to the publisher—who was not Blackwood but George Smith, of the firm Smith, Elder, who had offered her the unprecedented sum of £10,000. He did not make his money back—the book was universally praised, but heavy going for the ordinary reader—and George Eliot returned sheepishly to the Blackwood fold.

At this period, Marian was working her way through the hiatus in her career that followed the English "country" novels and preceded her dissection of town life during the Industrial Revolution. This change in theme was difficult because it involved abandoning the justification of her younger self and facing a more complex, more fully adult set of themes. Her retreat into scholarship was a necessary prelude to this major effort, but much of her difficulty with *Romola* stemmed from her knowledge that it *was* something of a retreat.

Lewes, too, was weathering a difficult crisis in his career. Anxious to pursue his scientific studies, he was still troubled by the need of providing (or helping to provide) for two households, and this implied continuing with periodical journalism. He had reluctantly consented to edit a new review, the *Fortnightly*, though he was plagued by headaches, fainting fits, and indigestion, all brought about by overwork and overstrain. Marian's morbid diffidence over her work, his sons' careers, and the continuing financial drama of Agnes all took their toll of his health. Marian wrote,

> Dear George is all activity, yet is in very frail health. How I worship his good humour, his good sense, his affectionate care for every one who has claims on him! That worship is my best life.[10]

George's multifarious activities kept Marian in touch with current opinion, with life itself, while she immersed herself in one titanic project after another. She read him her day's work in the evening, and heard his advice; he dealt with the post and the callers while she was at work on a book, and shielded her from too much social life. Her fame was beginning to overcome the scruples of the prudish, and isolation was now something she would have liked more of.

The Leweses moved to a new house, the Priory on the north bank of the Regent's Canal, where they were to live for the rest of their life together. Sumptuously decorated by Owen Jones, the house was comfortable and convenient, and the number of callers who attended their Sunday afternoons steadily grew, and even began to include wives and daughters. George Eliot's presence, like her novels, was undeniably edifying, and the women who met her adored her as Maria Lewis and Sara Hennell had done in the past. Even the Queen reported that she had enjoyed *Adam Bede*, to George Eliot's delight and Lewes's relative indifference.

In her next novel after the interlude of *Romola*, George Eliot returned for her setting to her native Midlands, though to a slightly later period and to the manufacturing towns rather than the regions of old-fashioned agriculture. *Felix Holt, the Radical* was scarcely the political tract that its name implied—even the thoroughly conservative John Blackwood could say, "I suspect I am a radical of the Felix Holt breed, and so was my father before me." He was delighted to have George Eliot back with the firm, and with a novel set in England—"It quite takes me back to the days when Adam Bede won the Derby."

Set at the time of the 1832 Reform Bill, *Felix Holt* combined two plots in the way that was characteristic of all George Eliot's later novels. She had always used pairs of contrasting characters—Dinah and Hetty, Arthur and Adam, Maggie and Lucy—but now she had both a "political" plot, built around Felix, and a classical tragedy, illustrating her doctrine of Nemesis, built around Mrs. Transome. This allowed her to treat several strata of society at once; it also allowed her to begin the exploration of the relation between individual morality and social structure that was to be her greatest theme.

Felix Holt won wide critical approval, but the novel has certain problems that show that the second great phase of George Eliot's career was not, even yet, fully under way. She was still immersing herself in scholarly study rather than writing spontaneously from her deepest self. She had consulted the lawyer Frederic Harrison to work out the details of inheritance in the book, and some of this complicated "scaffolding" had not been sufficiently dismantled. The mass of undigested legal detail sat uneasily with the emotional themes of the story, and diminished the power of their effect.

Her next academic exercise, again the product of study rather than of feeling, was a book-length poem, *The Spanish Gypsy*, partly sketched out during a trip through Spain. As she had predicted at the time of *Silas Marner*, her verse was resolutely humorless; but the theme foreshadowed later developments in her career—she was doing for the Gypsies what she had tried to do for the Florentine Renaissance in *Romola* and what she was to do for the Jews in *Daniel Deronda*.

Painful as this period of concentrated study and uncongenial tasks was to her, it was immensely valuable—and not only as an emotional resting place. All of the scholastic exercises she had set herself—in linguistics, verse, history, and (through Lewes) in science and philosophy—were widening her equipment as a novelist, and finally she was ready to begin *Middlemarch*, which is generally agreed to be the most complete picture of English society ever written. She was ready to wear both her erudition and her autobiographical inclinations more lightly than ever before, to put them to use with complete mastery.

Middlemarch began as two separate novels, which were joined early in their existence. But the dual structure did not split the novel apart, as it had done in the case of *Felix Holt*. The two stories were different aspects of the same theme, and in their entirety provide a sort of apologia for George Eliot's life with Lewes. One of the themes is the story of Lydgate, a talented and ambitious young doctor, whose career is ruined by the obstinate selfishness of his beautiful wife, Rosamund. Lydgate's susceptibility to female beauty is the weakness for which he is punished—a theme that reminds us of Hetty in *Adam Bede*, George Eliot's first treatment of the selfishness that pretty girls are liable to. Played off against this story is the portrait of Dorothea, an idealistic young woman who sees in the aging pedant Casaubon an opportunity to combine love with service. This tragic mistake, which George Eliot herself came close to making in the days of Dr. Brabant, is rectified by Casaubon's death and Dorothea's marriage to the talented, impecunious Ladislaw—the closest thing to a portrait of Lewes in any of her novels.

Middlemarch contains much more than these two stories. On the one hand, it is a long meditation on the themes of inheritance, families, social change, and how these things affect individual ambition; and on the other hand, it is about the difficulty of finding a role that confronts a young woman of unusual capabilities, and about how she is tempted to pour her energy and devotion into unworthy vessels. But it is clear that, for all the flaws of Dorothea and Ladislaw, George Eliot's imagined ideal was now very close to the situation that she herself achieved with Lewes.

It was during and after the writing of *Middlemarch* that George Eliot became recognized as a great moral teacher, a sort of wise woman or Sibyl. Lewes called her "Madonna," and enjoyed referring to their Sunday afternoons at the Priory as religious services. Her effect on women had always been of a kind to compel confessional outpourings; many said or wrote that in her presence they felt that finally someone understood everything about their lives and their sufferings. She had attracted fervid emotional disciples, and a woman she and Lewes visited on their way to Spain, Mrs. Frederick Lehmann, indicated in a letter to her husband something of how the effect was produced.

> I felt I must make an effort, because they told me it was solely on *my account* they came to Pau. "We look upon you as a sort of heroine, dear Mrs. Lehmann, parted so long from your husband and your home, and take a deep interest in you," for which I thanked her, and felt inexpressibly soothed in the idea that somebody had at last found out I was a heroine, which I had been suspecting all along myself. . . . She made me tell her the whole story of our courtship and marriage, which seemed to interest her intensely. In fact, she was like a dear, loving elder sister to me the whole time.[11]

Mrs. Lehmann and other competent, happy women were able to enjoy the effect without being bowled over by it. But there were others—unhappy, lonely women, whose emotional needs were acute—who fell in love with George Eliot in the full sense of the term.

Edith Simcox, an early organizer of women's trade unions, became one of the most ardent worshippers. Her biographer says,

> For years she celebrated 8 December, the day she first saw George Eliot's handwriting. . . . Though he probably did not suspect the depth of this pathological obsession, George Henry Lewes in general fostered the devotion of Edith and the others as an aid in his endless struggle against George Eliot's self-depreciation and diffidence.[12]

Edith sometimes met the other disciples on her visits to the Priory; far from feeling jealous, she was pleased to find that another "had loved my darling lover-wise too." Elma Stuart, who is buried next to George Eliot in Highgate cemetery, was liable to fling herself to the floor and kiss the feet of her idol—the nearest thing to a caress that any of them were generally permitted. Lewes wrote in his diary,

> Elma to lunch. She showed us the handkerchief with which she had wiped the tears from Polly's eyes, and henceforth has preserved as a relic. [13]

Alexander Main, a young Scot, carried his adoration far enough to compile a book, which went through many editions—the *Wise, Witty, and Tender Sayings of George Eliot*. Lewes approved the publicity, though he ridiculed Main's tendency to behave as if the *Sayings* were a more important book than the novels from which they came.

George Eliot and Lewes did not leave off traveling once they were settled at the Priory; on the contrary, their European travels during and after *Middlemarch* were longer than usual—the work had been utterly exhausting, and they had no domestic responsibilities to keep them in London. George Eliot was not yet looking for another theme, but at the Kursaal in Hamburg they watched the gambling, and saw an episode that was to be the "germ" of *Daniel Deronda*.

> The saddest thing to be witnessed is the play of Miss Leigh, Byron's grand niece, who is only 26 years old, and is completely in the grasp of this mean, money-raking demon. It made me cry to see her young fresh face among the hags and brutally stupid men around her. [14]

Deronda is to my mind her greatest book, flawed though it is. She never could quite bring herself to make her heroine plain-looking, as Charlotte Brontë did on principle; but in Gwendolen for the first time she can treat a beauty sympathetically, and examine her own feelings toward egotism in a complex way. Her deepest themes—the relation of heroism to domestic obligation and to success as an artist, the nature of marriage, the search for an ideal—receive their most powerful treatment in this book. It also contains what may be a portrait of the young Lewes in the character of Hans Meyrick, the impecunious idolater who combines domestic affections with inability to realize either his artistic ambitions or the kind of social commitment that his hero, Deronda, is capable of. The Ladislaw/Meyrick type is by no means everything that Lewes was, but its existence seems to indicate that while Lewes was to George Eliot the indispensable companion of her life, she never considered that he embodied her masculine ideal. This ideal, by the time she wrote *Deronda*, was indeed very far removed from earthly reality, and this is one of the book's flaws. Perhaps she, too, like Katherine Mansfield, mentally contrasted her husband's weakness with her father's strength—and though she had made her choice in life, and made it happily, she still felt a kind of regret for the strength and certainty that she had attributed to her father in her childhood.

Lewes, however, had by his own interest in psychology and in intellectual independence helped to guide her toward one of the main themes of *Deronda*—the revival of the Jewish nation. George Eliot's attraction to the Jews has baffled many people, beginning with Blackwood. She was known to admire *Uncle Tom's Cabin*, and in part she seems to have intended to do for the Jews what Harriet Beecher Stowe had done for the American Negro. Her treatment of Savonarola's Florence and of the Spanish Gypsies had begun her series of "exotic" backgrounds. Her evangelical days had left their legacy of sympathy for religious persecution. Above all, however, the Jewish intellectual tradition interested her and Lewes because it seemed to be carrying out their own lines of thought, lines that were still ignored by the conventional Anglo-Saxon establishment. They were well aware that this group was providing most of the impulses toward new interpretations of history and psychology, which were to culminate in the careers of Marx and Freud. Freud, indeed, was to sum up the psychological themes that Lewes devoted the latter part of his life to studying; and in 1926, Freud explained what his Jewish identification had meant for him.

. . . it was to my Jewish nature alone that I owed two characteristics that had become indispensable to me in the difficult course of my life. Because I was a Jew I found myself free from many prejudices which restricted others in the use of their intellect; and as a Jew I was prepared to join the Opposition, and to do without agreement with the "compact majority." [15]

These "two characteristics" were the very ones that George Eliot most ardently desired for herself. The Jews represented a more powerful theme for her than any other minority, because here she found an oppressed group who actually far surpassed their oppressors in the qualities that she valued most highly. She was identifying herself with those who were secretly superior. She felt that her own outcast status was somehow related to the established church, the structure of patriarchal authority, and that other forms of oppression by this same authority might illuminate her own condition. And was not anti-Semitism practised in an informal, unspoken way, like the conventional suppression of women? Was it not accepted in just as unthinking a fashion?

The Jewish part of *Deronda*, then, was much more than a picturesque setting—it summed up certain things about her intellectual life with Lewes, and her feelings about being a woman in an anomalous situation. In spite of the confidence that years of success had given her, *Deronda* was as deeply felt, and gave her as much suffering, as anything that had gone before. William Blackwood wrote to his brother John, after a visit during which he inquired whether she was pleased with the manuscript,

> She at once hung her head low and said "Oh no, it is detestable I think. . . ."

But when he suggested taking the first part to Edinburgh with him,

> if you had seen her face of horror and fright and meek expression you would have been startled. It was one of the most striking scenes I have ever seen and for a minute or two she would not speak. She seemed just to tremble at the idea of the M.S. being taken from her as if it were her baby. . . .[16]

Deronda was George Eliot's last novel, and the ordeal of its completion had exhausted Lewes as much as Marian. They bought a country house at Witley, Surrey, where they continued their old life of work and reading together at a more leisurely pace. Marian seemed to realize that her long engagement with the novel had reached a halt: she began work on a volume of philosophical essays,

Theophrastus Such, for which she adopted the persona of an aging misanthrope, reflecting with irony and sadness on the themes she had treated so much more excitingly in fiction.

After only two summers at Witley, the by now continually ailing Lewes declined rapidly in health. His diary reveals that he felt his own death to be imminent, though he concealed this knowledge from Marian. He feared the effect of his death on her far more than he feared death itself. Toward the end of 1878, after a week's acute illness, Lewes died, and the desolated Marian knew that her career as a novelist, their joint effort, was indeed at an end. It is such a commonplace of literary history for a writer to die soon after the completion of his life's work that it is interesting that Lewes himself was the first to die after the final act in the career of George Eliot; her own death, two years later, was, it seems, more closely related to the futility of life without Lewes than to life without novel-writing. Just as her real career had begun after her relationship with Lewes, so it did not survive his death.

She spent the first few months of her widowhood in revising and completing Lewes's last major book, *Problems of Life and Mind*. She began seeing a few friends. Then, with a precipitancy that surprised only those of her friends who had not known the young Marian, she announced that she planned to marry a man twenty years younger than herself—John Cross. He and his widowed mother had been neighbors of the Leweses in Surrey, and his mother's death, coinciding with that of Lewes, had created a bond of sympathy between him and Marian. For several years Marian had called John "Nephew." He had taken over from Lewes much of the business of managing George Eliot's money and investments, and he was the first friend she saw after Lewes's death. They began reading Dante together, and in the growing affection and tone of dependence in her letters to him, even before the death of Lewes, it is possible to see that she was preparing herself for the coming ordeal and looking around for possible supports when it came.

Her marriage, in May 1880, outraged many of her friends; but her brother Isaac wrote to her for the first time since she had cut herself off from society by living with Lewes. John Cross himself seems to have had a difficult time in making the adjustment from nephew and adorer to husband of this mother figure: in a fit of temporary insanity, he jumped into the Grand Canal during their Venetian honeymoon. He was to write a biography of George Eliot that suppressed all mention of the sexual nature that so alarmed him, and thus created a picture of her as the boring and sanctimonious Victorian Sibyl that later generations never got past, and that interfered for decades with a true appreciation of the nature of her achievement.

But public opinion and the stresses of her new life had little time to affect George Eliot: she died at the end of December, 1880, after a mere seven months of legal marriage.

CHAPTER 3

The Works of George Henry Lewes

The problem that perplexes any modern student of Lewes is his obscurity—his books are practically unknown, and his reputation rests solely on that of George Eliot. Yet to his contemporaries, it seemed certain that he was to be enduringly famous. Was he simply overshadowed by George Eliot? Did he leave his best work undone to be her aide-de-camp instead? Does a polymath like Lewes inevitably suffer eclipse by comparison with single-minded professionals?

There is some truth in all of these hypotheses. But there is also the fact that Lewes himself deliberately chose to be a man of his time, and to do work that would inevitably be superseded—that is to say, scientific work. In fact, Lewes's humility, his craftsman's mentality, insisted upon the temporal nature of all intellectual work: he believed that there are no eternal truths, and that art could only reveal the truth of one time. Ironically, his lifelong companion has—if anyone has—produced art for all time, and this achievement seems to be related to the strength of her ego. She preached humility, but Lewes practised it—and this is one clue to their relative reputations today. So much of his energy went into fueling her achievement that she was able to write with the power and concentration of two people. After his liaison with George Eliot began, Lewes was still capable of many kinds of intellectual work, but not of fictional creation. The story of his career shows a great deal of what went into her books, because so much of his vitality, brilliance, and versatility was absorbed by them.

Lewes's approach to his work was practical and free of cant. He turned his hand to anything that came along, and his ability to support himself by his pen was always his justification for wielding it. Not for him to hide behind degrees and sinecures; he ridiculed the pompous insistence on specialization:

> The public like a man to confine himself to one special topic. Division of labour is the grand thing: if you have made pins' heads, content yourself with that, and do not venture upon points.[1]

In fact, far from being the typical mid-Victorian man of letters, Lewes was in many respects an eighteenth-century figure: his prose is as direct as that of Tom Paine, occasionally as witty as Voltaire, and he had the courage and convictions of the French revolutionaries. Holyoake, his colleague on the *Leader*, said:

> Lewes was intellectually the bravest man I have known. . . . Men of natural intrepidity never take danger into account or, if they are conscious of it, it only influences them as an inspiration to action. Mr. Lewes had intellectual intrepidity of this kind.[2]

Intellectual liberty, he thought, was the great thing; he had no interest in bludgeoning his opponents into sharing or admitting his point of view. George Eliot enjoyed above all the sense of independence that this quality gave her life with him: she wrote to Sara Hennell (of whose silliness Lewes was one of the severest critics),

> . . . you must not impute *my* opinions to *him*, nor vice versa. The intense happiness of our union is derived in a high degree from the perfect freedom with which we each follow and declare our own impressions. In this respect I know *no* man so great as he—that difference of opinion rouses no egoistic irritation in him, and that he is ready to admit that

The Works of George Henry Lewes | 1 6 1

another's argument is the stronger, the moment his intellect recognizes it.[3]

Lewes's lack of egotism is the striking thing here—and indeed it seems that George Eliot early set out to play for the highest stakes that the ego could imagine, the status of great artist, while Lewes's self-abnegation was so much a part of his personality that the world took him at his own valuation, and awarded him a lower status and a less public role to play. Is "great artist" a choice of the ego as much as a choice dictated by natural gifts? Certainly this case seems to indicate as much. Lewes's sense of intellectual freedom was crucial to the developing George Eliot, who had suffered so much from spiritual dictatorship; and equally important was Lewes's early and clear recognition of the fact that he and she were playing quite different games. One way this choice worked itself out in practice is that from the first, George Eliot was exceptionally deliberate and conscious of the quality of every word she wrote, while Lewes was speedy and erratic and careless—at least until he came under her influence: she writes, again to Sara, of her effect on the insouciant Lewes:

> Rewriting is an excellent process frequently both for the book and its author, and to prevent you from grudging the toil, I will tell you that so old a writer as Mr. Lewes now re-writes everything of importance, though in all the earlier years of his authorship he would never take that trouble.[4]

In this we see not only the initial difference in their temperaments, but one reason why the books Lewes wrote after he met Marian are so much more solid and serious than the early ones. If his speediness helped to cut through her diffidence, his sense of the dignity of the printed word was certainly increased by her respect for it.

His choice of science and journalism over fiction was not difficult; his successes with the novel had not been so brilliant as to cause him much of a pang at giving it up. But there is no doubt that he deliberately left the field clear for George Eliot: when the editors of *Once a Week* pressed him for a serial novel, having agreed with Polly that it was desirable I should not swerve from Science any more, at least just now, I declined.[5]

His first and most enduring fame was won as a literary critic; and here he seems to have viewed himself as the educator of public taste rather than (like Murry) the empathetic interpreter or the critical theorist. Indeed, he objected to critical theory as strongly as to all dogma:

> My first objection to anything like a doctrine in Literature is, . . . at the best it could only exhibit the laws which great artists had followed, it could not embrace the laws which great artists to come would follow.[6]

This is an indication of the open-mindedness that enabled Lewes and Murry both to pass the acid test of the critic: the accurate valuation of the new. It also enabled them to perceive the gifts of their women long before sufficient proof had been offered to the outside world to establish their reputations.

All the same, Lewes held that literary values were objective facts; his relativism did not extend to leniency to ignorant or unformed taste. The republic of letters was open to anyone willing to do the work necessary to enter it; but it was a meritocracy. Acquiescing in ignorant judgments was as great a sin against truth as was the blind upholding of privilege.

> People talk of admiring or not admiring Racine, as if it were a matter of taste; but it is in truth a matter of knowledge. He has survived two centuries of criticism, and in spite of every change of taste; the admiration of Europe for two centuries is a pedestal whereon none but the highest can repose; those, therefore, who refuse their tribute to Racine are convicted of incompetence to judge him; convicted of want of sufficient knowledge of the language, or want of critical appreciation. . . . When we hear a Frenchman disparage Shakespeare, we invariably suspect his critical power, or his knowledge of our language. . . .[7]

This passage shows many of the fundamental characteristics of Lewes's literary criticism—his cosmopolitanism, his willingness to admire enthusiastically, his reliance on general acclaim as an index of quality, his insistence on competence. Popular success and critical consensus were for him unarguable evidences of literary quality; he is perhaps unique among critics in showing no inclination at all to separate success from merit. Is this practicality, democracy, or the absence of the inner certainty that makes a critic (or an artist) go against the crowd? Was the importance of success to George Eliot enhanced by the fact that it would prove something about her talent to Lewes as well as to the public at large?

He never, in fact, judges literature in the abstract—and his opinions on the Romantics are full of social and political considerations, which make his reliance on popularity seem related to his democratic ideology. Wordsworth he considered "the greatest egotist who ever lived" (which perhaps provides a clue to why he was George Eliot's favorite poet), and "as a *philosophical* poet, mediocrity itself." The reason was that Wordsworth's human sympathies had atrophied with the growth of his political conservatism: he espoused

> the wretched absurdity that man, to keep himself pure and pious, should shun cities and the haunts of men, to shut himself in mountain solitudes. . . . With all this tenderness for Nature not a heart-beat for Man! [8]

Wordsworth sought his own salvation at the expense of others (in true evangelical fashion), much as George Eliot was tempted to do during her "Holy War." This mingling of political and literary judgment is reminiscent of Murry's remarks on Fielding—the insistence of both critics on egalitarian morality in literature is related to their ability to admire Mansfield and Eliot; the two women, in turn, however appreciative of this admiration and support, have a sneaking sympathy with the egotism of other geniuses: it is interesting that Katherine Mansfield says of Wordsworth, "What a Pa man!" Though a fellow-genius could never have fostered the career of either woman, and this fact helped to dictate their choice of mate, the kind of dissatisfaction we find in so many of Katherine Mansfield's letters, and in George Eliot's portrayal of Ladislaw, indicates that some part of these women still wanted a man who was unquestionably stronger, a hero rather than a hero worshipper.

This common female desire was subordinate, in them, to the desire for independence; but the choice was not made wholly without regret.

Lewes was much less of a hero worshipper than Murry; the poets he admired were part of the fabric of his ideological stance. Shelley the atheist was to him the greatest of the Romantics:

> Shelley alone was the poet standing completely on his truth; giving up his life to it, and eternally preaching it.[9]

Toryism, said Lewes, wished to keep the world in long clothes; revolution was the seizure of adult clothes denied; and the Romantics were the expression of the French Revolution. But Shelley was greater as a man than as an artist (compare Murry's remarks on Lawrence) because of his sins against art: sins that involved moving beyond the accessible and intelligible, which alone were appropriate for a democratic age, to poetic flights that led him into error and obscurity.

> . . . he sometimes uses the epithet "*wingless* boat." A prosaic critic would say that boats not usually having wings, to call one wingless is superfluous; and although the prosaic critic would thereby prove himself, as he always does, to be a discoverer of mares' nests, and one might ask him if Shelley did not know that as well as he, yet his objection to the epithet would be well founded, though ill expressed. By "wingless" the student of Shelley knows that he means to intimate extreme swiftness by some supernatural means, but this meaning is too remote for poetry.[10]

The rationalism that served Lewes so well in this kind of close reading was joined with an acute psychological penetration, heightened by his scientific studies, that enabled him to see what so many of his contemporaries missed, for example in Dickens:

> Psychologists will understand both the extent and the limitation of the remark, when I say that in no other perfectly sane mind . . . have I observed vividness of imagination approaching so closely to hallucination. . . . my studies have led me to the conviction that nothing is less like genius than insanity. . . .[11]

This ability to recognize the quality of genius, and to distinguish it from the insanity with which it is often confused by more conventional minds, shows how remarkably equipped was Lewes to give George Eliot the kind of understanding she needed. His insistence that genius was healthy, that it was the most joyous and sane and human of qualities, served him not only in understanding her, but in his own work. Another great psychologist, Havelock Ellis, has analyzed the reasons for the success of Lewes's most important work, the *Life of Goethe,* in terms that recall descriptions of Middleton Murry as a Romantic poet manqué, and thus the man best equipped to understand and write about them. After detailing Lewes's outward qualifications—interest in the drama, knowledge of French and German literature, first-hand acquaintance with the Goethe circle at Weimar—Ellis goes on,

> There was another and even more important sense in which Lewes was near to Goethe. He was not a man of genius, but with his very various talents and aptitudes he had encountered the same problems of art and thought and life as Goethe had had to wrestle with. Goethe was a dilettante—that is to say, a lover of all things—on a more than heroic scale; Lewes was something of the same on a lower plane. He was an artist and a man of science, a thinker and a man of the world. It was an invaluable combination of qualities for approaching a personality of Goethe's immense scope. . . .[12]

When Lewes came to the moment in life when he had to confront the question of turning from these varied interests to one overriding interest (the moment, say, when Murry founded the *Adelphi*), he was enough of a Victorian to want to identify the most fundamental and unifying idea of all—and he was also enough of a Victorian to believe that the place to look was science. His later career is well summed up by the French author of a book on "English Psychology":

> Mr Lewes lacks the vocation of the scholar, which indeed is generally wanting in original minds. . . . Mr Lewes is a physiologist. But as all reflective spirits who please themselves with conceptions of entirety, find

philosophy at the end of every science, so Mr Lewes has found it there.[13]

Lewes began in science with his usual strong sense of his popular audience. He wrote directly for the reader of *Blackwood's*, whom he envisioned "on Wimbledon Common with net and jar." He says in the introduction to his collection of *Sea-Side Studies*,

> I have endeavoured to furnish the visitor to the sea-side with plain direc-
> tions, by means of which he may study and enjoy the marvels of ocean-
> life; and to present such descriptions of the animals and the wonders of
> their organisation, as may interest the reader by his own fireside.[14]

This is the book he was working on during the visit to Tenby when George Eliot conceived the idea for her first story—her own de-scription of the "wonders of organisation" of the human animal for her readers to enjoy by their firesides. And from this time forward, Lewes's scientific work proceeded in counterpoint to her novelistic work. His tools—the microscope and the handbook of species— were, metaphorically speaking, hers too; and his speciality of dissec-tion aroused her keenest excitement and interest, as she reveals in a letter to his son Charlie.

> I wish you could have seen today, as I did, the delicate spinal cord of a
> dragon fly—like a tiny thread with tiny beads on it—which your father
> has just dissected! He is so wonderfully clever now at the dissection of
> these delicate things and has attained this cleverness entirely by devoted
> practice during the last three years. I hope *you* have some of his resolu-
> tion and persistent regularity in work. . . .[15]

Lewes, like Murry, was an adept at the art of getting on with things: George Eliot says elsewhere that if he took it into his head to do a translation of Dante, he would take the book down and knock off the first couple of cantos while his tea was being made.

The culmination of his physiological studies was *The Physiology of Common Life*, which he published in 1860 and intended for the student as well as the general reader. This is his search for a unify-ing theory of life, and while Marx found it in economic deter-

minism, Lewes sees it in the physical necessities that underlie economics. Hunger is the motivating force:

> Look where we may, we see it as the motive power which sets the vast
> array of human machinery in action. . . . Nothing but the necessities
> of food will force man to that labour which he hates, and will always
> avoid when he can. And although this seems obvious only when applied
> to the labouring classes, it is equally though less obviously true when
> applied to all other classes, for the money we all labour to gain is
> nothing but food, and the surplus of food, which will buy other men's
> labour.[16]

But the high Marxian seriousness of this passage is not maintained:
Lewes the practical polymath creeps in, and gets sidetracked by
such questions as the miseries of indigestion, the effects of cooking,
"Are fish-eaters unusually prolific?," and "Pastry—is it injurious?"

Volume II of the book looks forward to Lewes's later concerns by
treating psychology as a branch of physiology. For it was in pursuit
of a science of mind that Lewes undertook his physiological researches, which concentrated on the spinal cord, the nervous system, and the brain itself.

His last book, *Problems of Life and Mind,* was a series of rather
disconnected volumes, two of which were edited by George Eliot
after Lewes's death. It is a melancholy, frustrating book in some
ways—he clearly saw the necessity for a great breakthrough in psychology, but he could not make it himself: the basic data were insufficient, Lewes himself was ill and near the end of his career, and
in any case he had not the utter concentration of mind to make
the great leap that was finally made by Freud. Nor did he live in
the milieu that was to prove itself most receptive to the new ideas—
it is no coincidence that the Jewish tradition which received George
Eliot's homage in *Daniel Deronda* was also to be the source of the
ideas Lewes was groping for in his own work.

Lewes's account of his own searches, and his vision of the necessity for Freud, came out clearly in the first volume.

> 1860 . . . I believed that my researches into the nervous system had
> placed in my hands a clue through the labyrinth of mental phenomena.

. . . In 1862 I began the investigation of the physiological mechanism of Feeling and Thought, and from that time forward have sought assistance in a wide range of research. . . . Psychology is still without the fundamental data necessary to its *constitution* as a science; it is very much in the condition of Chemistry before Lavoisier, or of Biology before Bichat.[17]

The effort to separate metaphysics from science had also preoccupied Lewes in his early years, but by this time, he saw that task as all but accomplished: "The expansion of knowledge is loosening the very earth clutched by the roots of creeds and churches. . . . Science is penetrating everywhere, and slowly changing men's conception of the world and of man's destiny."

Both Lewes and George Eliot, in their different ways, tried to discover a moral code for an age without faith—based on sociology, psychology, and the needs of human nature and society. One clue to why the novelist succeeded where the scientist failed, at least in England, is given by that incarnation of cultural conventionality, John Blackwood. He refused to publish *Problems of Life and Mind* on the grounds of its flippant impieties, and this is the example he cited:

Now surely it is no matter of exhilaration, but rather of deep regret, that we find ourselves in a universe of mystery, compelled to grope our way amid shadows, with terrible penalties affixed to each false step. To resign ourselves to this condition is one thing; another to exult in it, and claim the exultation as an act of piety. Among the many strange servilities mistaken for pieties, one of the least lovely is that which hopes to flatter God by despising the world, and vilifying human nature.*

* The Author of Creation is the only author who is supposed to be flattered by our lavish assurance that his works are imbecile.[18]

Blackwood was willing to publish George Eliot's search for the meaning of human nature, her questioning of God's design and indeed of his very existence, because these questions were cloaked in plot and character—her verisimilitude could be praised while her theology and sociology were ignored. The English terror of ideas is one reason why there was an English George Eliot, but never an English Freud.

Psychological researchers today are in some ways turning away from the legacy of Freud and using terms reminiscent of Lewes, who believed that "the psychologist's quest is one half physiology and one half sociology." Current beliefs that biological and chemical disorders are implicated in mental illness, as are the family and society, show us how audacious and prescient were some of the suggestions made by Lewes a hundred years ago.

The symbiosis of George Henry Lewes and George Eliot had many ramifications. The success of her novels meant that he could pursue unpopular and not very lucrative researches; the ideas he was working with influenced the depth psychology that is one of the most remarkable aspects of her novels. If she went deeper than he in penetrating the mystery of existence, it is partly because he gave her a thread to follow in the search.

CHAPTER 4

The Novels of
George Eliot

Critical and public opinion of George Eliot has not always been as uniformly high as it is today. In his biography, published not long after her death, John Cross emphasized the sibylline, moral aspect of her works—thus ensuring her unpopularity with the generations who rebelled against the "eminent Victorians." Her letters are uniformly sanctimonious, even hypocritical, in direct contrast to the stark honesty and self-revelation in her novels. And the inflicting of *Silas Marner* on schoolchildren provided the final obstacle to general appreciation of her work.

But even at its lowest, her reputation never suffered complete eclipse, though different aspects of her work have won admiration at different times. Today, she is valued as a (not wholly appropriate) hero of feminism as well as a great novelist; this may prove to be yet another misconception, but it also shows that more people are ready to understand her message today than ever before, and to sympathize with her major themes.

Today's obsession with biography has helped in the rehabilitation of George Eliot, for there are indeed ways in which her life was bolder than her work. She never allowed her heroines to escape from an unsuccessful marriage except by the death of the unwanted husband, nor could they have extramarital love affairs without retribution. Lewes's separation from Agnes, and his life with Marian, have no parallels in her books. Her closest imagining of her own life is in the character of Maggie, who never reaches adulthood: like Katherine Mansfield in her portrayal of Kezia, George Eliot has made a choice in life that none of her heroines are shown to have made. Romola, Dorothea, and Gwendolen, the heroines of the later novels, are all looking for a role, a métier; none of them is allowed the satisfying and healing practice of an art that George Eliot found for herself. She remains her own heroine, always greater and more complete than the female characters she imagines.

George Eliot's critique of marriage is nonetheless profound, even if it is acted out by women less capable than herself. The history of the gradual rise of her reputation is in part the history of acceptance of the ideas she propounds: that economic independence, and a métier, are necessary to women as to men; that marriage as an occupation and a means of support is legalized prostitution; that there is no "man question" nor "woman question," but only the human question.

Tracing her critical reputation thus tells us much about the subtle and slow development of feminism over the last century; and there is one critic who provides a link between the age of George Eliot and that of Katherine Mansfield, representing attitudes that both of them had to escape or come to terms with.

Leslie Stephen was one of the early biographers of George Eliot; he had been to one or two Sunday afternoons at the Priory, and he admired her (as so many men did) because, in contrast to other women writers, "It may safely be said that no novelist of mark ever possessed a wider intellectual culture." Leslie Stephen's daughter, Virginia Woolf, also admired George Eliot, whose struggles with patriarchy she saw as very close to her own. The character based on Sir Leslie in *To the Lighthouse* represents a complicated threat, because he is not the simple patriarch that George Eliot created in Mr. Brooke, Sir Hugo Mallinger, and many others, and that Katherine Mansfield showed as Stanley Burnell. He understands female genius, encourages it to an extent, and thus is very resourceful in controlling it. This may be a reason why Virginia Woolf found it so very difficult to get free of her father, and why the conflicts set up by this rebellion were so much more crippling then anything George Eliot or Katherine Mansfield experienced. The lesbian element in Virginia Woolf is much the most pronounced, though it appears in the other two; this is not only an attempt to get free of the father, but a reflection of his insistence that all real intellectual life is by its nature masculine, and that a woman takes part in it only insofar as she herself is masculine.

Sir Leslie points out that only after her father's death was George Eliot able to reach out for intellectual liberation—a remark that could equally well be made about his own daughter, whose famous Bloomsbury household could only be established after the death of the demanding, irascible Sir Leslie. Virginia Woolf was envious of her brother, who died as early as Chummie; and part of her participation in Bloomsbury was the assuming of his place in the lives of his friends.

Beneath these similarities, however, there are vast differences: the worlds from which George Eliot and Katherine Mansfield made their escape had a vitality undimmed by sophistication; the decadent liberality of Bloomsbury complicated matters. Sir Leslie confesses that he has a tendency to fall in love with Maggie, and to sympathize with her tribulations as an intelligent girl; he modestly asserts that, as far as feminism goes, "I should be afraid to express any opinion upon a question in which women must be the best judges." This openness and comprehension seem, superficially, to make things easier for his daughter: indeed, her famous dictum, that *Middlemarch* "is one of the few English novels written for grown-up people," derives from him:

> We are indeed told dogmatically that a novelist should never indulge in little asides to the reader. Why not? . . . A child, it is true, dislikes to have the illusion broken, and is angry if you try to persuade him that Giant Despair was not a real personage like his favourite Blunderbore. But the attempt to produce such illusions is really unworthy of work intended for full-grown readers.[1]

Many of Virginia Woolf's other attitudes show the extent to which she was unable to throw off the opinions that were the legacy of this enlightened patriarch. He prefers George Eliot's early novels to the later ones; *Felix Holt* disappoints him on the grounds that an artist of George Eliot's stature should be above the "long-lost heir" device. This foreshadows Virginia Woolf's denunciation of all plot as artificial, and of Katherine Mansfield's "cheap and obvious" plots in particular. *Middlemarch* seems to him to exude a charmless melancholy—a melancholy that many readers have noticed in such works as *To the Lighthouse*, and have attributed to the desperate struggles for independence that had to take place before these works could be written. Sir Leslie's remarks on the Jewish part of *Daniel Deronda* are delivered in as snobbish a vein as are some of Virginia Woolf's dismissals of Murry.

> Mordecai is devoted to the restoration of the Jewish nationality— a scheme which to the vulgar mind seems only one degree less chimerical than Zarca's plan for a gypsy nationality in Africa. . . . George Eliot's sympathy for the Jew, her aversion to Anti-Semitism, was thoroughly generous, and naturally welcomed by its objects. But taken as the motive of a hero it strikes one as showing a defective sense of humour.[2]

These similarities of opinion between the father and the daughter throw light on the anti-patriarchal struggles of all the women in this book. Virginia Woolf could not rebel completely against a father whose intellectual influence was so compelling; thus she never reached the attitude of forgiveness that Katherine Mansfield attains in her New Zealand stories, and that George Eliot showed in *Adam Bede*. Some of the psychological strength that permitted this forgiveness was derived from the simple and consistent identity of the patriarchal force, the fact that it could be separated from the daughter's subsequent artistic life. This is why, though Virginia Woolf is obviously akin to George Eliot and Katherine Mansfield in many ways, and provides an illuminating comparison to them, she is not really of their company. Her genius was as great as theirs, and her struggles as heroic—but she was psychologically incapable of using the strength derived from love and work to dispel the crippling emotional legacy of her early life; her fight for independence took too great a toll.

Writers whose psychological struggles with their parents go on into adulthood seem to establish a more formal art, in which self-revelation is subordinate to technical elaboration. Virginia Woolf and Henry James are two representatives of the modern aesthetic which has been based on such criteria, and their standards of artistic purity have become something of a critical religion. But in the appreciation of writers whose vitality has not been sapped by this kind of conflict, such elaborate critical methods are unnecessary. Katherine Mansfield always subordinated perfection of technique to perfection of attitude; Murry rightly said that the works we feel to be "great" are notorious for their technical imperfection. The unbiased reader of George Eliot, as of Fielding, quickly realizes that formal judgments are irrelevant: she is ready to use whatever device will serve her purpose, and objections to the "authorial voice" or to "insufficient distancing" are spurious.

George Eliot's gift was more than a "gift of expression," to use Lewes's strictures on most literary careers. It was a consciously developed ability to bring the real world into her novels—an ability that paralleled, and derived from, her ability to love and live fully in her relationship with Lewes. If we are to judge her perceptions about her characters, and her own judgments of them, we must first accept them as real people. George Eliot herself saw realism as the essential of her art; and where critics have identified her failings, they have usually pointed to them as lapses of realism.

Judgments of realism have changed in the century since she wrote. George Eliot's contemporaries, like Blackwood and almost all of her early critics, admired the Poysers more than anything else in *Adam Bede*, and the Dodson aunts more than anything else in *The Mill on the Floss*. Mrs. Poyser, the farmer's wife whose country aphorisms, domestic competence, and strict morality provide a running contrast to the other characters, is less believable nowadays: most modern critics would go along with John Bayley's description of "that rustic perfection of the Poysers, in which every confirming touch rings just too typical to be true." But George Eliot's "ideal" characters are not necessarily believable either: Dinah, the Methodist preacher who talks Hetty Sorrel into repentance of her infanticide, and who finally marries Adam Bede, induced Leslie Stephen to say that in creating her, George Eliot did not impress him as she intended to impress her readers.

These criticisms point to George Eliot's two characteristic lapses of realism. The first is the sentimentalizing of the lower classes and of the past—a tendency much less marked in her than in most novelists of her time and class; indeed her contemporaries praised her for her realism in this respect. Is it in part a political judgment that today condemns her nostalgia for agricultural England, for that society in which class distinctions implied no lack of mutual respect? Certainly she is no apologist for the aristocracy—from the days when she first decided that the "true drama of evangelicalism" lay among the middle and lower classes, her tendency had been to fall in with the "kind hearts are more than coronets" line. I suppose that finding Mrs. Poyser and the others enchanting or corny must remain a matter of taste; to say that George Eliot is less realistic than Hardy, for example, because her picture of rural England is more cheerful, may be bad history as well as bad literary criticism.

Her second failure of realism, and one from which it is hard to dissent, is in her presentation of "ideal" characters—Dinah, Felix Holt, Daniel Deronda, as well as Dorothea and Romola. Perhaps one reason for the similarity of the first three is that they all belong to categories with which she wished to feel thoroughly sympathetic, but could not quite manage it: Methodists, workingmen, Jews. These *ought* to be the good and genuine people she could oppose to her cynical aristocrats, deluded young beauties, sinners and time-servers of all kinds. But the only way she could present an "ideal" was by holding in abeyance her knowledge of what she knew to be psychologically true of every human being—the many failings, compromises, and dishonesties from which these characters are miraculously free. By the time of Deronda, she was striving mightily to attach some psychological roots to his unearthly bloom of saintliness, but she did not really succeed.

Why did she need these "ideal" characters, when her most successful episodes are those in which she opposes a relative human virtue to a relative human vice, with no reference to the ideal at all? Their inclusion seems to me to have been related to her scholarship: she spent two years studying the Florentine Renaissance before she began *Romola*, and her correspondence during the writing of *Felix Holt* consists largely of discussion of inheritance law, which the lawyer Frederic Harrison advised her on. She studied Judaism in the same intense way for *Daniel Deronda*. These were all subjects that she deliberately mugged up, just as she thought out for herself a scheme of human morals which must of necessity have an ideal to relate the rest to. The erudition and the ideal characters are alike parts of the scaffolding that never quite got dismantled, or incorporated into the real novel. Even more deeply, both the ideal characters and the scholarship represent a failure of nerve— something she is hiding behind to avoid telling all she knows. Daniel and Felix are related to her inability to imagine a strong man who is not an adversary: if they really did convincingly have the personal qualities she attributes to them, they would be her enemies, because they would be threats to her own autonomy. Thus their combination of strength and humility, of mastery and sacrifice, is puzzling and unconvincing. The heroines, too, come from her unwillingness to admit the power and ruthlessness of her own ego: Dinah, Romola, Dorothea achieve independence, but for George Eliot to approve of their doing so, they must sacrifice. They, too, have an unreal blending of strength and self-abnegation.

George Eliot's own deepest struggle, and therefore the most basic theme of her novels, was exactly this conflict between the needs of the self and the moral imperative of altruism. It is presented most convincingly in the form of her most realistic characters, because once the people and the situation are made unassailably real, she can have her say about them without being accused of cooking the evidence. And what she has to say generally involves the level of their moral intelligence, and the conditions, inner and outer, for its growth. John Bayley sums up,

> George Eliot's novels are about the coming of the kind of consciousness which Freud hoped for the human race: "Where Id was shall Ego be." [3]

Lewes's psychological studies undoubtedly contributed to her treatment of this theme, and he and George Eliot shared some ideas about the role of societal evolution in the development of the individual conscience. The most fascinating thing in this fascinating judgment is the use of the word "Ego." Perhaps Freud used it to mean rationality, while in George Eliot's world it is closer to the evangelical conscience; but for both, it is a recognition of wider necessities than the instinctual desires of the self. George Eliot judged her characters in terms of this social or moral nature, and opposed it to "egotism"—her own failing and the one she saw as posing the greatest dangers to character. Her view developed over the years, however, until by the time she created Gwendolen Harleth she was ready to see Ego as the complex thing Freud identified— that which gives the personality its strength, its power, everything that makes it valuable, as well as ringing it about with dangers.

Her failures of realism are related to the other major criticism that has been made of her work: failures of judgment. It has generally been felt that she is too hard on some of her women characters—Hetty and Rosamund in particular—and not hard enough on others—for example, Dorothea and perhaps Maggie. The distinction is, of course, between those characters who are identified with the author and those who represent her worst enemy in life: the pretty woman who unfairly snares the man who would have been happier with George Eliot.

Her rage against the pretty, selfish ones is solidly based: it is hard to dissent from her judgments of Hetty (for whom, after all, she feels intense pity as well as condemnation) and Rosamund, one of the most convincing villains in all her work. However, it could be said that she spends an inordinate amount of time and effort to demolish them. Perhaps she is too soft on Dorothea—but her spontaneous movement of sympathy for Casaubon, and her presentation of the foolish idealist as Dodo in name and nature, leave room for doubt. And Maggie is a special case—surely *The Mill on the Floss* is one of those books (Christina Stead's *The Man Who Loved Children* is another) unique in its author's career: the impassioned story of the writer's coming of age. Distanced judgment of the central character is not only impossible in such a case, it is wholly inappropriate.

The case of Gwendolen Harleth shows that by the end of her career, George Eliot's feelings about female egotism and female beauty had become extremely subtle and complicated. Gwendolen's use of her looks to catch a husband is not contrasted with the behavior of any "ideal" woman, searching for a useful social role; but with the serious demands of art, presented by Herr Klesmer. He tells her, indeed, that her beauty has helped to disqualify her for the life of the artist by making things too easy for her; but both he and the author pity the girl for whom everything has conspired to set such a fatal trap, which springs itself on her with tragic inevitability.

Daniel Deronda is George Eliot's final word on these themes which so much preoccupied her; and just as her life stands in contrast to Victorian convention, so this novel reverses the classic Victorian treatment of many of the same themes. Everything her life had been—emotionally bold and independent, refusing the wifely role for a unique kind of intellectual companionship—is brought into play and justified here. It is perhaps the ultimate statement of Lewes's influence on her, because had she not found him, and lived the life they shared, she could never have seen so clearly just what to refuse that was conventionally offered to women.

To see what she did in *Deronda*, we must contrast it with the whole school of novels to which it stands in opposition. There is a strange similarity, for example, between the plots of *Vanity Fair*, *Wuthering Heights*, and—in a sort of "trickling down" of the idea to the ultimate popular level—*Gone with the Wind*. The contrast between the wicked, ambitious woman, who makes a calculating marriage and is cold toward the child of that marriage, and the loving, submissive woman, presents the author with a difficult choice: he generally despises the "good" woman more or less openly, and sides with the fascinating temptress while explicitly condemning her. The wicked man, who ultimately has his revenge on the wicked woman for deserting him in favor of conventionality, is presented even more sympathetically. The nature/culture antitheses, which are also intelligence/stupidity and originality/convention, stem from the Protestant double-think that began with *Paradise Lost*.

The atheist George Eliot indulges in no such subterfuges. Gwendolen's damnation by her wicked husband, Grandcourt, and redemption by Deronda are described with conviction, all the more so because in the other novels, the blond, aristocratic Grandcourt would have been the "good" character and the dark, Jewish Deronda the "bad" one. In *Wuthering Heights* we are drawn to Heathcliff, the explicitly infernal; he is fascinating and sympathetic from the early moment when he implores the dead Cathy to come back. Grandcourt is also explicitly infernal, though outwardly he should be the good, fair-haired "Edgar" of the novel, and this time it is clear that the author is not at all on his side, nor are we tempted to be so.

By the time George Eliot came to write *Daniel Deronda*, her realism was so assured that here, alone among her novels, she flirts with the Gothic. Deronda's return of the necklace, the panel that opens to reveal the ghastly picture, all are hints that we are moving among forces imperfectly understood by the characters. There is something Shakespearean about her use of Gothic detail: Mirah's story of her escape is like the dumb-shows in *Hamlet* and *Macbeth* that prefigure the plot; and the image-clusters—water, jewels, pallor, and blackness—are Shakespearean in their resonance.

George Eliot has moved beyond realism to something more inclusive, more difficult. The setting of Gwendolen's unmarried life is pure Jane Austen—but her real story begins where Jane Austen leaves off: everything prior to the marriage choice is mere prologue. The movement of the novel is the massive, heroic struggle so characteristic of the greatest nineteenth-century art: the "out of suffering comes good" of Dostoevsky and Beethoven. It is as daemonic as *Wuthering Heights* or *Moby Dick*—both of which Lewes was among the first to recognize for what they were.

One of the great strengths of *Deronda* is that by this time, George Eliot has thoroughly exorcised her need for autobiography, her account of the struggles of Mary Ann Evans. She is no longer concerned, as she was in *The Mill on the Floss* and *Middlemarch*, with the accurate portrayal of her own conflicts—her jealousy of her brother, her mistaken dependence on an older man. There were living models for many of the characters in *Deronda* (with the notable exception of the saintly Daniel himself), but very many of them also contain aspects of the author's own experience. Klesmer's point of view clearly has her approval in his scene with Gwendolen—here George Eliot is no longer the young woman looking for a role in life; she is the assured and undoubted artist. At other moments, she is the Gwendolen who implicitly criticizes her mother's dependent attitude; she is Daniel's mother, leaving her child to pursue her own career; she is even Daniel himself, championing the poor and despised.

This fragmentation of her own personality means that she is not engaged in pitting a George Eliot-character against the world; and this is why, in Gwendolen, she is able to explore certain aspects of her own psychology at a deeper level than ever before. She is not distracted by the trivia of appearance and fortune; although Gwendolen's reluctance to marry has something to do with George Eliot's, and although at the time she was writing *Daniel Deronda* she was receiving the adoration of Edith, Elma, and the rest, she does not identify herself with Gwendolen. Gordon Haight has suggested that

> Some of the Leweses' interest in these morbidly passionate women may be attributed to their concern with psychology. Gwendolen Harleth, whose intricate character George Eliot was creating when she first knew Edith, has a similar physical aversion to men. Though Grandcourt is made frightful enough to justify it in his case, her rejection of Rex's love suggests a latent homosexual streak. Gwendolen confesses to having been jealous of her stepfather, and sleeps in her mother's bed till the day of her marriage. Traits like these obviously fascinate the novelist, George Eliot.[4]

None of this implies that George Eliot herself had their aversion to men; her whole life could equally well be seen as a story of dependence on men and attraction to them. But it was certainly one of the many aspects of her own psychology—and by this time she was a great enough artist to dissect some of the many aspects of her personality with the care, the detachment, the lack of special pleading, that she had always been able to bring to the examination of other people.

Thus it is not strictly accurate to say that George Eliot never presented a woman like herself in her novels. She drew on her own experience, as any novelist must do, in order to understand all the people in her books. And many of the choices she herself made are reflected in the choices made by her heroines.

As she saw it, the two central questions of a woman's life are work and children. She dissected marriage, and decided that it was not a career in itself, but instead a trap for the unwary or the complacent. However, to marry or not to marry was never the question. For an independent woman—Gwendolen or Dorothea at the end of the novels concerning them—it would have few dangers. They would keep their independence once they had won it, and marry someone who was not likely to imperil it: in this they are like their creator. The real question, still unsolved by them, is the choice of métier.

Motherhood is represented as the complacent option in the case of Celia Brooke; and the women who desert their children, Hetty and Lydia Glasher, are horribly punished. Only in *Deronda* is there a woman, Daniel's mother, who is vindicated in abandoning her parental role. Here is an obligation that, except in the case of an undoubted artist with another vocation, cannot be deserted with impunity. Though she toyed with the idea, George Eliot did not give Dorothea or Gwendolen a child; and Rosamund has a miscarriage. Allowing any of them to have children would end the argument about independence before it was properly begun, and obscure the issue of whether or not to continue with the marriage. A woman with children is in George Eliot's eyes precluded from seeking another career. Supporting her is another's responsibility.

How does George Eliot justify the evasion of this natural career in her own case? A very interesting answer is given by tracing the genesis of *The Spanish Gypsy*, whose heroine renounces love and chooses duty to her people. George Eliot thought of this theme while looking at a Titian painting of the Annunciation, and developed it in her notes:

> A young maiden, believing herself to be on the eve of the chief event of her life,—marriage,—about to share in the ordinary lot of womanhood, full of young hope, has suddenly announced to her that she is chosen to fulfil a great destiny, entailing a terribly different experience from that of ordinary womanhood. . . .[5]

Why does she set this story, which clearly was full of resonance for her, among the Spanish Gypsies? Dedication to a national idea is here, as it is in *Deronda*, a kind of substitute for an artistic vocation such as George Eliot justified herself by submitting to. The woman who experiences this "annunciation" need feel no other obligation. And she is a Gypsy, as Ruby Redinger so pertinently suggests, because Gypsies are symbols of freedom—Maggie's brief adventure with them, in *The Mill on the Floss*, is enough to establish that.

In Katherine Mansfield's early story, "How Pearl Button Was Kidnapped," this heroine, too, is briefly abducted by Gypsies, and recaptured and brought home to conventionality. Colette has a tale about the time she dreamed she was being abducted, and awoke to find that her mother had, in the night, transported her to a bed closer to the parents' room. Fantasies of abduction, escape from the mother, are in all three women closely related to the "annunciation" that sets them apart from the obligation of bearing children, and allows them to choose another task in life.

The moral intelligence that is only gained by earning one's own living is the major theme that George Eliot wishes her heroines to confront. Dorothea is a dodo because she has always been rich enough not to think about it; the wickedness of Rosamund is that she refuses to take any responsibility for it; Gwendolen's strength is that she makes her choice more or less consciously and takes the consequences "like a man." Throughout the books, the "good" characters work for a living; the bad ones expect it to be provided by someone else. Even Maggie's mother is morally blind because she bewails the loss of her possessions, but cannot do anything herself to save them—she is hopelessly dependent, a status only allowable in children.

In fact, the women of the "older" generation are always presented as people who accepted the conventions because in their time there was nothing else they could do, while the daughter's generation faces more complicated choices. Katherine Mansfield has this attitude toward *her* mother. It is interesting to see that each generation of daughters feels that it is the first to be given a choice—and feels its mothers to be the last of the old regime.

George Eliot's novels certainly foreshadowed, if they did not expressly delineate, the kind of relation that she herself had with Lewes. It is the choice open to the best of her heroines at the end of their moral struggles. Having escaped the pressures of conventionality (and here the themes of rebellion against parents, choice of a life work, and—in a more fantastic vein—abduction by Gypsies are relevant), they must enter into another kind of life: a life that starts out with independence but does not end there, that is able to maintain independence within a framework of loving commitment. This is what George Eliot herself was able to achieve, and this is the kind of choice she was trying to teach her heroines—and through them, other women—to make.

PART III

Colette

CHAPTER 1

Sido

*Les seuls vrais paradis sont les
paradis que l'on a perdus.*

—Marcel Proust

The childhood of Sidonie-Gabrielle Colette is one of the most exhaustively described in literary history—a circumstance that makes it more difficult, if anything, to determine the facts about it. Her parents, her house, the garden, the woods, the school: all figure in her re-creation of the quintessential French childhood which influenced a whole nation's ideas about itself. Because Colette herself came to be a legendary figure to her countrymen, they are the French equivalents of Lincoln's log cabin, Washington's cherry tree, Mark Twain's Mississippi.

For a writer who was, more than any other, to sum up France and Frenchness, Colette had an appropriately diverse yet curiously untypical background. Her mother's family came from the north of France, her father's from Toulon in the south. Adèle-Sidonie Landoy, the "Sido" of her daughter's mythmaking, was born in Paris. Sido's mother died soon after her birth; her father, Henri-Marie Landoy, from Charleville in the Marne, was a grocer and chocolate manufacturer who may have been part Negro. His peripatetic life has been explained as the consequence of membership in a secret society that was persecuted by Louis-Philippe's government. It was no life for a child, and the baby Sido was put to nurse at a farm in the Puisaye, a remote part of Burgundy.

After her father's death, the nineteen-year-old Sido went to Belgium to live with her two elder brothers, journalists who led a bohemian, artistic life. For several years, Sido imbibed an intellectual atmosphere far removed from the country air of her childhood. But on holiday visits to the Puisaye, she attracted the attention of a notorious local alcoholic and womanizer, Jules Robineau-Duclos. His family was eager to marry him off, for it was feared that his estates would pass into the hands of his many peasant mistresses and illegitimate children. Sido had no dowry; an arrangement was soon made between the two families, and she was in effect sold to this man who was twenty-one years her senior.

Inevitably unhappy in the family manor house, which was populated by cackling crones and voluptuous maids, Sido was nonetheless capable of defending herself: she threw a lamp-holder at her husband, scarring him for life, the first time he tried to beat her. Their daughter Juliette was a strange, withdrawn child, possibly autistic or even mongoloid; and by the time their son Achille was born, local opinion unanimously declared him to be the child of Captain Colette. Robineau-Duclos died of alcoholism and apoplexy soon after the birth of this second child, and Sido was free to marry her new admirer.

Jules-Joseph Colette came from a military family, possibly Italian in origin. He graduated from Saint-Cyr and was posted to a regiment of Zouaves. After service in Algeria and the Crimea, he was wounded at the battle of Marignan. With a leg amputated, he was invalided out of the army, awarded the Légion d'Honneur, and appointed tax collector at Saint-Sauveur-en-Puisaye. Here he dabbled in local politics, and married the rich widow of Robineau-Duclos. Sido had inherited the handsome stone house on the main village street which they were to occupy for the next few years, and it was there that their two children, Léopold and Sidonie-Gabrielle, were born, the latter in 1873.

The garden at the back of the house, completely concealed by a high wall, was to become the center of Colette's personal mythology. Here Sido established her mysterious rapport with plants, animals, and her own children. Here the young Colette began her intense examination of the natural world. Almost Islamic in its concealment, completeness, and sense of luxuriance, it was as female as a harem: the older brothers escaped to the woods, the Captain could sometimes be heard singing upstairs, but Sido and her youngest daughter were the inhabitants of the garden. Colette's mother called her Minet-Chéri, "dear kitten," and treated her with the same watchful possessiveness that she accorded to the rest of her kingdom. Sido's mystic union with plants and animals, amounting almost to pantheism; her constant exhortations to "Look!"; her excessively maternal quality—these were the components of the "earthly paradise" that Colette, like the Persian miniaturists, never stopped trying to re-create.

There were objective reasons for Sido's definition of her family as an intensely self-contained unit. Their mixed background, the oddness of Juliette, and their lack of roots in what was still an agricultural society, all helped to cut them off from their neighbors. Nothing seemed to alleviate this isolation: even when Juliette married into a neighboring family, it narrowed, rather than widened, the Colette circle: apparently because the Captain could not pay the agreed dowry, Juliette was prevented from communicating with her own relations. Colette's childhood memories are of solitude, of the woods and ponds in the wild country that began beyond the garden, and of a sensual alertness unspoiled by too many impressions.

This enclosed world, however, also aroused the temptation to escape. George Eliot wrote, in "Brother and Sister," of how she and Isaac evaded their mother's admonitions as they set out toward the countryside:

> Then with the benediction of her gaze
> Clung to us lessening, and pursued us still
> Across the homestead to the rookery elms. . . .[1]

Similarly, Colette recounts her own reactions:

—Ne passe pas par les prés du Petit-Moulin, ils sont inondés! Ne vas pas du côté de Thury, il y a des voitures de bohémiens! Surtout, reviens avant la tombée de la nuit! Ne mange pas les prunelles sur les haies, ni les sinelles! Ne mets pas à même tes poches la salade pleine de terre! . . .

. . . Passée la limite où la voix maternelle—un soprano nuancé, étendu, qui n'était jamais discordant—pouvait m'attendre, je me dirigeais avec décision vers le Petit-Moulin et ses prés inondés. . . .[2]

("Don't go by way of the Petit-Moulin fields, they're flooded! And don't go toward Thury—there are gypsy wagons there! And see that you get back before dark! Mind you don't eat any spindle berries or sloes in the hedges! And don't put the lettuce in your pockets with all its dirt!" . . .

. . . Beyond the reach of the maternal voice—a modulated soprano with a wide range but never harsh—I determinedly went toward Petit-Moulin and its flooded meadows. . . .)

Sido's voice and personality seem to have had the "penetrating omnipresence" that Erikson identifies as the characteristic of the possessive mother; resentment of any indication that the child identifies with the other parent is another classic attribute. The relationship between her parents fascinated Colette: the curious coexistence of Sido's disillusionment and the Captain's romanticism.

Whatever the pantheistic influence of Sido, it was Colette's father who fed her knowledge of literature and language. Closeted in his study, he worked for years on a series of large, handsomely bound volumes that all his family assumed to be his collected works in manuscript. It was only after his death that they looked into the books, and found that they were all composed of blank pages. Sido, enraged and humiliated by the deception, couldn't seem to use the paper up fast enough—as a frill for the leg of lamb, a shopping list, to light the fire. Colette, on the other hand, seems to have felt the pathos of the situation more keenly than the betrayal, and to have taken it to heart by assuming the task of writing her father's unrealized works. But to Sido, it confirmed the suspicion that literature was unreal and life was real—and that men were on the unreal side of things.

In spite of his impotence before the blank page, the Captain recited to his daughter reams of his own poetry—in the style of Victor Hugo—and that of the French classical poets. Her mother wondered why it took children so long to appreciate good writing (her own favorite bedside book was Saint-Simon), but in the mean-time, Colette was becoming imbued with a sense of the classical style that was to baffle later readers, who could not see any source for it in her education. In her father's study, the shelves of dusty tomes were open for her inspection, and she has described how

> J'ai grandi au creux du berceau énorme, du puissant vaisseau qui pro-page son rythme sur l'infini lyrique,—ainsi j'appelle, ainsi je vois l'alex-andrin. Aux pieds de mon père, ma première enfance ramassait des hémistiches, tombés de lui comme des copeaux frisés que le rabot en-lève au bois précieux.[3]

> (I grew up nestled in an enormous cradle, that powerful vessel which projects its rhythm on lyrical infinity—that is the name, the image that I give to the alexandrine. At my father's feet, my early childhood gathered up half-lines that fell from him like curly shavings planed from the precious wood.)

If her literary education, in these basic and influential ways, was carried out by her father, Colette's emotional bent was determined by Sido. Disillusioned by two husbands, and pinning all her hopes on her youngest child, she made Colette feel singled out for a special destiny, which could only be achieved if she did not give herself over into the hands of a man.

The disillusionment of Sido was complete by the time Colette reached the age of sixteen, for it was in that year that the family went bankrupt. Sido had brought a considerable fortune to her sec-ond marriage, mostly in the form of tenanted property; but the feckless Captain had managed things so badly that he was in debt to all the tenants for sums exceeding the value of the land. A cabal of locals, led by the family into which Juliette had married, seems to have formed to ruin the interloper from Toulon, and everything was lost. Portable possessions were put out into the street, and the family took refuge with Achille, the eldest son, who had become a doctor in nearby Châtillon-Coligny. Thus the event that George Eliot imagined happening to her own family, in *The Mill on the Floss,* actually happened to Colette; and the imagined grievances of Christiana Evans became the real grievances of Sido.

Colette herself dated her passionate interest in earning money from this event: not only had she lost her beloved house and garden, but she could see no immediate means of escape from the overcrowded new situation. There was money neither for education nor for a dowry. Colette had left school, after gaining the Brevet Elémentaire, when the family left Saint-Sauveur; and in spite of the memories with which she was to fill the Claudine books, there does not seem to have been anything exceptional about her schooldays. Her classmates and teachers were important to her who had so few human beings in her life; she excelled in French composition; but, like Katherine Mansfield, she was more interested in the "pattern that was weaving," in atmosphere and human relations, than in the curriculum. But one aspect of her education stayed with her: the school taught French history, French geography, the French language—and this chauvinistic emphasis, inculcating patriotism rather than widening horizons, is one source of the way Colette as a writer came to identify herself with her own country.

Little is known about Colette's life in Châtillon-Coligny. She already had the literary tastes of an adult, and she systematically raided her father's library. She accompanied Achille on his rounds, waiting with a book in the carriage while he visited his patients. In fact, altogether, she waited.

What Colette herself thought she was waiting for at this time is unknown. She describes the conflicting pulls of love and solitude, the hesitation she already felt between the two: "To become only a woman—how paltry. Yet I hastened eagerly toward that common goal." Her own published memories are of communion with nature, books, and her mother; but it was already clear that the young Colette was not part of the society immediately around her—cut off by the peculiarities of her family, by their abrupt departure from her natal village, and by the romantic fantasies that both parents had built around the future of their youngest child. She would have welcomed some kind of "annunciation," inviting her to a destiny other than the common lot of womanhood, which was already made suspect to her by her mother's precept and example.

Colette later claimed that writing was the last thing she would have thought of doing—that she was alone among professional writers in never having filled notebooks with adolescent scribblings;

that she had never touched pen to paper until told to do so, first by her teachers and then by Willy. One can see in this the hostility of Sido to the idea of writing—an idea that had diverted her husband from managing his property, and left nothing but a shelf of blank books instead of the solid land and houses with which he should have occupied himself. Colette was following her mother's unspoken dictates when she occupied herself with the real, the physical, instead of with the reflections and mirages to be found in books. This resistance to literariness was later to become, famously, one of Colette's most valuable qualities as a writer, and to make her work accessible to even the most unintellectual reader. But it was formed in an atmosphere of tension between the ambitions and interests fed by her father and the attempts of Sido to keep her captive in the real world.

How did Colette really feel about her mother? The carefully edited memories in Colette's published reminiscences set up a smoke screen; but beneath the haze of emotion, the actual memories carry a message very different from the overt one. Perhaps the most famous memory is of the letter Sido wrote to her then son-in-law, Jouvenel, refusing an invitation to visit on the grounds that her pink cactus is about to bloom, which happens only once every four years. Already an old woman, Sido must stay and witness the flowering for the last time. The moral drawn by Colette is that her mother "herself never ceased to flower, untiringly. . . ." Another famous incident in the memoirs recalls the time Colette repeated to Sido what the schoolchildren had told her about Christmas, and gifts brought by the Christ Child. Sido, who had resolutely banished all such nonsense from her household, was concerned that Minet-Chéri really believed such tales. But in the night, she silently came to her room with parcels—only to think a while by the window, and then take them away again, to give them herself as usual on New Year's morning. This is told as an example of how Sido was almost ready to sacrifice principle for love of her child.

There are many other such stories in these glowing memoirs, and they leave the reader wondering what they are really about. For although they are presented admiringly, they are all stories of rejection, of the self-willed force of that smothering, powerful personality. The further Colette gets from the days when she was under its influence, the more lovingly she can remember Sido's ambitions for her, Sido's care of her, and Sido's attempts to keep her from experiencing the pain of life for herself. The daughter's guilt at her resistance of the maternal influence is so strong that she cannot criticize her overtly; she can only tell these stories if she coats them with sanctimonious praise.

If Sido stood in the way of Colette's escape, she was only one of many obstacles. Colette herself was suspicious of marriage—Sido spoke witheringly of its supposed advantages, and her daughter was afraid of losing her status as "precious child" and becoming that everyday thing, a wife. As she indicated by creating the persona of Claudine, Colette had a streak of fierce, masculine independence, a tomboy element in her nature that was bound to find certain things about the France of her day disconcerting. She was a shy, attractive girl, with large, thoughtful eyes and a thick plait of hair that reached to her knees; but her shyness was not that of the submissive village child, but rather the calm certainty and instinct for self-preservation of the wild animal. She could not see herself taking one of the few roads to metropolitan independence that were open to women at the time. She was not a bluestocking, a courtesan, or an aristocrat; in the era of the *grandes cocottes*, such "professional" careers as the stage usually turned out to be varieties of prostitution. Colette had to invent an original role for herself, one that would get her out of provincial life without exposing her to the even greater dangers of life in the capital.

Her self-contained family was suspicious of strangers, of intruders of any kind, and the young Colette does not seem to have had any local suitors. Friends of her older brothers came to stay occasionally, and Colette has recorded in *La Maison de Claudine* a conversation with one of them—a young lawyer, engaged to be married: "But what will she do, your wife, while you're being a lawyer?" "How funny you are! Why, she'll be my wife!"

Colette, triumphant, thought she detected a note of regret for the camaraderie he had enjoyed with her and her brothers, and apprehensiveness about dooming himself to the company of a woman who was only his wife. She was almost as suspicious of marriage as was Sido herself—but like Sido, she would have to accept it in order to begin her own life. She was ready to feel active interest in any young man who came along; and it was a fortunate chance that this crucial visitor turned out to be acceptable enough, and clever enough, to penetrate the defenses thrown up by Sido around her daughter.

In *La Maison de Claudine*, published in 1922, Colette has made of her childhood one of the classic childhoods in all literature. The key to it is her recognition that every childhood is enchanted, that it exists in a separate world, a world that was only intensified, but not created, by the walled garden of Sido. Though its title is derived from her fictional persona, the book is probably as close to straight nonfiction as anything Colette ever wrote. She is remembering real events and real people, and organizing them to form a psychologically meaningful whole. The events are less important in themselves than for what they reveal about Colette's developing perceptions. The series of subtly modulated anecdotes—the animals, the garden, the marriage of Juliette, the servant's wedding, the raucous schoolgirls, the yellowed books in the library—all represent the filtering of experience from the outer world through the windows of childhood.

What Colette saw through those windows came to be the unifying themes for all her work, her distinctive point of view. The boyish little girls (they seem to have used each other's surnames, so that she called herself "Colette" long before she started to write), the epicene visiting actors, and the sense that the mysteries of love and sex are essentially corrupting, and that reticence is the only appropriate attitude before them—these are the constants of Colette's vision. There is also the faintly contemptuous, patronizing attitude toward men; like the handsome "Second Empire" red setter beloved of their yellow bulldog, like the romantic Captain himself, they are extravagant, luxurious decorations, ornaments to life but not part of the seriousness of life, which is the province of the female who bears children, makes gardens, and organizes the whole household around herself. The climax of this vision is Colette's dream of abduction, inspired by a picture on the wall of her bedroom—but it turns out that her mother, worried by her being so far away, has moved her during the night closer to her own room.

This is the technique, indirect but clear, by which Colette turns a portrait of provincial life into a revelation of the determining influences on her own psyche. The sensuous texture of the book is strong and compelling, and the episodes never draw a moral nor insist on their message—but the picture that emerges is coherent. The young Colette faced the dilemma of escaping from her mother without submitting to a traditional marriage. But there was no way in which she could devise her own escape, in the provincial France of the Belle Epoque. Hers had to be the feminine art of waiting for her opportunity and then taking it.

Sido, of course, was ready to resist any candidate who came along. Her view of happiness seems to have been total possession of the beloved object—something she only achieved with her children, and only temporarily with her daughters. The marriage of Juliette had led to a family feud, after which mother and daughter never saw each other again; clearly the policy of total possession could lead to total resistance. With men, this need produced an inevitably unhappy situation—it only worked with dependent men, who were willing to be engulfed; and this was the kind of man who would prove ultimately unsatisfying to the strong Sido. She chose a weak man, knowing that she could direct him; then when this had been accomplished, she was disillusioned by his weakness. She turned to her sons for consolation; neither of them ever married.

It is a not uncommon feminine mentality, a leitmotif of the stories of George Eliot and Katherine Mansfield as well as Colette, evident in the personalities of the mothers and (particularly in the case of Katherine Mansfield) showing up in the daughters as well. Perhaps this is the kind of mother who produces an exceptional daughter, out of her own frustration and her accumulated hostility to men. But while the mothers tried to solve the situation through their children, the daughters tried (because they did not want to emulate the mothers they had resisted) to achieve a more complex balance between love and independence. And their first task was to deal with the mother.

The only solution was escape; but since the possessiveness had worn the guise of love, resistance left a residue of guilt. As a result, Colette spent the rest of her life in idealizing her mother and asserting their closeness. Another consequence of these tangled emotions was that Colette probably did not expect from her first marriage the kind of romantic happiness sometimes attributed to brides. She had a strong suspicion that Sido's doubts were well founded, especially in the case of a girl formed by Sido herself. Perhaps if she made the wrong choice, and married a man who disappointed her, she could keep something closer to freedom than if love were enclosing her completely.

CHAPTER 2

Willy

He loves to sit and hear me sing,
*   Then, laughing, sports and plays with me;*
Then stretches out my golden wing,
*   And mocks my loss of liberty.*

—William Blake

Captain Colette, entombed in his study, may not have been filling the volumes of his collected works, but he did keep up his interest in the literary and scientific passions of his youth and his correspondence with friends from the past. One of these friends was Albert Gauthier-Villars, whom he had met in the Italian campaign. A brilliant graduate of the Ecole Polytechnique, Gauthier-Villars had organized the telegraphic systems for several military campaigns, been awarded the Légion d'Honneur, and bought up the scientific publishing firm of Bachelier. Renamed for its new owner, the firm was to publish Auguste Comte, Louis Pasteur, Bertrand Russell, Marie Curie, and Albert Einstein, as well as many government and scientific periodicals. The work was lucrative and exacting.

Gauthier-Villars had two sons. Henri, the younger, had broken away from the family firm, for his interests were literary and musical rather than scientific, and his father's intense respectability had produced in him an intense desire to shock. A brilliant student, he had published Parnassian poetry, light novels, and music criticism. He was beginning to be known, even caricatured, as "Willy," a fashionable intellectual of the demi-monde.

In 1891, he visited the family of his father's old friend Captain Colette. At thirty-two, Willy had a son, but had never been married; he was a popular success, but perpetually worried about money; he was an entertaining raconteur, and knew the great world of bohemian Paris. Willy was interested in the young Colette—he could see that she was an original, and that marrying her could be one of the most original things he had ever done. Bored with elaborate courtesans and overdressed actresses, the Parisian world was ready for something fresh, original, unspoiled, and therefore slightly shocking. But as well as calculating the effect of this feeling on the taste of others, Willy was capable of being swayed by it himself, and it is hard to doubt that he was genuinely captivated by the simple, audacious, intelligent girl with the long plait of hair and the schoolgirl dresses. Colette later denied that she had really loved Willy, preferring to describe her emotions as a blend of rebelliousness, curiosity, and the practical need to escape by marrying someone, anyone—but she was fascinated by his quick wit and his sophistication, and flattered by his interest in her.

Willy and Colette were engaged for two years, during which they rarely saw each other. Their correspondence from this time has never come to light, but the long letters Colette speaks of must have been her first really consistent practice at writing. Already, Willy was having his effect on the ambitious but motiveless young girl.

Willy's indecision may have been one reason for the long engagement; he was constantly being distracted by the vagaries of work, money, fashion, and his own unaccountable impulses. Colette's youth was another barrier. But the really insurmountable obstacle was undoubtedly the opposition of Sido. Her views on marriage were scathing; and she was capable of combining them with wounding remarks about Willy in particular in a way that even her daughter's later hagiography cannot conceal. To her, marriage meant her daughter going off with a man "whom you don't even know"; love was a temporary illusion, followed by the awful recognition that you had let a stranger into the family and were legally bound to him. Her predictions about her daughter's unhappiness in marriage turned out to be well founded, but they were the kind of prophecy that tends to be self-fulfilling. She had implanted enough of herself in her daughter to make her isolated, suspicious, and all but incapable of surrender to a man.

There were some things about Willy that seemed to recommend him as the knight who could cut through this particular briar patch to rescue the sleeping beauty. He inhabited a world that was as egalitarian as any to be found at the time—the women he knew were at least semi-independent beings, and he valued his own freedom so much that he was relatively uninterested in enslaving other people. He provided an entree into that great world about which Colette's curiosity was wholly unsatisfied. The bohemianism of Sido's brothers found an echo in him; so did the literary fantasies of the Captain.

Willy's most curious quality, and one known to few at this period of his life, was that his enormous literary output was almost entirely written by ghosts—scribblers to whom he gave assignments, from whom he collected the manuscripts, and whom he paid a mere fraction of what he got for the work, which he signed with his own name or with one of his many pseudonyms. Here was a worthy successor to the Captain's bound volumes of blank pages. In Willy's case the works actually existed, which made the hoax more plausible and profitable, but the mentality was the same—both men were paralyzed by the sight of a sheet of blank paper.

Colette, then, in a sense chose her father's frustrated vocation, and acted out the literary fantasies of both Willy and the Captain. Her denial of any sense of literary vocation must be taken with a grain of salt: both her parents regarded literary ambition as the summit of all ambition (even Sido's contempt for her husband's failure as a writer was partly conditioned by her admiration for great and successful writers), and treated her as an exceptional child, capable of anything. Her specialness in their eyes gave her the self-confidence to assault what she knew they saw as the heights. For the Willy to whom they handed her over, writing was necessary but impossible. Far from being the accident that she implies, her career as a writer was something toward which every influence was pushing her.

The epistolary relationship with Willy was her first test as a writer. He was not so deeply committed that he could not have broken off the engagement at any time, but her letters must have

had something of the fresh charm of her personality, and they kept
him interested. For the first time in her career, but not the last, she
was writing for her very life. Willy became more and more enrap-
tured with the idea of showing up in blasé Paris with this talented
country girl, until the day came when he sent the famous, characteristic telegram to the mayor of Châtillon-Coligny: "Publiez bans
Gauthier-Villars–Colette. Salutations empressées. Gauthier-
Villars." ("Publish banns for Gauthier-Villars–Colette. Hasty
regards.")

Colette was married in white muslin, with dark red carnations at
her bosom that made her look "like a dove with a dagger in its
breast." Sido, in black, was desperately, obviously unhappy. After a
night at the bride's home, the newly married pair, accompanied by
Willy's two witnesses, took the train for Paris.

Colette's teacher at Saint-Sauveur had percipiently remarked, in
the margin of one of her essays, "De l'imagination; mais on sent un
parti-pris de se singulariser." ("Has imagination; but also a desire to
be conspicuous.") Now was her chance to "se singulariser"—to use
the assurance of the favored child, the instinctive sense of timing of
Sido's daughter, to learn what she could from her new situation.

The young couple settled down in a dark, gloomy flat in the Rue
Jacob, near the Seine on the Left Bank. Ugly, depressing, and ec-
centrically decorated by the previous tenant with tiny pieces of con-
fetti glued in mosaic all over the walls, the flat was soon full of
Willy's piles of yellowed newspapers, obscene postcards, manuscripts, and cardboard files. The lack of money, of sunlight, of
good air and good food, were as depressing to Colette as was her
discovery of the "difference . . . between love and the laborious,
exhausting pastime of sex."

Colette's survival strategies were not equal, at first, to the strains
of her new existence. She missed Sido to the point of desperation,
and wrote to her every day, though she refused to admit the truth
about her feelings toward her husband. Finally she became ill with
"brain fever"—an inexact contemporary term used for several
serious illnesses, including typhus—which she describes in *Claudine à Paris*. In that book, she says that her plait of long hair, her
mother's pride and joy, was cut off at the time of her illness, which
was grave enough to bring Sido to Paris to nurse her. But contem-

porary accounts say that Colette herself cut it off as an assertive act of liberation. This is the kind of discrepancy that is often to be found in her descriptions of this period of her life: her acts of rebellion against her mother, in particular, are generally suppressed, and her husbands are made to look worse than they were.

Her descriptions, in memoirs as well as in the Claudine novels, certainly leave out the exhilaration she felt at her liberation from the provinces, her pleasure in being able to shock and amuse bohemian Paris. She was noticed at the theater, early in her marriage— her youth, her loud laugh, and her long plait of hair set her apart from the crowd. Photographs of her among Willy's fat, German-looking family, at their country house in the Jura, show an ironic, audacious young face, utterly self-assured.

She went to see Willy's young son at his boarding school in England; he records that his "seductive stepmother" caused a sensation. By this time, she had begun the assiduous physical culture that was her response to an enervating city life. She installed a gymnasium, first at the Rue Jacob, then at the larger, more elegant flat they took in the Rue de Courcelles. Photographs of Colette on her swing, in black maillot, track shoes, and a broad white ribbon with a coquettish rosette over one eye, have a kinky charm. She told her stepson Jacques, "La santé, vois-tu, mon garçon, c'est la seule chose qui nous appartienne en propre." [1] ("You see, my boy, health is the only thing that really belongs to us.")

Jacques remained with his grandparents, and never lived with Willy and Colette. But his description of his father is very different from anything Colette gives us. Willy, he says, was "the most secretive of men," and "very much in love with his young wife"; in fact, he was "a cultivated, well-bred man," different from the "legendary and droll Willy, the effervescent turn-of-the-century *boulevardier.*"

If it is difficult to get a clear impression of this secretive man, he himself is largely to blame: much of his feverish activity was devoted to elaborate hoaxes and foolery, to obscuring his real nature behind pseudonyms and stylistic masks. Among his writing names were Henry (or Henri) Maugis, Jim Smiley, Boris Zichine, and— for himself and his wife—Silly and Jeannette. He claimed that in an age when everyone from courtesans (Liane de Pougy) to writers

(Anatole France) took pseudonyms, he was simply doing the accepted thing.

Even his life was treated as a joke. His "souvenirs littéraires . . . et autres," supposedly an autobiography, is a mass of facetious innuendo. He starts out,

> Le kaiser Guillaume II est né en 1859. Moi aussi. Il a quitté sa patrie pour vivre à l'étranger. Moi aussi. Il signe toute sa correspondance "Willy." Moi aussi. Mais là s'arrête la ressemblance.[2]

> (Kaiser William II was born in 1859. Me too. He left his homeland to live abroad. Me too. He signs all his correspondence "Willy." Me too. But there the resemblance ends.)

On the question of his "nègres," or ghost writers, the story of whom could not be indefinitely concealed, he says, "I have ghosts, but I have also been a ghost. Many times."

The book is full of miscellaneous unrelated jokes; e.g. Cocteau was so inconsolable after the death of Radiguet that the Dadaists called him "le veuf sur le toit." *

A description of Willy in a 1904 pamphlet, part of a series called "Les célébrités d'aujourd'hui," has the same tone as the memoirs, and may well have come from the same pen:

> Talent: multiforme, helléniste, latiniste, Wagnériste.
> Style truculent. Willy est un blond clairsemé, poupin, un peu fat, de grosses lèvres de jouisseur, des yeux de myope, frais encore. A des succès féminins nombreux et le laisse savoir. En musique, ne possède que des notions délicieusement vagues. . . .[3]

> (Talent: various, hellenist, latinist, Wagnerist.
> Truculent style. Willy is a sparse blond, foppish, a bit vain, with thick sensualist's lips, near-sighted, still fresh. Has numerous successes with women and lets it be known. As for music, has nothing but deliciously vague ideas.)

---

* *Le Boeuf sur le toit* ("the ox on the roof") was the title of one of Cocteau's plays, after which a famous Paris nightclub was later named: "veuf" means "widower."

Among the works that probably came from Willy's own pen are several poems—one is a flowery sonnet on the beauties of music, which he sent to a paper edited by a rival of his called Mangeot; the sonnet was accepted and printed before the hapless editor realized that it was an acrostic in which the first letters of the lines spelled "Mangeot est bête" ("Mangeot is a fool").

The Willy establishment was, according to his son Jacques, "a Catherine wheel of jokes, not very charitable on the whole but very amusing." A lifelong friend of Colette's, the painter Jacques-Emile Blanche, said that the young bride with her short hair "was in the vanguard of fashion." Willy was a sort of father figure to her: "Her lord and master . . . treated her like a child." He goes on to describe the milieu:

> Le studio Gauthier-Villars aura été le berceau des arts modernes, un lieu de libre discussion entre jeunes gens et vieux maîtres, entre artistes et femmes du monde.[4]

> (The Gauthier-Villars studio will prove to have been the cradle of modern art, a scene of free discussion among young men and old masters, among artists and women of the world.)

What was Colette's role to be in this ménage? Apparently she was early disillusioned about the importance of the adored young wife; Willy was constantly preoccupied, hatching schemes and visiting contributors and trying to make sense out of his tangled accounts. Colette had to be on show from time to time, at the theater and in cafés, but it was not long before Willy tried to put her to work in his literary sweatshop.

Colette's own description of the event is the only one we have—how Willy, ever on the search for new ideas, asked her to write down some of the stories she told him of her schooldays; how she found some ruled school notebooks that activated her memory like the *madeleine* dipped in *tilleul*; how Willy at first thought her scribblings worthless, then, going through his desk drawers a few months later, said "I'm mad!" and rushed off to the printers with the first of the "Claudine" novels.

The books were touched up by Willy and signed by him (though

he confidentially admitted that his young wife had been a great
help with them). They created a greater sensation than anything
Willy had done up to that time. As he suspected when he married
Colette and brought her to Paris, the sophisticated demi-monde
was ready to be shocked by innocence. Claudine became a type—
there was *parfum Claudine, gâteau Claudine,* and to this day
French fashion magazines show the *"col Claudine."* Something of
the appeal of this audacious schoolgirl, who prefigured "la
garçonne" of the 1920s, is summed up by Colette's friend Régis
Leroi:

> Claudine apporte à un siècle nouveau une femme nouvelle: les che-
> veux courts, la robe simple et sportive, le naïf col rond de l'enfance,
> devenu perverse parure de coquette.[5]

> (Claudine presents a new century with a new woman: her short hair, her
> plain, casual dress, her ingenuous, childlike round collar that trans-
> formed into a perversely coquettish costume.)

In the series, the schoolgirl Claudine, after uncovering lesbianism among both the girls and the teachers in her village
school, marries the much older Renaud. In Paris, she falls in love
with Rézi, a glamorous and sophisticated woman; the affair is condoned by Renaud, but Claudine discovers that he, too, is Rézi's
lover. Shocked, she retreats to the beloved country home of her
childhood; Renaud gradually wins her back, and they remain a
devoted couple until his death. The simplicity of Claudine was
made piquant by the suggestion of perversion—the lesbian air of
the school, the interest of older men in the young girls, and, eventually, Claudine's complicity with her homosexual stepson Marcel
and her affair with the glamorous Rézi. Many of these devices seem
to have been the direct suggestions of Willy, who was constantly
urging Colette to spice it up a bit; but the character of Claudine
herself is so characteristic of Colette's view of herself throughout
her life that it is hard to believe that she was much influenced in its
creation. Claudine has a reticence, a *pudeur,* that is contrasted
with the corrupt, commercial sexual liaisons of some of the other
characters.

The portrait of Claudine herself is one of the strengths of these slight books. The other is Colette's feeling for the natural world of her childhood, the powerful nostalgia she felt during her early years with Willy. Willy attempted to assuage this longing by buying Colette a country house: Les Monts-Bouçons, near Besançon. He was not entirely to blame for the fact that his young wife was so ill-at-ease in his life—her longing for Sido and the country were probably as difficult for him to cope with as his eccentricities were for her. She returned, for weeks at a time, to her beloved rural pursuits—though, says her implacable stepson Jacques, "There was nothing she did not know about the land; nonetheless, for her farmers, she was nothing but a 'lady from Paris' playing the countrywoman." Her country life was always to have a somewhat theatrical element about it—as was her alienation from the *vie de Bohème*. Her later insistence that the bohemianism of Willy's life disgusted and dismayed her, and that she longed for the provincial order of her mother's lavender-scented wardrobes, preserve cupboards, and kitchen garden, is belied by contemporary observers. The Rue de Courcelles flat was furnished with white leather and pale green paint in the slickest modern fashion; Colette lay in bed most of the morning, then monopolized the bathroom until it was time to go out to lunch. Her room was littered with dirty lingerie, old powder puffs, and the rest of the paraphernalia of a raffish and fashionable young woman.

As early as the Claudines, one can see a split between the real Colette and the literary persona—and it is difficult to tell which comes closer to anything that can be called the truth. In the midst of the life she had so longed for as a provincial girl, she writes of her nostalgia for the country; while participating fully in the life around her, she dreams of retreat to childhood, to sexual innocence, to solitude. This was to be one of the characteristic paradoxes of all her work—no one had a more eager appetite for life, and no one wrote more sadly and nostalgically about withdrawing from it.

The Claudines contain one episode that most critics have found convincing: the affair with Rézi, and Claudine's dismay when it is condoned by her husband on the grounds that lesbian love is mere play, not to be taken seriously. Whether or not Colette fell in love with a woman like Rézi cannot be known—but like the character of Claudine, the affair with Rézi introduces a theme that was to be characteristic of all her work, and it is impossible not to believe that it reflected something in her own nature rather than the "spicy" interpolations of Willy. In fact the Rézi episode is written in a hurried scribble, with few corrections from Willy's pen—it has an air of less deliberation, and more emotion, than the rest of the neatly filled notebooks.

Most of Willy's interpolations concern Maugis, the music critic, who was in part a caricature of Willy himself—far from resenting this line, Willy participated in it enthusiastically, writing much of Maugis's dialogue himself. He also corrects Colette's exuberant style—his famous marginal remark, "Have I married the last of the lyric poets?" brought her up short and corrected her tendency to effusion. He crosses out repeated words—mostly color words—and adds notes about literary soirées, foreign writers, and English and German terms, most of which Colette ignores. He also used the inside covers of her notebooks for his interminable lists of accounts, in which payments to various "nègres" are mingled with purchases of stamps, cologne, and hired carriages. There is something obsessive about these lists, in tiny, cramped writing—and when Colette surprised him with one of his mistresses, they were not in bed, but going over the accounts.

After the success of the Claudines, Willy adapted them for the theater, and the actress chosen to play the lead was the young Polaire, famous for her wasp waist and huge dark eyes. Willy dressed Colette and Polaire alike, went about with one "Claudine" on each arm, and spread the story that the two girls were in love—showing more than a passing resemblance to the Renaud who countenances Claudine's affair with Rézi. The "père de Claudine"—Willy—may himself have been Polaire's lover; in any case, Colette said that by the end of her marriage to Willy, there was nothing she did not know about jealousy.

But sexual jealousy was only part of her unhappiness: she was also envious of the actresses she knew, free to earn their own living and to have affairs with young men. The "elegant, intelligent companion . . . smiling in the shadow of the flat-brimmed hat," as one observer described Willy's young wife, was ready to try her own wings, and the father figure who had nurtured her was beginning to stand in her way.

Willy had appropriated the money and the credit for the Claudines. It was clear that as long as Colette lived with him, any money she earned would be his; and it was doubtful whether her own name would appear on anything she wrote. The "nègre" system, as operated by Willy, did not allow such things to happen, especially in the case of a wife whose earnings were legally his in any event. Colette claimed that Willy's infidelities were at the root of their separation, but her search for financial and artistic independence was obviously crucial as well. The two things, in fact, are subtly related: throughout her books, she condemns all the kinds of love that turn out to be commercial transactions, and elevates whatever curious liaison manages—often by its very unacceptability—to escape this stigma. Her marriage to Willy was sexually unfulfilling partly because it was becoming a mutual commercial exploitation.

It was becoming widely known in literary and theatrical Paris that Colette was in fact the author of the Claudines. She knew that as soon as she achieved her independence from Willy, there were people willing to publish her books. She was preparing the ground carefully for the eventual break.

But simply writing books and handing them over to publishing friends was a move that could have been easily foiled by Willy. He was to go on for years using the idea of Claudine in a number of different series, and would have done anything in his power to prevent Colette from setting up shop as a competitor. She had to devise a more tortuous route to freedom, one that he condoned at first. She had kept up her gymnastics; as her mother sourly wrote, "You are becoming more supple, both physically and morally." She began taking lessons in the art of mime—the one branch of the theater in which she felt she might be able to cope professionally with a minimum of training. Willy encouraged her to go on tour, leaving him free to pursue his own complicated love life—and Colette took his permission as a tactful dismissal.

So began Colette's "vagabondage," and the end of her life with the man she had called "Doucette," and who had written, probably by his own hand,

Et, dans un rêve, je me vois
Près de Claudine aux yeux magiques,
Oubliant toutes les musiques
Pour écouter rire sa voix.

(And, in a dream, I see myself
Near Claudine of the magic eyes,
Forgetting all music
To hear her laughing voice.)

It had been a real marriage, in spite of Colette's many disillusionments and later disclaimers. Willy, impresario to so many people, had brought out something genuine in Colette's personality rather than simply imposing a role on her. Did he invent Claudine by discovering Colette? Perhaps it would never have happened without him; but the aspects of Colette that appeared in the early books—the ambiguous sexuality, the tension between love and retreat—were there already, and Willy recognized and developed them.

Colette the vagabond took refuge in friendship from the risks inherent in love. Her mime teacher, Georges Wague, was one of her comrades; another was the Anglophile writer Marcel Schwob, who had translated Kipling and probably had an influence on Colette's developing technique. Katherine Mansfield, too, had read Schwob's translation of *Plain Tales from the Hills*—which he called *Simples Contes des Collines*—while she was staying in Francis Carco's apartment on the Quai aux Fleurs; both she and Colette were interested in Kipling's use of the short story, and in a way they were cultivating the same kind of sensibility. Mansfield wrote in her Paris journal, in 1914,

It's very quiet. I've re-read *L'Entrave*. I suppose Colette is the only woman in France who does just this. I don't care a fig at present for anyone I know except her.

Carco, the friend they had in common, represented the same thing for them both. Katherine Mansfield's description of him, as the epicene young Frenchman in "Je ne parle pas français," sheds some light on Colette's world. The charming but opportunistic Carco, twice married and continually involved in liaisons with both sexes, horrifed the idealistic, puritanical Katherine, who meant to indicate by her title that she did not speak the language of sexual exploitation and dishonesty that Carco came to represent for her.

The growing discipline and native idealism of Colette, too, were offended by the bohemian world—and perhaps this is one source of her insistence on the theme of retreat, escape, solitude. But one of her refuges proved to be as complex a trap as marriage itself.

Schwob's wife, the beautiful and distinguished actress Marguerite Moreno, had become Colette's closest friend, and they agreed that they were both the kind of woman who represented a "temptation of homosexuality" for some men; young homosexuals were attracted to them throughout their lives. But Colette was only thirty-one when she left Willy, and the group to whom she was most interesting at that stage was composed of older lesbians.

Colette was described as one of the *amphibies* "in that amiably anarchic society frequented by fashionable pleasure-seekers no less than by the free world of letters." [6] This world was partly composed of the rich lesbians Colette describes in *Le Pur et l'Impur*. Overlapping with the literary world, and seceding from the conventional high society of the era, this particular aspect of the demi-monde went in for travesty, for exoticism, and for secret codes of membership. Natalie Clifford Barney, the poet Renée Vivien, and other literary Sapphists formed a circle whose elegance was solidly based on the aristocratic incomes of some of its members, one of whom fell in love with Colette.

The Marquise de Belbeuf was the youngest daughter of the Duc de Morny; an unattractive child, her mother had made no secret of her distaste for her, and called her "the tapir." "Missy," as she was known to her friends, had been raised by servants, and her arranged marriage to the marquis had been brief and unhappy. By the time Colette met her, she was a dignified and extremely masculine figure who wore well-tailored smoking jackets and cropped hair. (Her resemblance to Gertrude Stein was striking.) Colette, who had seen herself as the "male" partner to the ultrafeminine Rézi, changed roles in order to play Missy's "petite amie"—a game that she entered into with amusement for a while, even wearing a gold ankle bracelet engraved with the words "I belong to Missy." Missy took mime lessons too, and the pair appeared together in a piece called *Rêve d'Egypte*—but their passionate kiss on stage was interrupted by the enraged relatives of the marquis, who considered it a public scandal, and Missy's part had to be played by Wague.

For Colette, belonging to Missy turned out to be just another form of unacceptable dependence—a question of power and possession, all too similar to marriage. The marquise was jealous, and it was she who paid the bills. But she did provide comfort and company, and though she appears in none of Colette's writings of the time, the letters are full of references to Missy accompanying her on tour, nursing her through the flu, and buying her Rozven, the house on the Breton coast where she was to spend her summers for the next fifteen years.

A clue to what Colette's life was like in this period may be found in *La Vagabonde*, published in 1911, which is even further from Colette's direct emotional experience than were the Claudines, but which represents the way she wanted to see herself. Renée Néré, the heroine, makes her peace with solitude, and learns to live without dependence, in the way that Colette desired for herself. This theme of renunciation was much more than a pose, or Colette would not have returned to it again and again, as if it were something she could not help. Marriage had disappointed her, but she had also found that in many ways it was not what she had wanted in the first place. Marriage was a question of power, and when it extended itself to power over her professional life, it was intolerable. The desire for independence through work was something few women had; even fewer managed to achieve it. It forced Colette into the theater, a world where she did not feel very much at home, but which was more sympathetic to female independence than was conventional society.

The first pieces she signed with her own name were the "Dialogues de Bêtes," slightly arch conversations between a dog and a cat about their human masters. These productions seemed slight enough for Willy not to attempt to co-opt them; and they indicated one route by which Colette was to approach the direct treatment of human emotions. Her animal personae also appeared in her acting—her animal impersonations cloaked some of her ineptitude on the stage, and provided an excuse for seminudity. But her nudity, like that of an animal, seems to have had a very unerotic effect: she herself later defended noble, honest nudity against salacious half-undress; it is like the relation of her disciplined, classical style to her amorous subject matter. In all her works, on and off the stage, Colette demystified love and eroticism and faced them squarely and fully illuminated. Her nudity was startling only in its *pudeur*, or modesty.

In the "Dialogues de Bêtes," but also in the other books with their many animal characters, the reactions of animals to human beings are an important revelation of character. In fact, there is no sharp line of demarcation between man and the other animals, and "Il n'y a qu'*une* bête" was as characteristic a saying of Colette's as "Il n'y a qu'*un* amour." The unity of all varieties of love, whether between man and beast, man and woman, woman and woman, was something that her emotional career during the years with Willy had thoroughly demonstrated to her. At this point, she was open to the idea that perhaps conjugal love was not to be, for her, the most important variety. For a while, she would try to do without it.

Colette had gained from Willy the strength that enabled her to attempt life on her own; he had demystified the world of the professional artist and writer, and started her on the exploitation of her own talent. For all Willy's selfishness, he had given her much—the proof is that his only lasting fame has been through the creation of Colette.

CHAPTER 3

Jouvenel

La Vagabonde is Colette's account of the years after she left Willy; but like her accounts of life with him, it has only an oblique relation to the truth. Solitude, punctuated by refusal of the security offered by rich suitors, was her fictional pose at this time; in fact her liaison with Missy protected her from the hazards of independent life right up to the moment when she met her second husband. Her habit of introducing real names into her fiction—a habit dating from the very first Claudines, where it was perhaps introduced by the roguish Willy—obscures the issue; and the compilation in English of *Earthly Paradise*, a sort of autobiography edited from her own writings, has reinforced the misconception that most of her novels are thinly disguised fact. Colette herself would never have claimed as much, and to say that her life was different from her fiction is not to disagree with any of her own statements on the matter. But even where her books are not "true to life" in this narrow sense, they reflect feelings that lay deeper than her overt behavior.

Independence was something she longed for precisely because it was so difficult to achieve; because she was constantly being tempted away from "ton cher fantôme, solitude" by "l'ombre menaçante de l'amour."

Her disillusion with Willy deepened her native mistrust of men; she continued to see him, to quarrel with him over her rights in the books she had written, and at first her stage publicity was managed by him. In 1909 she wrote to her friend and protector, Léon Hamel,

C'est encore Willy de qui j'ai appris des choses pas belles, . . . il a vendu, à mon insu, *toutes* les Claudines aux Editeurs, pour presque rien et que ces livres qui m'appartenaient si entièrement (moralement) sont à jamais perdus pour lui et pour moi . . . jamais, même après sa mort, je ne rentrerai en possession de ces livres qui sont miens. J'en ai éprouvé un profond bouleversement, cher ami, je le lui ai écrit. Il a répondu à mon cri de désespoir par une lettre froide, presque menaçante, et je pense qu'après l'explication nécessaire qui aura lieu à son retour de Monte-Carlo (après-demain) tout sera fini entre nous.

Songez qu'après 3 ans de séparation, j'apprends encore, trop souvent, de nouvelles trahisons que j'ignorais . . .[1]

(Once again I have learned some things about Willy that aren't at all nice . . . he has sold *all* the Claudines to their publishers, for almost nothing, without my knowledge—and these books which belong to me so entirely (morally) are lost forever to him and to me . . . never, even after his death, will I regain possession of these books which are mine. I have been profoundly upset by this, dear friend, and I've written him to tell him so. He has responded to my hopeless cry with a cold, almost threatening, letter, and I think that after the necessary explanations, which will take place when he gets back from Monte Carlo [the day after tomorrow], everything will be over between us.

Just think, after three years of separation, I am still learning, all too often, of new betrayals I didn't know about.)

Willy had not been jealous of Missy, and the marquise in turn was not jealous of the young playboys who were interested in her protégée. As long as things stayed on the level of amusement, she knew that she had little competition. But in July 1911, a new tone enters the letters as a serious contender appears on the scene.

Henry de Jouvenel was co-editor of *Le Matin*, one of the big Paris dailies. He had been married once, was attractive to women, and was an important figure in the world of journalism that Colette saw as one possible escape from the grind of theatrical touring. He was arrogant, energetic, and masculine, and came from a world more central and powerful in French life than either the faded bohemia of the Belle Epoque or the ultimately rather depressing circle of Missy and her friends. But he was not too respectable or stuffy to be seriously interested in the notorious Colette, as several of her rich admirers, such as the young Auguste Hériot, had been.

Missy and Colette were spending the summer at Rozven, amid the peace and solitude she was to use as the background for *Le Blé en herbe.* Perhaps their retreat was consciously modeled on that of the Ladies of Llangollen, the famous couple who had escaped from their families into the Welsh mountains a century before, and whose story Colette retells in *Le Pur et l'Impur.* Colette occasionally abandoned the idyll to go on music-hall tours, and in Lausanne, at the conclusion of one such tour, she was joined by Jouvenel, who abruptly declared that he couldn't live without her any longer. Missy and Hériot were wildly jealous, as was Jouvenel's previous mistress, Madame de Comminges, known as "La Panthère." Colette announced to La Panthère that she was the "other woman"; the rejected one threatened to assassinate her, and Colette was placed under a guard of journalists from *Le Matin.* After a month of tension and drama, La Panthère and Hériot departed together on a cruise, and Colette and Jouvenel set up housekeeping together.

Colette seems to have treated Missy rather badly, adopting a tone of hard unconcern; she wrote to Wague's wife,

Tu veux des nouvelles de Missy? je n'en ai pas, et elle continue à détenir tout ce qui m'appartient. J'aime bien qu'on me fasse bénéficier d'un traitement d'exception, et je serai la première à avoir vu "la marquise" demander de l'argent à une femme qu'elle quitte. [2]

(Do you want news of Missy? I don't have any, and she continues to hang onto everything that belongs to me. I like it when I get special treatment, and I shall be the first to have seen "the marquise" ask for money from a woman whom she is abandoning.)

Missy in fact was exceptionally generous: she removed her furniture from Rozven, but she left Colette the house, renting one for herself just around the point. By this time a pattern was emerging: Colette had a capacity for allying herself with people on the way up, and for jettisoning those whose moment had passed. The casualties she left behind regretted her desertion, and never recovered the élan that had attracted her to them in the first place.

The affair with Jouvenel was serious enough to supersede all others; but it seemed clear to Colette that this love, like previous ones, was merely temporary. Sidi, as she called him (in a surprising reminiscence of Sido), exhibited an "egotism . . . so naïve and so childish that one wants to laugh and cry." She told Hamel that "We have good moments and lousy quarters of an hour. This can't go on for long. . . . " [3] But their agreements to part always ended in postponement; Sidi's business trips and long hours at the paper, and Colette's theatrical tours, refreshed them for the fray.

The imagery that recurs in Colette's description of Sidi is that of a sultan, a pasha, a Muslim. Ever since her days in Sido's walled garden, this was the only civilization outside the French that seems to have interested her at all (she had none of the Anglophilia of Schwob or of the French aristocracy, and none of Willy's interest in German culture); and Sidi the Pasha, surrounded by his harem of adoring females, had the kind of male chauvinism that she understood. There was no point in disguising the fact that this was the way of the world: as she expressed it in a fictional dialogue with "Mon amie Valentine,"

—Le retour à la vie de famille, ma chère, il n'y a que ça! Et la vie de famille comme la comprenaient nos grand'mères! On ne se souciait pas de baccalauréats pour les jeunes filles, dans ce temps-là, et personne ne s'en portait plus mal, au contraire!

Je lève un instant les yeux sur ma houri en caftan vert, cherchant en vain sur elle la trace morbide d'un baccalauréat mal guéri. . . .[4]

(—The return to family life, my dear, there's nothing like it! And family life as our grandmothers knew it! One didn't worry about degrees for girls, in those days, and nobody was the worse for it, on the contrary!

I raise my eyes for a moment to my houri in her green caftan, looking in vain for the deadly signs of a badly-healed degree. . . .)

This subtle critique of antifeminism implies that it comes from those who have no right to speak on the subject—but it also recognizes that even in a society where degrees for women exist, women are still dependent on men for their living. The "houri in her green caftan" is using the same strategies as Moslem women, and her attack on female baccalaureates is a clumsy defense of these strategies.

The affair with Sidi was one aspect of Colette's own practical strategy. He appointed her literary editor of *Le Matin*, and she was responsible for choosing a daily feuilleton to appear under the rubric "Mille et un Matins" (the Muslim imagery again), and for writing one a week herself. Her afternoons in the ancient and crumbling "Maison Rouge" which the newspaper inhabited in the Boulevard Poissonière introduced her to a new life—political journalism, smart publishers, and literary hostesses. Her reputation had preceded her at the paper: one of Sidi's co-editors said, "If that woman's name appears in this paper, I'm leaving!" Asked if he knew the lady, according to Colette he "blushed for the first time in his life and said 'Certainly not! I don't go to brothels!' " Colette never tried to undo her reputation as a salacious and immoral writer: it was better box-office than anything else; but there was nonetheless a satisfaction in entering a world that had been closed to her.

The difficult relation between Colette and Sidi was cemented into marriage by a series of fortuitous events. Colette's mother had been ill during the summer of 1912, and Colette had therefore depended much more heavily than usual upon Sidi, who responded affectionately. On September 25, Sido died. Colette wrote: "I am tormented by the stupid idea that I won't be able to write to Mother anymore, as I used to do so often." [5] Colette's relation with Sido had, as she indicates, long been an epistolary one, but the guilt induced by that realization was possibly harder to bear than the loss of a real person would have been. Sido had feared for Colette's second marriage, saying that two husbands had not done *her* any good, and that life with the dominating Jouvenel would prevent her from doing her own writing. Colette was impressed enough by these remarks to remember and repeat them. But the surest evidence of the continuing link between Colette and her mother, and the extent to which it directed Colette's behavior, is that within one week of her mother's death Colette became pregnant for the first time, at the age of forty.

Colette and Sidi were married in the sixth month of her pregnancy, after an exhausting music-hall tour and amid a fever of parties, dinners, and festivities. The birth was difficult—"thirty hours with *no* respite, chloroform and forceps" [6]—and however much Colette may have wished to play the role of the earth mother in later life, maternity was not a role she took to easily. She watched the expertise of the baby nurse with amazement, and never seems to have contemplated making the baby a part of her own Parisian life. The Jouvenel château in the Corrèze was clearly the place for babies.

Within a few months, the war broke out—and its effect on Colette's life was to ease the potential strains of marriage and motherhood, and to postpone the possibility of their becoming burdensome. Sidi was in uniform, first at the front and then participating in the political negotiations, and Colette's journalistic pose was simple pride in her soldier husband. Safety dictated that her daughter stay in the country, while the national effort demanded that Colette herself continue to work. For a while, things were clear and straightforward.

Like Katherine Mansfield, Colette was burning with curiosity about the battle front, and managed to talk her way there with the help of her journalist's credentials. But most of the time she was in Paris, and her reporting of the conditions of life for ordinary people in wartime gained her an affectionate mass audience that she had never had before.

With the end of the war, the interests of Colette and Sidi began to diverge fatally. Though she had been drawn back into conjugal love even after her disillusion with Willy, and though Sidi had been an indispensable professional help to her, Colette was still suspicious of love, still resistant to the idea that she might commit herself wholly to a man. Though her work seemed still to require an emotional basis in her life, it also provided a retreat from an in-creasingly difficult marriage, and Colette began to immerse herself in literary tasks of all kinds.

As well as writing her own novels and working at *Le Matin*, she chose the novels published by Ferenczi in the "Collection Co-lette." She wrote advertising. She collaborated in the stage adapta-tions of her own books. She wrote for magazines, wrote coffee-table books, and did theater criticism. She still went on tour, often in productions of her own works. Money was important to her, as was the establishment of a solid safety net of contacts, royalties, and reputation, a net that would catch her whatever happened to her shaky marriage.

Sidi, in the meantime, was beginning to carve out his political career. In 1921 he was elected senator from the Corrèze. In 1922 he led the French delegation to the League of Nations. Colette viewed politics with amused skepticism: in September 1922, after his disarmament proposal at the League was ratified by 44 nations, she wrote to a friend, "Que penses-tu de Sidi? Si on ne le f . . . pas roi de France après ça!" ("What do you think of Sidi? If they don't effing well make him King of France after that!") She had no desire to be a politician's wife, nor to entertain on the scale and in the manner that were becoming necessary at Castel-Novel, the family château. And in his turn, Sidi was undoubtedly anxious about the effect Colette's louche bohemian reputation would have on the glacially conventional world he was entering.

There is something defensive in Colette's jeers at Sidi's ambi-tions; also something proud. As Marguerite Moreno had written when she was making futile preparations for the visit of some rich friends, "There is a hell of a difference between Palaces, Villas, and other places, and my vaulted houses . . ." [7]

Colette was sure of the superiority of her own values and those of her friends; several years later, after her divorce from Sidi, she spelled out her philosophy in a letter to Marguerite:

Je n'ai jamais été riche d'argent, il n'y a pas de probabilité que je le sois jamais. Pour moi, être riche, ça veut dire posséder—outre la tendresse d'un être aimé et de mes amis—un bout de terre, une voiture qui roule, de la santé, la liberté de ne pas travailler au moment où je ne veux ou ne puis travailler. J'entends parler avec terreur des embellissements et modernités que Jouvenel fait à Castel-Novel. Réparer et moderniser—électricité, eau chaude, salles de bains partout—une demeure de cette taille, ça signifie, d'abord un demi-million disponible, puis la joie délirante de mener, enfin, enfin, la "Vie de château" . . . O Marguerite! tu m'entends claquer des dents? [8]

(I have never been rich in money, and it's not likely I ever shall be. For me, being rich means having—apart from the tenderness of a beloved being and of my friends—a bit of land, a car that goes, health, freedom not to work when I don't want to or can't work. I am horrified to hear about the embellishments and modernizations that Jouvenel is doing at Castel-Novel. Repair and modernize—electricity, hot water, bathrooms everywhere—life on this scale means, first of all, half a million in ready cash, and then the delirious joy of leading, finally, finally, the "vie de chateau" . . . Oh, Marguerite! Do you hear me gnashing my teeth?)

Colette, with her sharp sense of money, can be accused of opportunism; but she was not as closely implicated in the high life as were most French writers of her time. The French literary scene has always played the role of court jester to the aristocracy, and Colette did not entirely escape this temptation. But she also continued to write about outsiders—sometimes even working girls, like Mitsou; her wartime reporting, throughout two wars, was to win her a special place in the affections of the people of Paris. The village girl from Burgundy was a part of her literary persona that she valued very highly, and to which the "vie de château" was inimical.

Sidi, on the other hand, was intent on being an insider, and on founding a political dynasty. When his brother Robert died, Colette said that Sidi had lost the only great love of his life in the form of the "brilliant, blond, irritable editor of L'Oeuvre." Sidi's two sons, Bertrand and Renaud, had precociously brilliant careers as political writers; when Bertrand had two sons by two different wives, Colette remarked on the family likeness to the Sultan. In fact, there was something about a family dynasty that warred against marriage, as Colette understood very well herself. The matriarchy established by Sido had no place for male interlopers; they were irrelevant, just as women were in the Jouvenel scheme of things. Sido had said, at the time of her daughter's first marriage,

> la vérité, c'est qu'il faudrait épouser son propre frère, si l'on voulait se marier en connaissance de cause, et encore! Tout ce sang étranger qui entre dans une famille, et qui fait qu'on regarde son propre fils en se disant: "D'où m'amène-t-il ces yeux-là, et ce front, et ces colères de fou, et cette aptitude au mensonge? . . ." Ah! mon pauvre toutou chéri, je ne cherche pas à expliquer, ni à refaire, comme ils disent, une société nouvelle, mais tout est si mal arrangé! [9]

> (The truth is that you would have to marry your own brother if you wanted to marry with full awareness, and more! All this foreign blood that comes into a family, and makes you say as you look at your own son, "Where does he get those eyes, and that forehead, and those mad rages, and that talent for lying? . . ." Oh! my poor dear puppy, I'm not trying to explain, nor to refashion, as they say, a new society, but everything is so badly organized!)

Her unflattering description of Willy cannot have made Colette's life with him any easier; altogether, her hostility to men from outside the family seems to have been passed on to her daughter and then to her granddaughter: when the young Colette de Jouvenel married in 1935, she left her husband almost immediately, giving as the reason "horreur physique."

The idea that a brother is closer than a husband, and that incest is the only way round the insuperable problem of marrying a stranger, is interesting in view of the strong brother-sister attachments felt by Colette, as well as by George Eliot and Katherine Mansfield. *Julie de Carneilhan* is the novel Colette wrote, much later, about her second marriage—and as she had done with Willy, she revenged herself on Jouvenel by asserting in fiction what was taken as fact. In the book, she accuses Jouvenel of needing a rich wife to finance his political career, and of deliberately getting rid of Colette in order to find someone more suitable. In the novel, the disillusioned Julie behaves magnanimously to her successor, then rides away with her brother to the country of their childhood.

Sidi's arrogance as a public man is perfectly expressed by a letter he wrote a journalist who had submitted for his approval an article about him: on Sénat writing paper and signed "Jouvenel" in lordly style, in a large, bold hand, he remarks that he has deleted several passages, but that

> J'ai laissé celle où vous parlez de mon "ambition terrible et limée," parce que je ne vous cacherai pas qu'elle m'a paru fort amusante.
> Mais, au fait, il n'est peut-être pas mauvais de faire croire qu'on est ambitieux, même quand on ne l'est pas. Ça répond à l'idée que les gens se font des hommes politiques et il ne faut pas troubler les habitudes.[10]

> (I have left in that bit where you speak of my "terrible and glittering ambition" because I will not hide from you the fact that I found it very amusing.
> But, in fact, perhaps it is no bad thing to have people believe that one is ambitious, even when one is not. It corresponds to the idea that people have of politicians, and one must not disturb their habits.)

Sidi's absences grew more frequent and prolonged, his love affairs more flagrant. Colette took refuge in the summers at Rozven, where the Jouvenel children came, as well as a large cast of friends and colleagues and dependents. Like George Eliot, Colette was beginning to be the focus of adoration by a number of lonely, often talented women, who saw in her the rapport with life and the psychological strength that they lacked. The poet Hélène Picard, who wrote a book called *Pour un mauvais garçon* under the influence of her unhappy passion for Francis Carco, was one such—and of the inevitable accusation that such women were Colette's lovers, Colette herself had this to say:

> Féminine avec exclusivité, presque avec emportement, cette Hélène lettrée se taisait, gênée, quand il était question devant elle de perversions homosexuelles. Elle se refusait même à admettre qu'elles existassent. De deux femmes, qui singeaient le couple, et que nous jugions sans sévérité: "Non, non," s'écria Hélène, "c'est laid! Ou bien c'est pour rire. Elles font semblant, elles sont ridicules." L'un de nous lui remontra que l'autre sexe n'était ni exempt ni dédaigneux d'errements analogues. Hélène s'apaisa: "Entre garçons, oui, ça peut aller." [11]

(Exclusively feminine, almost furiously so, well-read Hélène became speechless with embarrassment when homosexual perversions were discussed in front of her. She even refused to admit they existed. Of two women, who aped a couple, and whom we judged without severity: "No, no," cried Hélène, "it is ugly! Or else it's laughable. They are alike, they are ridiculous." One of us remonstrated that the other sex was neither exempt from nor disdainful of analogous errors. Hélène said peaceably, "Between boys, yes, all right.")

This is an interesting reversal of the Willy/Renaud view that lesbianism is trivial: clearly Colette finds it more flattering for female perversion to be judged the greater sin. Certainly female affection had a solidity that the love of men seemed to lack, especially the love of such men as Sidi. As she had done after her first marriage, Colette took refuge with women from the perfidy of her husband. Colette remarks of his latest mistress,

> Amour, amour . . . Anagramme d'amour: rouma. Ajoute "nia" et
> . . . tu trouves au bout une dame qui a des os de cheval et qui pond des livres en deux volumes. Il n'a pas de chance, notre Sidi . . .[12]

> (Love, love . . . Anagram of love: "Rouma." Add "nia" and . . . you find at the end a lady with the bones of a horse, who pens two-volume books. He's not lucky, our Sidi. . . .)

The divergence of Sidi and Colette took several years to accomplish; but it was irrevocable. Years after their parting, Colette looked at a photograph of Sidi and said, "Ah, il est perdu." When he died suddenly of a heart attack in 1935, she had not seen him for a dozen years, and said that she would not have recognized him on the street.

While she was with Sidi, Colette wrote the books that male critics, in particular, prefer of all her oeuvre—straight novels, in which direct autobiography is disguised and the copious, overblown *style Colette* more tightly controlled than usual. This was the period of strict, classical short novels, treating themes that had always been considered salacious in serious and reticent fashion. Women often prefer her first-person books, the later volumes of reminiscence and meditation in which her style reaches its most luxuriant flowering. But the controlled, objective novels won praise from established men of letters, including Proust and Gide; even the misogynist Montherlant said that one could not criticize *Chéri*, one could only say "That's it."

Sidi may have been one influence in the direction of objectivity. Colette records that he asked irritably, "Can't you write about anything but love?"—but that he was in too much of a hurry to meet his latest mistress to stop and explain what he thought she should do instead. The discrepancy between style and theme is what gives the novels of this period their fascination: *Chéri, Le Blé en herbe, Mitsou, La Seconde*—all treat "unacceptable" themes in a severe fashion that brings them closer to the philosophical fable than to the magazine story. Colette was living up to the idea Sidi's world had of what a writer was supposed to do, and she was beginning to receive the serious homage of that world.

Even at this period, her fiction reflected her life with great fidelity. *La Seconde*, for example, is thought to be one of her least autobiographical novels; but the theme of the charismatic man with a houseful of women, and the complicity between his wife and his mistress, has obvious parallels with Colette's life at the time. The theme of sexual tension between wife and stepson, too, is carried over from the Claudine books: Colette had played the role of stepmother in both her marriages, and the suggestion has been made (though never substantiated) that an incestuous affair of this kind caused the final rupture with Sidi.

Colette's interest in the stepson theme is, however, close to what was becoming her prevailing role in life as in her books. As she aged, Colette had abandoned the theme of the Claudines and *La Vagabonde*—a young woman's search for independence. The father figure, earlier represented by Renaud and Hamel, disappeared from her stories. Instead, she gradually began to see herself as an older woman loved by younger men. *Le Blé en herbe* touches on this theme; *Chéri*—the story of the son of a *grande cocotte*, who falls in love with one of the famous courtesans of his mother's generation but is unwillingly married off to a girl his own age—is the classic statement of it, as *Lolita* is of the reverse situation. Both are stark tragedies of time, inevitable and final. Lolita grows up; Léa grows old; the men who loved them can do nothing to bring them back. Colette may have already been seeing herself as Léa, a character she created on the stage; she had gone from being Claudine to being Léa with no intervening role in which she felt emotionally at home. The years with Sidi, productive though they were, produced no fictional persona with whom Colette completely identified herself.

To Colette, it was clear that the era of the *grandes cocottes* had ended only to be replaced by the same thing in a different guise. Women still depended on the favors of men, only now they bought those favors with their talents and their wits as well as with their bodies. Writers and actresses were in the same game as the courtesans—and what happened to aging courtesans? They did not marry respectable politicians of their own age; they took handsome, feckless young lovers, while the respectable politicians were marrying for money and having affairs with younger women. This is the background against which she saw her own life; she was disillusioned about men and contemptuous of them. She was drawing closer to Sido, because she now felt that her mother had been right—what use were husbands? Her fictional re-creation of Sido began at this period of her life.

Colette could not express her feelings directly in her books—surface charm was an essential of the courtesan's art, in words as in every other way. Preaching was forbidden; ideas were out of place. Her many disclaimers, her insistence that she had no moral to propound and no capacity for serious thought, are coquettish; her third husband was to point out that they belonged to the same mentality that led her to conceal her high, domed forehead, the forehead of a Beethoven, beneath a mass of curly hair.

Her contempt shows in her male characters: they are either desirable pieces of flesh (Jean in *L'Entrave*, and Chéri himself), exploiters, or innocent young boys being initiated to corruption by older women. And yet even in this time of disillusion, the focus of her books and of her own life remained the male-female relationship. The love of women was no more than a recuperative interlude; she had to find some way to reconcile her need for men with her desire to be independent of them. Her task was more difficult than that of George Eliot or Katherine Mansfield, perhaps because it was harder to find a Frenchman with the egalitarianism of Murry or Lewes.

Professionally, Sidi had done a great deal for Colette—her position in the world of serious letters, and of mass journalism, was assured. She had borne a daughter, and been (more or less) mistress of a château. But she still felt an impulse to withdraw to the periphery of life, to pull out of the maelstrom; and this impulse appears even in her most "objective" books. Like Katherine Mansfield, she was the kind of writer who worked with complete concentration, and who was most deeply in touch with herself in the privacy of her work sessions. Far from being a means of self-disguise, her stories are vehicles of self-revelation, and show the emotional imperatives that she felt most strongly. Though it may not be true to say that they are accurate biography, her books show what she sensed about her own personality: the more fully she entered into love, the more she desired to be free of it.

CHAPTER 4

Goudeket

The long disentanglement from Sidi was Colette's second "retreat from love." With the approach of physical old age, could it be that finally she was to enact this persistent fantasy? that the solitude she had longed for in so many books was at last to be hers? Or did it lose all its savor if it were not enjoyed in the face of importunings? Now that it was a real possibility, was it still so attractive?

These questions seemed to evaporate a mere two years later, in the spring of 1925, when Colette, for the first time in her life, fell unashamedly and joyously in love. It was as if, now that her career was established, now that the serious and threatening part of her life as a woman was over—she had married twice, produced a child, and reached the menopause—now that she had made peace with the ghost of her mother, she could at last feel free to love with the irresponsible gusto that we mistakenly associate with youth.

Maurice Goudeket was twenty years younger than Colette, good-looking and popular in the society of actresses, dress designers, and writers from which most of her friends came. A *courtier en perles*, or pearl merchant, he was the son of a Dutch diamond merchant and a Frenchwoman. He has described his own uneasiness in his parents' petit-bourgeois Jewish household, and the precarious social-climbing dinners they gave, where "the inevitable false countess confronted the ineluctable faux-filet." The family had spent several years in Amsterdam during his childhood—an uprooting that necessitated education by governesses, and that left him so alienated from boys of his own age that he never afterward felt at ease in the company of men. When they moved back to Paris and he entered the Lycée Condorcet (in the same year as Jean Cocteau), his French was ultra-precise, his personality romantic and solitary, his sexuality strong but repressed. He dreamed of a great love, a Juliet or Héloïse—and when he read his first few pages of Colette, he told his parents, "I am going to marry that woman. She is the only one in the world who can understand me."

Maurice and Colette met at Marguerite Moreno's house on the Cap d'Ail. He felt that she was playing the role of Colette a bit to excess, with her feline reclinings and Burgundian "r"s—but he also felt that he was face to face with his destiny. And he was later to say, "At first, I thought you were playing the part of Colette. But after thirty years with you, I now believe that you *are* Colette." He offered to drive her back to Paris, and by the end of the glorious excursion through the spring sunshine, her interest was thoroughly awakened. Having failed to establish the egalitarian relation she sought with Jouvenel, who was her counterpart in age and prestige, she was ready to look for it with someone whose adoration of her made chauvinistic behavior less likely. Soon they were meeting in the evening in Paris, for conversations that began at midnight and finished at 4 A.M., described by Colette as "orgies of Vittel, oranges and grapefruits, and cigarettes." She wrote to Marguerite,

Le garçon est exquis. J'aime mieux ne rien ajouter. Quelle grâce masculine il y a dans certains amollissements, et comme on est touché de voir le feu intérieur fondre l'enveloppe. Est-ce que tu ne crois pas qu'il y a peu d'hommes qui sachent, sans hausser la voix, ni changer le ton, dire . . . ce qu'il faut dire? [1]

(The boy is exquisite. I prefer to say no more. What masculine grace there is in certain softnesses, and how touching it is to see the internal fire melt the crust. Don't you agree that there are few men who know,

without raising their voice, or changing their tone, how to say . . .
what must be said?)

Her tone is still a bit objective and appraising, the tone of Léa as
she evaluates the beauty of Chéri. There is also something of practised toughness in her own description of how she fought off the
competition, represented by a woman she refers to as "la Chi-
wawa":

Cette malheureuse femme, *sentant* ce qui se passe, est entrée dans la
peau d'une harpie et a montré sa passion déchaînée pour ce garçon.
. . . j'ai tout apaisé avec beaucoup de sang-froid, sans cris ni pugilats.
Ç'a été très simple.
—Mon Dieu, où étiez-vous à telle, telle, telle heure?
—Où je veux.
—Mais vos amis m'ont dit . . .
—Mes amis n'ont rien de commun avec des inquisiteurs.
. . . Nous n'avons prononcé aucun nom. Elle a dit:
—C'est bien, je partirai. Mais promettez-moi que si vous êtes
heureuse, je le saurai?
—Je n'aurai pas seulement achevé de l'être que je quitterai le lieu de
ma félicité pour courir au télégraphe.[2]

(This unhappy woman, *feeling* what is going on, has turned into a
harpy and displayed her unbridled passion for this boy. . . . I have
calmed everything down very coolly, without cries or blows. It has been
very simple.
—My God, where were you at such, and such, and such a time?
—Where I wished.
—But your friends told me . . .
—My friends have nothing in common with inquisitors.
. . . We didn't mention any names. She said,
—Very well, I'm leaving. But promise me that if you are happy, I
shall know of it?
—As soon as I've succeeded, I shall leave the scene of my felicity to
rush and send a telegram.)

The progress of the affair was faithfully reported to Marguerite; in fact she knew much more about Colette's feelings than did Maurice himself, who says that not until he read the letters to Marguerite after the death of Colette did he realize that she was already in love with him while he was still awed and nervous in her presence. By June, Colette was writing,

> Acacias, acacias, et encore acacias, et roses, et eau rapide, et heures plus rapides que l'eau . . .
>
> Ah! la la, et encore la la! Et jamais assez la la! Elle est propre, ton amie, va. Elle est dans un beau pétrin agréable, jusqu'aux yeux, jusqu'aux lèvres, jusque plus loin que ça! Oh! le satanisme des gens tranquilles—je dis ça pour le gars Maurice.—Veux-tu savoir ce que c'est que le gars Maurice? C'est un salaud, et un ci et un ça, et même un chic type, et une peau de satin. C'est là que j'en suis.

> (Acacias, acacias, and again acacias, and roses, and quick flowing water, and hours that flow by quicker than the water . . .
>
> Oh! la la, and again la la! And never enough la la! She's a proper one, your friend. She's in a lovely fix, up to her eyes, up to her lips, and even further than that! Oh! the devilishness of quiet men—I refer to that lad Maurice.—Would you like to know what he is, that lad Maurice? He's a skunk, and a this and a that, and a nice guy, and an exquisite creature. And that's the state I'm in.)

Marguerite responded severely, "You've fallen into a fit! That's all there is to it."

But Colette assured her, "No, I'm not crazy—it's much more serious."

Still, Colette was not at all sure that this was to be more than a passing affair. Her first two marriages had convinced her that love did not last; and because of the difference in age, she was even less sanguine than usual about this love.

The first book she wrote after meeting Maurice was *La Fin de Chéri*, in which the hero of the earlier book retreats from the disillusioned world after World War I and attempts to rediscover his beloved Léa, but age has made her unrecognizable. Obsessed by a past that no longer exists, he commits suicide. It is Colette's most tragic, severe treatment of the theme of the retreat from love. Many critics have called it the most masculine of her books, and she herself speaks of the "vieux garçon" who was her writing self at this time, and who could not be influenced by the emotions of the female body he happened to inhabit.

Colette continued to play the role of Léa on the stage, and her many descriptions of both Maurice and Chéri as "Satan classique" indicate that in some sense she had finally begun to play in real life the role she had so often imagined for herself. Her own aging was, she feared, the thing that would put an end to the relation with Maurice, as it had ended the love of Chéri and Léa: when Chéri returns, no longer tempted by the uninteresting charms of younger women, he finds that the Léa he loved is now an old woman—she has disappeared beneath fat and gray hair.

The role of Léa, however, was in many ways a self-protective one. It is she who has the upper hand throughout: she directs the affair, she decides how long it should go on, and she is invulnerable. Chéri, the suppliant, thinks that time is on his side, but he discovers that Léa has escaped him, and he has nothing left. The older women throughout Colette's books have this strength, this vision of themselves as the givers of love and therefore the ones who cannot lose their independence.

But Maurice was no Chéri, no spoiled sensualist, but an intensely literary young man with an idealistic notion of love. Like Middleton Murry, he sought contact with life through the medium of a woman who was more vitally in touch with the natural world than was he himself. He was ready to accept life with Colette on any terms she named, including friendship and partnership after the end of physical love.

He and Colette spent their summers at Saint-Tropez, in a house she had bought and named "La Treille Muscate." It was Maurice who convinced Colette to transfer her allegiance from Brittany to his beloved Mediterranean, and in the years before the little fishing port became crowded with the beautiful people and their Ferraris, Colette, Maurice, and their painter friends lived the idyllic life of beach, garden, local wine, and Provençal cooking that searchers for the "good life" have been trying to emulate ever since.

Maurice claims that he would have been ashamed to mind being called "Monsieur Colette"—that it is given to few people to find a satisfying vocation in serving genius, and that one can only be grateful for the opportunity. But he resented Colette's implication that the "retreat from love" had happened much earlier than it did. *La Naissance du jour* is set in Saint-Tropez, and Colette uses real names for most of the characters, including herself—but she regretfully sends away the young man who wants to become her lover, and resigns herself to a solitary old age. Maurice has protested several times in print that this book was written at the very time when they were living ardent and passionate summers in the Mediterranean heat; that it was merely Colette's imagining of a role she felt she must eventually play.

Vial, in the book, is an uninteresting young man, beautiful but without much to say. Colette does not renounce much when she hands him over to a girl of his own age. Like Jean in *L'Entrave,* he is treated almost contemptuously, as a possible vehicle of pleasure, but a second-rate human being. Colette may have found love easier to renounce in books than in life because the male characters she created were much less interesting than those she married.

For Maurice was already proving that he was more than a "peau de satin." With the advent of the Depression, his business, like so much of the luxury trade, ceased to exist, and he took up journalism, "the dream of my life." To Colette's undisguised astonishment, it turned out that he could write—and soon he was working for *Match, Marie-Claire* (where he became literary editor), and any other magazine that wanted miscellaneous articles turned out quickly. Professional camaraderie was the last thing Colette expected from her Chéri, but it helped to make the change from love to companionship possible. Because he was a novice, not to be mentioned in the same breath with the great Colette, his professional activities were no threat to hers—unlike her first two husbands, he was in no position to exert any influence on what she wrote. The sense of reluctant submission that she had felt with them, and that had spoiled the possibility of comradeship, did not exist any more.

By this time, Colette needed a shield from her public and a business adviser. Maurice, no longer preoccupied by his own business, was the ideal candidate. He knew her world, was a sharp negotiator, and also gave her the pride of a woman who is able to attract and keep a younger man—as Maurice was very conscious, this scenario held an important place in the French sexual mythology described (if not created) by Colette.

In many ways, his guardianship was like that provided by Lewes for George Eliot. Their routine of companionable reading and writing, and criticism of each other's work, was similar. Maurice says that they spoke of their work like two carpenters, an image that continues Colette's description of her childhood days in her father's study, where the Alexandrines fell like shavings from the workman's bench. Like Lewes, Maurice encouraged female adorers—Renée Hamon, the "petit corsaire" whose correspondence with Colette has been collected, brought Colette souvenirs from her exotic travels, and furnished her small white Breton fisherman's cottage with photographs of her idol.

The companionship of Colette and Maurice proceeded by gradual stages, as Colette grew more used to the idea of its permanence. They took adjoining flats in a building on the Champs-Elysées, with a balcony where Colette envisioned herself growing strawberries, though she only harvested half a dozen each year. When Colette was invited on the maiden crossing of the Normandie, they decided to get married—how else could they travel together in "prude America"? Maurice has ungallantly written that when he proposed to Colette, he saw by her intense glance how much it meant to her—and that he realized how continually afraid she had been of losing her young man, the event that Léa found so humiliating.

La Treille Muscate was sold when Saint-Tropez became crowded in the summer, and inquisitive visitors could not be kept out of the garden. Colette felt the first twinges of the arthritis that was eventually to cripple her, and the idea of setting up a permanent home with Maurice became more and more attractive. They found a flat in the Palais-Royal, at 9 Rue de Beaujolais, that was to be their window on the world until the death of Colette. Pauline, the woman who had kept house for Colette since her second marriage, completed the establishment, and for several years Colette had a secretary, Claude Chauvière, who published a book describing the household and its ways. Pauline seems to have been a reminder of the world of Sido—a countrywoman from the Limousin, she was a cook and housekeeper according to the best provincial tradition. Maurice's role seems to have been more ornamental than functional, though he gradually took on himself the tasks of organizing Colette's visitors, and the increasingly complicated logistics of her travels, which came to require crutches and then wheelchairs.

When war broke out, Colette and Maurice were away from Paris, though they soon returned, for Colette had no desire to escape the common experience of her "village" in the heart of the city. The full horror of war reached them with the inevitable knock on the door, and Maurice was taken off to an internment camp, from which he was only released as a result of weeks of frantic effort on the part of Colette. Thereafter, he made his way to the south, and when the occupation was extended, slipped through the lines and returned to Paris, where he slept in a hidden attic room. Colette was by this time a national monument, untouchable as Notre Dame; though she broadcast over the Free French network, and sent the manuscripts of her books to be published in Switzerland, she was not troubled by the Nazis.

During and after the war, Colette found herself in the role she had waited for so long: the wise French grandmother, advising her people with strategies of survival that dated from the Franco-Prussian war of 1871; sympathetically observing and reporting their struggles. In the postwar years, the honors bestowed on her included membership in the Belgian Academy, the Légion d'Honneur, and the Académie Goncourt. She reveled in being the only woman among "mes petits Goncourts."

Her books, for the first time, began to have happy endings. *Gigi*, her wartime novel that was almost a work of propaganda, so nostalgically does it analyze the art of the French courtesan, ends triumphantly: like earlier Colette heroines, Gigi defends love against commercial sexual transactions; but instead of dooming her to loneliness, this stand gains the acquiescence of the other characters. *L'Etoile Vesper* and *Le Fanal bleu*, the later volumes of reminiscence, record Colette's acceptance of her life, her work, and the pain that is her companion in the sleepless hours of the night.

The image of Colette in these final years is inseparable from the apartment in the Palais-Royal that was her final stage setting. Colette on the divan, which she referred to as her "raft," covered with cushions and fur rugs and spanned by a movable writing tray, gazing out at "Paris de ma fenêtre," and lighting the lamp with its shade of blue writing paper, was a familiar symbol of the survival of France itself. The bibelots, flowered paperweights, porcelain lamps, tapestry chairs—many worked by Colette herself—the polished wood and flower pictures—the whole was described by Renée Hamon as "très 1830, très SIDO." The "petit corsaire" recorded a visit in 1940:

Des roses rouges dans un baquet. Des tulipes cramoisies, veinées de blanc, narcisses, roses trémières et lilas. Joli mois de mai . . . La tapisserie qui attend.

Et sur la table longue et étroite, le jeu de stylos, la loupe, le pot de colle, les longs ciseaux et les lunettes. Et cet admirable papier bleu bien à elle.

Tout est ordonné: chaque objet a sa vraie place.

Pourtant, tout-à-l'heure, Colette s'écriera: "Pau . . . li . . . ne, où sont donc mes lunettes? Pau . . . li . . . ne, qu'ai-je donc fait de la lettre de X?"

Et la silencieuse, la secrète, la mystérieuse Pauline découvrira sans la moindre hésitation l'objet désiré . . .

Joli mois de mai . . .

Le soleil entre dans le studio, joue avec les rideaux de percale cirée, les boules de verre: miraflores somptueux.[3]

(Red roses in a tub. Crimson tulips, veined with white, narcissi, hollyhocks, and lilacs. Lovely month of May . . . The waiting tapestry.

And on the long, narrow table, the set of pens, the magnifying glass, the pot of glue, the long scissors and the spectacles. And that wonderful blue paper that is so much a part of her.

All is in order: every object has its proper place.

Presently, however, Colette will cry, "Pau . . . li . . . ne, where on earth are my glasses? Pau . . . li . . . ne, what in the world have I done with X's letter?"

And without the least hesitation, the silent, the secret, the mysterious Pauline will unearth the desired object. . . .

Lovely month of May . . .

The sun shines into the studio, plays with the glazed chintz curtains,
the glass paperweights: sumptuous blossomings.)

This passage is more than a demonstration that Colette's style is
catching. It is an evocation of the almost-lost world of Colette's
childhood, recaptured at last: the roses, the tulips, the light. When
Colette died in 1954, Maurice felt that she had at last returned to
the enchanted garden of Sido, and that the radiant look on her face
as she whispered "Regard. . . ." was a look of recognition.

The presence of Colette herself continued to linger with
Maurice. As he sat alone in the Palais-Royal apartment, writing the
memories that he was to include in *Près de Colette*, he felt that she
was personally guiding his work. And indeed the book could almost
have been written by Colette herself: it is divided into telling episodes, like *La Maison de Claudine*, and narrative and time perspective are skillfully used to bring out a psychological point.

Maurice married again; his second wife was the widow of the
couturier Lucien Lelong. At the age of seventy, he had a son. And
his second book, *Les Plaisirs de la Vieillesse*, contains a message
that Colette would have agreed with: that old age has a serenity and
completeness that make it incomparably happier than tormented,
ambivalent youth.

C H A P T E R 5

The Style of Colette

Caught in that sensual music all neglect
Monuments of unageing intellect.

—*William Butler Yeats*

The *style Colette* is one of the national possessions of France: it represents a fusion of the two most striking French cultural preoccupations, rigid intellectual formality and immersion in the life of the senses. Colette's stories are as stark and self-contained as a drama by Racine, with no unnecessary characters or action. But what are they about? She has abandoned the conflict between love and duty, between the intellect and the senses, that the classical French dramatists took as their theme; her books are about the many varieties of love, and the unending conflict between men and women. This results in a dilemma for her critics and readers—in which category are they to place her? Is she a classic, or a disgrace? Is she to be read openly or secretly, for pleasure or for duty?

The dilemma appears in its most acute form in the French school system, which can hardly ignore one of the ornaments of the nation's literature, but which equally feels that it can hardly assign the Claudine books or *Le Blé en herbe* to adolescents. The only book on the syllabus is likely to be *La Maison de Claudine*, and even that may appear in extracts to be read and then copied at dictation (the story of the Presbytère, a word which the young Colette thought described a snail's shell rather than the priest's house, is perhaps the favorite one); one French child observed, "What a funny writer Colette must have been, to write nothing but *dictées.*"

The heroines in Colette's books are often actresses or courtesans, and it seemed to her that making one's living by writing was essentially similar. The reader, the client, must be charmed and even bamboozled; self-revelation, though crucial, must take place on the performer's own terms; there must be a careful control underlying even the most apparently spontaneous moments.

This tension is part of what gives Colette's books their fascination, their mesmerizing quality. But it also means there is something ultimately unsatisfying about them, once the immediate spell dissipates. Just as she was always too guarded with men to be completely happy in marriage, so she is guarded in her work. The stories she tells are strangely at odds with the way she tells them. This is why the influence of the men in her life is difficult to assess: the presence of the adversary, the audience, was necessary, but it was also something to be manipulated and resisted. Only at the end, with Goudeket, was the man's presence so unthreatening that it could be admitted without fear.

Thus Goudeket was the one who has most interestingly analyzed her style, who got closest to understanding what she did and how she did it. He selected, out of many possibilities, one sentence of Colette to make his point:

L'idée de métamorphose est liée, depuis hier, à son destin, et plus d'un spectateur, en voyant cette comédienne à la haute stature, étreinte par une magnifique robe d'un bleu de flamme, appuyer les deux mains à sa taille comme pour se hisser hors d'elle-même, songea, comme moi, à la dernière éclosion de la libellule des étangs qui crève son dernier forreau, projette autour d'elle le regard de ses yeux bombés et mesure, en reflétant l'univers, le mal et le bien qu'elle y pourra répandre.

(The idea of metamorphosis is, after yesterday, bound up with her destiny, and more than one spectator, seeing this tall actress, squeezed into a magnificent gown of fiery blue, pressing her two hands to her waist as if to pull herself up out of herself, was, like me, reminded of the final hatching of the pond dragonfly who bursts his final casing, stares around him with bulging eyes and measures, reflecting the universe, all the evil and all the good that he can project out into it.)

Goudeket says of this sentence,

C'est la grande phrase du XVIIe siècle, avec ses incidentes, ses suspens, sa marche rythmée, enfin sa chute ample et sapide. . . . C'est une phrase bien virile, que sans doute aucun homme n'eut pu écrire, parce qu'il y manquerait le détail de la toilette, le geste de l'actrice.

(This is the great seventeenth-century sentence, with its descriptions, its moments of suspense, its rhythmic march, and the way it falls away, full and savory. . . . It is a very virile sentence which undoubtedly no man could have written, because he would have missed the detail of the dress, the gesture of the actress.)

The presence of the actress, and the combination of femininity and virility in the description, are the noteworthy points. But what interests Goudeket is the fact that Colette has so thoroughly mastered the *grande phrase*. It is a phenomenon that he cannot explain:

pourquoi une ancienne petite villageoise, munie du seul brevet élémentaire, écrivait, au courant de la plume, la langue des dieux, si les dieux sont français.

(why a little old village lady, endowed only with an elementary certificate, could turn out at a stroke of the pen the language of the gods, if the gods are French.)

He can only suggest that her style is, as she herself said of Cocteau, "the rhythm of a small sea creature who, far from the sea, follows the rhythm of his native tides." [1] There is a grain of truth in this, and Colette herself explained it more fully when she cited what Casanova recounted of one of his friends, a writer, who said, "My book is finished. All I have left to do is to cut out the Alexandrines." [2]

French falls as naturally into the *grand style*, the twelve-syllable line, as English does into what has been called the "iambic strait-jacket." But it falls into these rhythms most easily in the works of those writers who are also assiduous readers, and Colette, in spite of her "seul brevet élémentaire," certainly belonged to this category. Even Maurice, however, seems to have been fooled by her reticence about her own intellectualism, and to have taken the (male) line that outward forms, degrees and academic status, have something to do with what one actually knows. He may or may not have believed in Colette's pose as "une ancienne petite villageoise," but by the time he met her, it was nothing but a pose. She cultivated this appearance partly out of coquetry, partly because she knew that it made her achievement seem even more startling, but her learning in the French language was immense. Like George Eliot during the years when she was not "received," Colette had made use of her time—the years spent waiting for Willy, the sleepless nights after arthritis confined her to her "raft." But she never used her learning without an apology, as in her description of her meeting with Gabilla, the perfume chemist:

—"Liquidambar, styrax, citrons et citronnelles . . ." répétai-je. Est-ce le premier vers d'une *Ode Gabilline*, Monsieur, que cet alexandrin? . . . Souffrez qu'en vous quittant je montre le pédantisme d'un bas-bleu, et gardez en souvenir de moi, pour l'écrire au fronton de votre laboratoire, cette phrase de Jean-Jacques: "Les secrets, les doux parfums d'un cabinet de toilette ne sont pas un piège si faible qu'on pense . . ." [3]

(—"Liquid amber, styrax, lemon, citronella . . ." I repeated. Is this the first verse of a *Gabilline Ode*, sir, this Alexandrine? . . . Permit me, as I take my leave of you, to exhibit the pedantry of a bluestocking and ask you to write over the door of your laboratory, in memory of me this sentence of Jean-Jacques: "The secrets, the sweet perfumes of a dressing room are not such a feeble trap as one would think . . .")

Only Colette would believe (or pretend to believe) that a quotation from Rousseau, even about perfume, would brand her a bluestocking.

This passage relates to two of the most striking things about the *style Colette.* First, it shows her propensity for "feminine" imagery where it is least expected, an entirely open mind about appropriate metaphors that gives her imagery its freshness. Nothing is too humble to be used: she has the freedom trained out of most writers by the very academic process that supposedly qualifies them to write. In one of her frequent descriptions of the French countryside, she speaks of

> . . . quelques saules à grosse tête, chevelus d'un feuillage tendre que le vent peigne, divise, écarte et referme.[4]

> (. . . a few large-headed willows, with tresses of tender leaves which the wind combs, divides, parts, and rejoins.)

The second important thing about the perfume episode is that Colette goes on to say that, far from being trivial or frivolous, the blending of a scent is the embodiment of French civilization, as important as any other manifestation:

> Notre gastronomie célèbre se garde d'exagérer; la grande couture répudie les orgies colorées. . . . A la fortune d'une essence en vogue il ne faut pas seulement une clientèle de femmes fortunées, mais encore l'approbation populaire, l'assentiment d'une civilisation très vieille qui exerce, sur toutes choses de son ressort, la forme critique de l'esprit. . . . Tout parfum qui ne se réclame pas d'une origine végétale ne peut compter que sur un caprice bref de la mode.[5]

> Our celebrated gastronomy shuns hyperbole; the great couture repudiates orgies of color. . . . The success of a fashionable scent requires not only a clientele of rich women, but also popular acclaim, the assent of a very old civilization which exercises over everything that pertains to it the judgment of a critical spirit. . . . Any perfume that does not have a vegetable base can rely on no more than a brief caprice of fashion.

This sense of balance, of the blending of disparate elements into a unified whole, is as typical of the *style Colette* as it is of Frenchness; so is the emphasis on rapport with a popular audience. Here is Colette's own credo of nationality: balance, organic relation with the natural world, and the popular basis of the arts of living. The things she discusses—wine, cheese, cuisine, couture, perfume —are all matters of art and nature combined, and to Colette's public all are universally accessible, have their basis in the fact that they are necessities of life.

All the world agrees that the French painters, too, practised their art in this way, and Colette always felt closer kinship with painters than with the writers who have given France a reputation for literary coldness and formality. The Impressionists and their successors were her spiritual kin:

> Le foin fleuri de Monet, le Bonnard congestionné de végétation et de couleurs, un Derain d'une précision enchanteresse, la vigoureuse flexion qu'imprime Segonzac à des troncs puissants, un petit Leprin meilleur qu'un grand Utrillo, tout ici me semble intelligible, salubre, surprenant et familier. . . . Voici les traits ravissants de la terre française, chaude d'avoir, dans chacun de ses plis, bercé, nourri et enseveli un être humain.[6]

> (The flowered hayfields of Monet, the Bonnard crammed with vegetation and colors, a Derain of enchanting precision, the vigorous way that Segonzac bends powerful tree trunks, a little Leprin better than a large Utrillo, everything here seems to me intelligible, healthy, surprising, and familiar. . . . Here are the ravishing features of the French countryside, warm from having cradled, nourished, and buried in every one of its folds a human being.)

Her bond with the painters is that she celebrates the same France, the same rich and fruitful world. The male writers of France, from whom she consciously dissociates herself, have been sidetracked and misled by the cold and classical intellectual tradition of the country: the tendency to systematize, categorize, and work with antitheses. Although Colette too has a taste for antithesis—which appears in such facile Colette-ish phrases as "cette Bretagne doux et amer"—her terror of general ideas helps to save her from it, as it saves her from falling into the tendency to intellectualize of such writers as Gide, Sartre, and Camus.

Colette felt the strongest bond with the few French writers who also escaped this trap—Balzac, Baudelaire, and (among her own contemporaries) Proust. Outsiders, satanists, renegades, they saved their own spontaneity and capacity to respond to life by remaining alienated from the intellectual establishment. Telling the truth about money and sex preoccupied them, as it did Colette; they all saw conventional high culture as an attempt to cover up these truths.

Proust and Colette admired each other's work (Proust addressed her as "Maître"), and in a way they are counterparts: Colette was the Gomorrah to Proust's Sodom. Homosexuality was a source of freedom for them both, a refuge against conventionality. But Proust's homosexuality tended to set him apart, to make of him a kind of "special case," and to impair his universality. For Colette, it was part of that universality. Is this difference explained by Colette's assertion that "there is no Gomorrah," that female homosexuality does not really exist? After denying this idea, which in the Claudine stories she attributes to the patronizing husband, she seems to have embraced it in her own way. Or is it simply that she saw an aversion to men as an inescapable part of the female mentality, the slaves banding together against the oppressor as they do in La Seconde, while an aversion to women could only be pathological in a man? Her own preference for women—as subjects, friends, people with whom she felt a genuine rapport—seems to indicate this.

Colette's mental set can be best explained by starting with one of her most florid "set pieces" of prose, the kind of passage that repels her stricter male critics, and makes more tolerant male critics say "vive la différence," in the belief that it is Colette's "femininity" that enabled her to write it. Beneath its smoke screen of colors and sense descriptions, it conceals some of Colette's most profound analysis of the nature of her work.

Long automne nuancé, fructification obstinée . . . Il est l'achevé, le fort, le fragrant qui a si longtemps assemblé sur ma tête les sansonnets, leurs sifflements de bise et de soie égratignée, si longtemps étiré le grand V des canards, le vol des grues et des oies sauvages, agrégé, puis emporté des conseils massifs d'hirondelles . . . Commentés par les floraisons les plus brûlantes qui soient, par la sauge qui arde, le chrysanthème à

chevelure romantique, les dahlias plus noirs que la rose noire, les bali-
siers écarlates, pouvais-je, à de tels mouvements, associer l'idée de som-
meil et d'abdication? Ajoutez-y la prodigalité qui nous assure la possession des biens gratuits comme l'alise rousse, la mûre, le cèpe, la faine
triangulaire, la châtaigne d'eau à quatre cornes . . .[7]

(Long, nuanced autumn, prolonged fruitfulness . . . It is the consum-
mate, the strong, the fragrant which has for so long assembled the starlings
above my head, their whistlings of the north wind and of scratched silk,
for so long stretched out the great V of ducks, the flight of the cranes
and of the wild geese, collected, then swept away the massive councils
of swallows . . . Annotated by the most burning flowerings that may
be, by the glowing sage, the chrysanthemum with its romantic tresses,
the dahlias that are blacker than the black rose, the scarlet cannas, can I
associate with such movements the ideas of sleep and abdication? Add to
that the prodigality that assures us of the possession of free gifts like the
rust-colored hazelnut, the blackberry, the wild mushroom, the triangu-
lar beechnut, the four-horned water chestnut . . .)

The fruitful autumn of Colette's life was the time when she began
to identify with her mother, whom she re-created in terms of her
own needs. The mother whose disapproval of her daughter's husbands, of her daughter's life, of anything that diverted her from acting out Sido's own frustrated vocation and independence, had so
deeply directed Colette up to her fortieth year, was the source of a
pattern embedded in Colette's view of the world. Colette was born
when Sido was forty; and she in turn produced a daughter in her
own fortieth year, which also marked the death of Sido. Autumn—
rebirth—fruitfulness—the assumption by Colette of the earth-
mother role that her own mother had left vacant—this is the pattern we can discern in these passages.

Quarante années ne pesaient guère au personnage principal de toute ma
vie, à Sido, quand elle me mit au monde. Mais, après ma naissance,
elle engraissa, devint ronde sans enlaidir, dut renoncer à des robes qui
soulignaient sa taille de jeune fille. . . . C'est donc à cause de moi
qu'elle entra dans son automne de femme, et qu'elle s'y établit sereine-
ment. . . .[8]

(Forty years were scarcely a burden on the principal character in my whole life, Sido, when she brought me into the world. But, after my birth, she put on weight, became round without becoming ugly, and had to give up the dresses that pointed up her girlish figure. So it was on my account that she entered the autumn of her womanhood, and serenely settled down there. . . .)

Here we see her passionate desire to have been of crucial importance in the life of the mother whom she calls, justly, the "personnage principal de toute ma vie," and who seems to have so entirely encompassed her daughter's emotional life that the rest of her history is one long remembrance of "the endearments of a love that perhaps made us hard on other loves: Minet-Chéri . . . My shining sun. . . ." [9]

Sido's principal love objects were her children, perhaps particularly her son Achille, in whose house she eventually took up residence (after her husband's financial failure) and who never married. The desire to be in control, to be the giver of love and the director of the situation, was strong in Colette too—and in her own autumn, she, too, found a love object in the form of a much younger man. When she and Maurice went to Morocco, she responded to the Muslim pattern of sexuality in terms that are deeply related to her own life—Sido's Persian garden, the Mohammedan behavior of Sidi the pasha, and her own persona of "vieux garçon" with an eye for pretty boys: the pattern she embodied in Léa and Chéri, and that she recognized when she said that she represented a "temptation of homosexuality" for men. Her description of renting a mule in Morocco shows how she saw the world in terms of this pattern, and was interested in things that carried it out.

Pour gagner les souks par les ruelles, l'intendant me fit seller une mule noire à pompons rouges. Le meneur de la mule avait dix-sept ans d'age environ, et il était pareil aux adolescents qu'on voit, sur les miniatures persanes, entrer par le toit, descendre auprès d'une jeune femme dont le vieux mari dort dans sa barbe. Qu'eut été son sourire? Mais il ne souriait pas. Ce que voyant, l'intendant marocain lui prit d'une main le menton, appuya son autre main sur le front, et ouvrit l'adolescent comme on ouvre un fruit pourpre à pépins blancs, pour nous montrer qu'il était

beau jusqu'au fond, jusqu'au gosier rouge comme la gorge d'un glaieul.
Il vient de loin, ce geste de marchand d'éphèbes. Mais il n'a pas perdu
sa sensualité maquignonne, son habileté a troubler le spectateur.[10]

(To get to the souks by way of the alleys, the manager had saddled me a
black mule with red pompoms. The muleteer was about seventeen, and
he looked like the adolescents in Persian miniatures who come in
through the roof and get down next to a young wife whose old husband
is sleeping behind his beard. What would his smile be like? But he did
not smile. Seeing this, the Moroccan manager took his chin in one
hand, placed the other hand on his forehead, and opened up the youth
as one opens a purple fruit with white pips, to show us that he was beautiful all the way down to his red-gladiolus throat. It comes from a long
way back, this gesture of the ephebe-seller. But it has not lost its horse-
trading sensuality, its ability to disturb the spectator.)

This contains much of Colette's emotional history, from the
time when, married to an older man, she saw and envied Polaire
with her young lover; to the time that she herself was the appraiser
of youthful masculine beauty. She has been the young boy,
the androgynous Claudine; now she looks for her young self in
masculine guise.

The boy is compared to a fruit, an animal; the unity of all love
and of all organic life is asserted here, as it is throughout Colette's
works. This is why homosexuality can be one aspect of her universality, part of her inclusiveness. She is not turning against one
side of emotional or sexual experience, just including the other
facets.

If you confine yourself to one kind of love, the conventional
kind, says Colette, the chances are that you are incapable of love,
that sheer conventionality has taken its place. Every kind of love
has its particularity, its abnormality, and to recognize this is to love
fully. Her relation with Goudeket was possible in part because she
was ready to accept the idea that no love can be all-inclusive and
all-important; it coexists with other emotions and with the irreduc-
ible core of independence that Colette valued so highly.

Perhaps this is a clue to why Colette, like George Eliot and

Katherine Mansfield, has been accused of having difficulty in describing love between men and women in its most complete manifestation. Anthony Powell said that in *The Music of Time*, his series of novels portraying a whole stratum of English society, the only thing he deliberately excluded was his narrator's marriage—because it is impossible to describe a relation that includes so much. Katherine Mansfield confined herself to a child's-eye view of her parents' marriage, but in her stories as in her life, the primal happiness of childhood was always closer to her ideal than was the adult love she had so much trouble in accepting. George Eliot came closest of the three to describing it, as she came closest to approximating it in her own life; but the choice between love and work, and the possibility of combining the two, is something she resolves more fully than do any of her heroines.

The theme of renunciation in Colette's novels, and her persona as the old wise woman, enable her to treat the many varieties of love dispassionately; they also enable her to create happiness out of a marriage that the other two would have seen as a failure of the egalitarian idea. Sexual role-playing in France, more rigidly conventional than in the Anglo-Saxon countries, prevented her from finding real companionship and independence in her first two marriages; she had to invent a solution, to find a sexual stereotype (the older woman/younger man) that gave her what she needed—total love and total freedom.

By separating "total" love into its component parts, Colette was able to face head-on the fact that the relation of marriage includes most of the hues in the emotional spectrum, and to paint these hues one by one. This is why she always seems to stay on the periphery of her great subject, to circle around it, viewing it from one angle after another, and never to sum it up. She sees quite clearly that there is never an ideal that is more or less approximated, but spoiled by the failures and paradoxes of imperfect human beings; instead, each human relation is a summing up of various needs, drives, influences; the mixture is different in each case; and there is no such thing as a "norm." There are conventions, true enough—but adherence to them can be the most abnormal thing of all, the essence of hypocrisy, cruelty, and exploitation. The "conventional" man who keeps Luce as his mistress is a monster compared to the moral but unconventional Claudine; the "conventional" politician in *Julie de Carneilhan* is far less admirable than the straightforward Julie, even though it is she who is the outcast of society. In one of her subtlest books, *La Chatte*, it is the husband who behaves properly, and the wife who gives way to bizarre and unaccountable behavior—but it is he who is the monster of the two.

To say that love of a sexual nature has elements of parental love, homosexual love, hostility, dependence, ambiguity, is to express a truism of psychoanalysis; but to place these elements at the center of the stage, and to say that instead of being flaws in some nebulous, perfect love, they are love itself—this is Colette's profoundest insight.

Colette's best work achieves its strength by making no distinction between the normal and the abnormal, by reversing the categories of the pure and the impure.

Though Colette has often been considered one of those writers totally unrelated to her own time, who could have existed in any era, these psychological techniques make her very surely part of the modern movement that was the ultimate heir of romanticism. Her exploration of the world by means of her own psyche, her search for the roots of human experience and emotion, her broadening of the definition of literary subject matter, are the main characteristics of the literary history of the first half of this century. She is in the same class as Katherine Mansfield and Virginia Woolf—and as in their case, the fact that she was a woman has something to do with her modernism. The "feminine" sphere of psychological understanding, of human relations, was at the center of the literary stage; and women who had been barred from the aridities of conventional male letters were superbly equipped to delineate it.

The first English romantics were outsiders for class reasons, and the political analogies to their works were the French and American revolutions. Their literary device was the pastoral mode, a sophisticated way of seeming simpler than they were. The primitive painting of Gauguin and Picasso was another device of this kind; and the "spontaneity" of Katherine Mansfield and Colette is another. In Colette, this spontaneity is related to her many disclaimers of literary vocation, her insistence that

Mais dans ma jeunesse, je n'ai jamais, *jamais* désiré écrire . . . Car je sentais, chaque jour mieux, je sentais que j'étais justement faite pour ne *pas* écrire. . . . J'étais donc bien la seule de mon espèce, la seule mise au monde pour ne pas écrire.[11]

(But in my youth, I never, *never* wanted to write . . . Because I sensed, more clearly each day, I sensed that I was made precisely *not* to write. . . . So I was the only one of my kind, the only one sent into this world not to write.)

It is also related to her "feminine" desire not to appear a bluestocking or an intellectual, to dissemble her learning like her high forehead. Her "Sido" furnishings and provincial cupboards and country recipes are part of the pose, too—how much so we realize when we see how late in her life they were adopted.

This spontaneous primitivism was a necessary part of Colette's equipment as a writer, and this is why cutting herself off from love would have proved fatal to her gift. Her anti-intellectualism was perhaps not necessary to keep the springs of emotion available to her; but it is understandable when one notes the place that intellectualism has held in French literary life. It has indeed been the enemy of the kind of perception for which we value Colette. Thus John Weightman, perhaps the most astute English critic of French literature, is not necessarily correct when he argues that if she had had the education of Simone de Beauvoir, she would have been a novelist worth reckoning with. Perhaps so—but the other side of this equation is that Colette retained the very qualities Simone de Beauvoir conspicuously lacks, the insight, the spontaneity, of someone very much in touch with her own unconscious. As in art, so in life: Beauvoir and her lifelong companion, Jean-Paul Sartre, have equality, of a kind—but in their very self-conscious decision to live apart, to refuse children or marriage, there is something childlike and prim. And Beauvoir seems to realize this, and to reach out for what she does not have, when she constantly uses Colette's works to exemplify her description of the female life cycle in *The Second Sex*.

Colette's desire to confront experience directly, and not through the medium of literature, was as important for her as it was for

Katherine Mansfield. Their insistence on facing things, on choosing the difficult path, was similar—how much so we realize when we hear Colette say, in the very tones of Mansfield,

La fièvre, quand elle ne signifie pas pour moi le réveil d'un vieux point de pleurésie et la toux, est une sorte de fête, et je suis loin de l'accueillir d'un esprit effrayé, de courir à l'aspirine. Un tel enchantement ne mérite-t-il que des antidotes grossiers? [12]

(Fever, when it does not mean for me the reawakening of an old spot of pleurisy and a cough, is a kind of carnival, and I by no means approach it as if I were afraid, or run for the aspirin. Does such an enchanting thing deserve no better than vulgar antidotes?)

Goudeket recounts that she gave up smoking because she was beginning to enjoy it. As a sign that she is still unchanged by the horrors of war, she says that yes, thank God, she is still afraid of the air raids. The pain of her long battle with arthritis is also an occasion for thanks—it is her companion in the dead hours of the night, her proof that she can still feel.

There is a sort of thrift in this kind of thing that is typical of the bourgeoisie to which all three women belonged. Katherine Mansfield says that the emotional struggle with one's parents must be used—one cannot, as a writer, afford to waste such a store of experience. Colette turned her experiences to profit financially, artistically, and in terms of the discipline of her long life. The most characteristic utterance of a French bourgeoise is "Profitez"—an injunction that combines "Seize the day," "Economize," and "Drive a hard bargain."

The relation in Colette's work between money, sex, and fame or notoriety is very central. The transactions of a writer are implicitly compared to those of an actress, or a wife, or a mistress; some are conventionally moral and socially acceptable; others, and usually the purest, are outside of convention, law, or acceptability. In fact, she seems to say that one touchstone of pure emotion is its freedom from any taint of business—and marriage, sex, and the exercise of an artistic profession are all businesses. Only among the "pure" outcasts in Le Pur et l'Impur do we find emotion for its own sake, sufficient unto itself; there is no doubt in her mind who are the pure and who the corrupt.

Her critique of relations with men (including marriage) as business transactions of a more or less sordid kind is as strong as that of the other two women; like them, she tries to isolate the transcendent theme of love between men and women from its accretions of worldliness. How can she purify it, isolate it, and see it in its most basic form? Only in the loves of outsiders, unisexuals, or those mismatched in the world's eyes by disparity of age (*Chéri*), social standing (*Gigi*), experience (*Le Blé en herbe*), is love at all pure. This is why the purest love in her own life, her marriage to Goudeket, was also the most "inappropriate": relations with more eligible husbands were always essentially commercial.

Thus in the life of this typically French bourgeoise profiteer, there was a passionate desire to find and isolate something outside the range of profit—though of course this urge was the source of her greatest artistic profits.

Goudeket records that visitors used to hear him and Colette laughing as they came up the stairs—and the only explanation they could give for their hilarity was that "I was with her, and she was with me"—a remark that recalls Montaigne's description of his love for his friend, "because it was he, because it was I." This was the love sought by the young girl Colette, and her disillusion was the discovery that her first two marriages were more to do with money and sex than with love. Purged of money and sex, her life with Goudeket finally came close to fulfilling the idealistic fantasies of her youth. She reentered the enchanted garden from which she had been banished by contact with conventional role-playing, the variety of commercial sex that marriage often turned out to be, and the rest of the world's attacks on her independence and her vocation. Like the marriages of George Eliot and Katherine Mansfield, there was something innocent about Colette's life with Goudeket—a sense in which the two of them, purified by their love, banded together against disillusion. This is how love kept her creative gift alive.

CONCLUSION

The Muse at Work

The main theme of poetry is, properly,
the relations of man and woman. . . .

—Robert Graves, The White Goddess

The three heroines of this book were prose writers, but their relation with poetry was more complex than at first appears. In their
different ways, they all tried to make prose approach the condition
of poetry, in exactly the fashion that Virginia Woolf describes in
her diary:

> Why admit anything to literature that is not poetry—by which I mean
> saturated? Is that not my grudge against novelists? that they select noth-
> ing? The poets succeeding by simplifying: practically everything is left
> out. I want to put practically everything in: yet to saturate. [1]

George Eliot said that only Wordsworth came to mind as a possible audience for *Silas Marner;* indeed many of the themes in her
novels were Wordsworthian narratives translated into prose to fit
the changing tastes of the educated public. Her Browningesque poetry was less successful, because verse was no longer the dominant
mode of literary utterance.

Katherine Mansfield moved toward poetry as the modern poets
moved toward prose; she and Eliot and Virginia Woolf met on
some middle ground between the two. Murry certainly considered

her (and himself) to be the direct heirs of the Romantic poets, rather than of any prose tradition.

Colette asserted,

> Mais un écrivain en prose qui, ni pendant l'adolescence, ni pendant sa maturité, ni par abandon irrésistible, ni par gourmandise, par amour ou par douleur, ne s'est confié à la poésie versifiée, ne pensez-vous pas que c'est presque introuvable? [2]

> (But any prose writer who has never, either in his youth or in his maturity, either through some irresistible urge or through greed, out of love or out of grief, gone over to poetry in verse, don't you think that's unheard of?)

But she qualifies the poetry she hasn't written as "versifiée," knowing very well that much of her work has more in common with poetry (in the full sense of the word) than with prose.

The reason for emphasizing this link with poetry is that all three had the "daemonic" quality of the poet—the sense of writing from deeper impulses than are usually tapped in prose; in other words, they were serious artists. To relate them to the poetic tradition, and to approach them with terms derived from the study of poetry, reveals more about their lives and works than does any other approach.

The most comprehensive, convincing, and altogether explanatory poetic theory written in our time is that of Robert Graves, which has offended many by its apparent obscurity, its wealth of seemingly irrelevant and cranky detail from Celtic myth and pre-Socratic ritual and so on, and its link with the rather suspect anthropology of Frazer and his followers. Whether or not it is historically true that poetry is the voice of matriarchy, which in classical times was suppressed by patriarchal religion, it is an important and difficult matter to advance at least some theory about how a woman can fit into the traditional role of poet. It is a problem that these three women felt very keenly themselves, and their solution seems to me to corroborate what Graves has to say on the subject.

The idea he starts out with is uncompromising enough.

My thesis is that the language of poetic myth anciently current in the Mediterranean and Northern Europe was a magical language bound up with popular religious ceremonies in honour of the Moon-goddess, or Muse, some of them dating from the Old Stone Age, and that this remains the language of true poetry—"true" in the nostalgic modern sense of "the unimprovable original, not a synthetic substitute." [3]

This at once raises the crucial question—if woman is the Muse, can she also be the poet? Did Sappho, for example, gain her lesbian reputation because it was thought that a woman could only be the poet by renouncing her status as the Muse, in other words by becoming masculine? Graves believes that Sappho wrote as the Muse rather than as an imitation man, and that this is the task of any woman who becomes a poet:

That woman must not be excluded from the company of poets was one of the wise rules at the Devil Tavern in Fleet Street, just before the Puritan Revolution, when Ben Jonson laid down the laws of poetry for his young contemporaries. He knew the risk run by Apollonians who try to be wholly independent of women: they fall into sentimental homosexuality. Once poetic fashions begin to be set by the homosexual, and "Platonic love"—homosexual idealism—is introduced, the Goddess takes vengeance. Socrates, remember, would have banished poets from his dreary Republic. The alternative evasion of woman-love is monastic asceticism, the results of which are tragic rather than comic. However, woman is not a poet: she is either a Muse or she is nothing. This is not to say that a woman should refrain from writing poems; only, that she should write as a woman, not as if she were an honorary man. . . . She should be the visible moon: impartial, loving, severe, wise. [4]

Read in this light, the lives of these women seem quite remarkably to fall into Graves's pattern of descriptions of the Goddess: from androgynous and reticent maidenhood, to "femme fatale," to sibyl. The guardian of the earthly paradise is there, as well as the devourer of men. In Gravesian hyperbole,

She is the Flower-goddess Olwen or Blodeuwedd; but she is also Blodeuwedd the Owl, lamp-eyed, hooting dismally, with her foul nest in the hollow of a dead tree, or Circe the pitiless falcon, or Lamia with her flickering tongue, or the snarling-chopped Sow-goddess, or the mare-headed Rhiannon who feeds on raw flesh. *Odi atque amo:* "to be in love with" is also to hate. Determined to escape from the dilemma, the Apollonian teaches himself to despise woman, and teaches woman to despise herself.[5]

Beneath this rigmarole are some important themes: the hostility of men to the power of women, the fear that succumbing to this power will be a kind of self-immolation, and the ability of some men to joyfully accept the bargain.

The men who were able to make this daring leap were not poets themselves, though they all had literary ambitions. They were all impecunious. They faced the problem of combining their frustrated ambition with the necessity of getting a living; and their solution was in service to a Muse who would both write the poetry and get the money. This of course kept the women from feeling the usual temptations to domesticity—instead of being necessary for the family existence that they take up a domestic role, it was necessary that they *not* do so. They did have to find an audience, which meant that they had to write in prose. But their solution of this problem contributed much to the strength and immediacy of what they wrote: it was no bad thing to find a popular audience, since the intellectual audience had been corrupted by Apollonian literariness. Katherine Mansfield said that the greatest tribute she ever received was when the printer setting type for "At the Bay" said "These kids are real!" Similarly, George Eliot was delighted and gratified when a blacksmith said that *Adam Bede* must have been written by a man who knew the blacksmithing trade. And Colette went on and on about her rapport with the people, down to the crêpe-seller in the Palais-Royal who would bring her stuffed crêpes—"Goûtez-moi ça, Madame Colette!"

The books of all three are about antidomestic women trying to find a role, about antipoetic men's attempts to domesticate them. The chief enemies of the heroines are other women, who are enslaved themselves and have become the instruments of the enslavement of rebellious women. Only incidentally is society implicated in the struggle, though the structure of domestication is embedded in every aspect of society, and love of the real kind is always a subversive force.

These women valued an organic relation with life far above any participation in a literary establishment. Katherine Mansfield with her dream of the Heron, and her idylls at the Villa Pauline and Montana-sur-Sierre; Colette with her Breton and Côte d'Azur havens, and her "village" of the Palais-Royal; George Eliot's flights from London to the refreshment of the country—all found the urban scene that is stimulating to so many lesser talents to be clamorous, irrelevant, and deadly. The sense of natural religion was related to this love of the country: as Erikson says,

> . . . I have heard very clever men (but never a woman) claim that in principle there is nothing in nature that man cannot now learn to understand.[6]

Nor were they careful of their literary reputations in the way of people who are husbanding and exploiting a superficial talent. Colette began selling cosmetics to get back into touch with her female audience; like her music-hall performances, this was against the advice of the literary professionals. George Eliot's last defiant gesture, her marriage to Johnnie Cross, was certainly the act of a superbly independent and inner-directed Muse rather than of an aging litterateur. These surprising actions, and many more, can be understood in the Gravesian context, while they are baffling when viewed simply in terms of a professional career.

The life of the poet, Graves says, is discovered and acted out by a few people in every age. The age can be more or less hostile to it—the Romantic period was one of the most favorable periods for poetry, modern industrial civilization may ultimately be the death of it (though in the fifteen years since he published the last revised and enlarged edition of *The White Goddess*, many people have come around to Graves's point of view, and are looking for the kind of organic relation with life that the muse and the poet instinctively feel). But to commit oneself fully to this vocation seems to demand a confidence, a sureness in oneself and disregard for outside approval, which is more easily accessible when the world at large is receptive to one's aims. The "favored child," set apart by her gift as well as admired for it, must be able to find a sufficiently unconventional milieu to develop her talent and begin to use it, until she acquires the confidence to do without any support but that of her masculine worshipper.

The process of what Erikson calls "cultural consolidation" was one of the forces moving each of these women to the center of her particular national stage. George Eliot, at first an outsider, was part of the movement to centrality of the new Midlands middle class, supported and given power by the early industrial revolution. Coventry was one of the centers of this new power, which grew rapidly during George Eliot's early adulthood. Thus she felt herself swept to the center of things—and the themes of her early life, evangelical Christianity, rural nostalgia, the dispossessed rural landholder and the crass inheritors—all this became the theme of England itself, and gave her an audience.

Colette's career spanned a period when the power of France was declining rapidly, from the affluence and philistinism of the early part of the Third Republic to the spiritual and literal bankruptcy that followed both World Wars. In this period of decadence, certain themes were emphasized with which Colette identified herself at the outset of her career—themes of artistic bohemianism, sexual ambiguity, and a general inability to participate in the overt goals of the dominant class.

The collapse of English imperial power produced the "decadent" manifestation of Bloomsbury, and pulled to the center various regenerating elements, whose chance had come now that the previous establishment was routed. These disparate voices included such outsiders as Lawrence the miner's son, Eliot the American, Joyce the Irishman, and Katherine Mansfield the colonial.

How did the women in this book manage to find voices that still seem central, relevant, convincing? Though we can see in each case evidence of the influence and encouragement of their men, we cannot (without being unduly speculative) say what they would have done with other partners. The real link between their emotional lives and their work is more subtle and complicated—the problem of the woman artist was (and still is) to find a way to combine the battle for independence, violating social convention as it does, with a love relationship which by its nature limits independence. The woman politician, the businesswoman, may cripple her emotional life and still do her work, but for the "daemonic" writer, it is artistic death to do so.

These women's insistence on open-eyed confrontation with life, their determination to see things truly and the intelligence that enabled them to do so, operated to produce unconventional relationships with men, relationships far more egalitarian than the conventional mode. Contrasted with traditional marriage, in which the woman is often a victim or servant, these stories may make the men seem weak and submissive, and the women seem dominating. In fact, the men, too, had the courage to defy convention, and to treat their successful wives as beloved equals. They knew, of course, that to what we might call the *macho* majority they would be objects of derision or condescension, but they were able to endure that. If the conventional kind of marriage were not so widely accepted, it would be seen as the unjust and crippling situation that it is, and men like Murry, Lewes, and Goudeket would seem normal.

In such a relationship it is not always the woman who has the greater artistic success—the reverse was true of George Sand and Chopin. But at least the woman is not prevented from working as well as she can. Of course, the relationship of any couple that includes a very famous and successful artist will be affected by that, no matter which partner has the greater success. The temptation is to look at the work of the successful partner as the thing to be "explained" by the relationship; in fact, the strength and insight that made the work possible also makes the egalitarian marriage a reality.

Another clue to these women's success in love is, paradoxically, their insistence on the primacy of work. They knew that without the self-respect gained by following the dictates of their own intelligence and talent, they would never be able to insist on the kind of love relationship they were to find so satisfactory. All would have agreed with Katherine Mansfield, who wrote in her *Journal*,

Would life be worth living without work? NO. Therefore work is more important than life.

At the end *truth* is the only thing *worth having*: it's more thrilling than love, more joyful and more passionate.

The diffidence about the approach of love that we have noticed in these stories, the hesitancy in the face of such a dangerous and overwhelming commitment, is the best demonstration that it was taken seriously and, finally, entered into wholeheartedly. By approaching work and love realistically, these heroines triumphed in both.

NOTES

INTRODUCTION

1. Elizabeth Hardwick, *Seduction and Betrayal* (New York: Random House, 1974).
2. Erik H. Erikson, *Identity, Youth and Crisis* (New York: W. W. Norton, 1968).
3. Erikson, op. cit.

PART I

CHAPTER 1

1. Antony Alpers, *The Life of Katherine Mansfield* (New York: Knopf, 1953).
2. *The Journal of Katherine Mansfield*, ed. John Middleton Murry (London: Constable, 1967).
3. Alpers, op. cit.
4. *The Journal of Katherine Mansfield*, op. cit.
5. *Katherine Mansfield: The Memories of LM* (London: Michael Joseph, 1971).
6. Katherine Mansfield, *Letters to John Middleton Murry* (London: Constable, 1951).
7. Quoted in Frank Lea, *The Life of John Middleton Murry* (New York: Oxford University Press, 1960).

CHAPTER 2

1. *Katherine Mansfield: The Memories of LM*, op. cit.
2. Beatrice Lady Glenavy, *Today We Will Only Gossip* (London: Constable, 1964).

3. *The Journal of Katherine Mansfield*, op. cit.
4. *Katherine Mansfield: The Memories of LM*, op. cit.
5. Quoted in Alpers, op. cit.
6. Mansfield, *Letters to John Middleton Murry*, op. cit.
7. *The Letters of D. H. Lawrence*, ed. Aldous Huxley (London: Heinemann, 1932).
8. Ibid.
9. *The Letters of Katherine Mansfield*, 2 vols., ed. John Middleton Murry (London: Constable, 1928).
10. Ibid.
11. Glenavy, op. cit.
12. Francis Carco, *Souvenirs sur Katherine Mansfield* (Paris: Le Divan, 1934).
13. *The Journal of Katherine Mansfield*, op. cit.
14. Mansfield, *Letters to John Middleton Murry*, op. cit.
15. Ibid.
16. *The Journal of Katherine Mansfield*, op. cit.
17. Ibid.
18. *The Letters of D. H. Lawrence*, op. cit.
19. *Frieda Lawrence: The Memoirs and Correspondence*, ed. E. W. Tedlock (London: Heinemann, 1961).
20. Mansfield, *Letters to John Middleton Murry*, op. cit.
21. John Middleton Murry, *Cinnamon and Angelica* (Thavies Inn, London: Richard Cobden-Sanderson, 1920).
22. Carco, op. cit.
23. Mansfield, *Letters to John Middleton Murry*, op. cit.
24. Ibid.
25. *The Journal of Katherine Mansfield*, op. cit.
26. Letter to LM, quoted in *Katherine Mansfield: The Memories of LM*, op. cit.
27. Ibid.
28. *The Journal of Katherine Mansfield*, op. cit.
29. Letter to Koteliansky, in British Museum.
30. Mansfield, *Letters to John Middleton Murry*, op. cit.
31. Ibid., editorial note.
32. *The Journal of Katherine Mansfield*, op. cit.
33. Ibid.
34. Ibid.
35. Mansfield, *Letters to John Middleton Murry*, op. cit.
36. Ibid.
37. Ibid.
38. Ibid.
39. Ibid.
40. Letter from Mansfield to Sydney Schiff, in British Museum.
41. Quoted in *Adam: International Review*, vol. 38, nos. 370–75 (October 1973).
42. *The Journal of Katherine Mansfield*, op. cit.
43. Letter to Lady Ottoline Morrell, in *The Letters of Katherine Mansfield*, op. cit.

44. Mansfield, *Letters to John Middleton Murry*, op. cit.
45. *The Letters of Katherine Mansfield*, op. cit.
46. Edmund Wilson, *The Shores of Light* (New York: Farrar, Straus and Young, 1952).
47. *Katherine Mansfield: The Memories of LM*, op. cit.
48. *The Letters of Katherine Mansfield*, op. cit.
49. Ibid.
50. Letter to Koteliansky, in British Museum.
51. Mansfield, *Letters to John Middleton Murry*, op. cit., editorial note.
52. LM, op. cit.

CHAPTER 3
1. John Middleton Murry, *To the Unknown God—Essays Towards a Religion* (London: Jonathan Cape Ltd., 1924).
2. Ibid.
3. Quoted in Lea, op. cit.
4. Mary Middleton Murry, *To Keep Faith* (London: Constable, 1959).
5. Quoted in ibid.
6. John Middleton Murry, *Adam and Eve* (London: Andrew Dakers, 1944).
7. Lea, op. cit.
8. Quoted in Lea, op. cit.
9. John Middleton Murry, *Unprofessional Essays* (London: Jonathan Cape, 1956).
10. John Middleton Murry, *The Problem of Style* (Oxford: Oxford University Press, 1922).
11. *Frieda Lawrence*, op. cit.
12. Quentin Bell, *Virginia Woolf: A Biography* (London: The Hogarth Press, 1972).
13. *Collected Stories of D. H. Lawrence* (New York: Viking).
14. *The Letters of D. H. Lawrence*, op. cit.
15. Ibid.
16. Quoted in Lea, op. cit.

CHAPTER 4
1. Quoted in *Adam*, op. cit.
2. *The Journal of Katherine Mansfield*, op. cit.
3. *The Letters of Katherine Mansfield*, op. cit.
4. Ibid.
5. Ibid.
6. Ibid.
7. Ibid.
8. Ibid.
9. Quoted in *Adam*, op. cit.
10. Mansfield, *Letters to John Middleton Murry*, op. cit.
11. Katherine Mansfield, *Novels and Novelists* (London: Constable, 1930).
12. Mansfield, *Letters to John Middleton Murry*, op. cit.
13. Letter to Koteliansky, in *The Letters of Katherine Mansfield*, op. cit.

14. D. H. Lawrence, *Fantasia of the Unconscious* (New York: T. Seltzer, 1922).
15. *The Letters of Katherine Mansfield*, op. cit.
16. *The Scrapbook of Katherine Mansfield*, ed. John Middleton Murry (London: Constable, 1939).
17. *The Letters of D. H. Lawrence*, op. cit.
18. *Katherine Mansfield: The Memories of LM*, op. cit.
19. Mansfield, *Letters to John Middleton Murry*, op. cit.
20. *The Plumed Serpent* (New York: Viking, 1926).
21. Mansfield, *Novels and Novelists*, op. cit.
22. Mansfield, *Letters to John Middleton Murry*, op. cit.
23. *The Letters of Katherine Mansfield*, op. cit.
24. *The Journal of Katherine Mansfield*, op. cit.
25. Ibid.
26. Ibid.
27. Mansfield, *Letters to John Middleton Murry*, op. cit.
28. John Middleton Murry, *Katherine Mansfield and Other Literary Studies* (London: Constable, 1959).

PART II

CHAPTER 1

1. Ruby V. Redinger, *George Eliot: The Emergent Self* (New York: Alfred A. Knopf, 1975).
2. Quoted in Redinger, op. cit.
3. Charles Bray, *Phases of Opinions and Experience during a Long Life: An Autobiography* (London: Longmans, Green, 1885).
4. *The George Eliot Letters*, 7 vols., ed. Gordon S. Haight (New Haven: Yale University Press and London: Oxford University Press, 1954–1955), Vol. I, 22 February 1843.
5. *Strauss's Life of Jesus* (London, 1835).
6. Redinger, op. cit.
7. *The George Eliot Letters*, op. cit., Vol. II, 16 April 1853.
8. George Henry Lewes, *Rose, Blanche, and Violet* (London: Smith, Elder & Co., 1848).
9. Quoted in Gordon S. Haight, *George Eliot* (New York: Oxford University Press, 1968).
10. Quoted in Anna Theresa Kitchel, *George Lewes and George Eliot* (New York: John Day, 1933).
11. Ibid.
12. Quoted in Kitchel, op. cit.
13. Quoted in Haight, op. cit.
14. *The George Eliot Letters*, op. cit., Vol. I, 18 February 1842.
15. Erikson, *Identity, Youth and Crisis* (New York: W. W. Norton, 1968).
16. Letters, II, 166.
17. Letters, II, 179.

CHAPTER 2

1. George Eliot, *Essays*, ed. Charles Lee Lewes (London: Blackwood, 1884).
2. Haight, op. cit.
3. *The George Eliot Letters*, op. cit., Vol. II, GE Journal, 6 December 1857.
4. Ibid., Vol. III, 21 May 1859.
5. Ibid., 7 June 1860.
6. Ibid., 28 June 1859.
7. Ibid., Vol. IV, 15 August 1866.
8. Ibid., Vol. III, 24 February 1861.
9. George Henry Lewes, *Ranthorpe* (London, 1847).
10. *The George Eliot Letters*, op. cit., Vol. IV, GE Journal, 25–29 March 1865.
11. Ibid., Vol. IV, 22 January 1867.
12. K. A. McKenzie, *Edith Simcox and George Eliot* (New York: Oxford University Press, 1961).
13. *The George Eliot Letters*, op. cit., Vol. VI, 18 February 1875.
14. Ibid., Vol. V, 4 October 1872.
15. Quoted in Erikson, op. cit.
16. *The George Eliot Letters*, op. cit., Vol. VI, 21 April 1875.

CHAPTER 3

1. Quoted in Alice R. Kaminsky, *Literary Criticism of George Henry Lewes* (Lincoln: University of Nebraska Press, 1964).
2. Ibid.
3. *The George Eliot Letters*, op. cit., Vol. III, 13 November 1860.
4. Ibid., 19 April 1859.
5. Ibid., Vol. III, GHL Journal, 15 November 1859.
6. Quoted in Kaminsky, op. cit.
7. Quoted in Kaminsky, op. cit.
8. Quoted in ibid.
9. Quoted in ibid.
10. Quoted in ibid.
11. Quoted in ibid.
12. Introduction by Havelock Ellis to George Henry Lewes, *The Life of Goethe*, Everyman Edition (London: Geo. Rutledge & Sons Ltd., 1855).
13. T. Ribot, *English Psychology* (London: Henry S. King, 1873).
14. George Henry Lewes, *Sea-Side Studies* (Edinburgh: William Blackwood & Sons, 1858).
15. *The George Eliot Letters*, op. cit., Vol. III, 7 October 1859.
16. George Henry Lewes, *The Physiology of Common Life* (London: Tauchnitz, 1860).
17. George Henry Lewes, *Problems of Life and Mind* (London: Trübner, 1874).
18. Ibid.

CHAPTER 4

1. Quoted in Gordon S. Haight, A *Century of George Eliot Criticism* (Boston: Houghton Mifflin, 1965).
2. Leslie Stephen, *George Eliot* (London: Macmillan & Co. Ltd., 1902) in English Men of Letters series.
3. John Bayley, "The Pastoral of Intellect" in Hardy, *Critical Essays on George Eliot* (London: Routledge & Kegan Paul, 1970).
4. Haight, *George Eliot*, op. cit.
5. J. W. Cross, *George Eliot's Life as Related in Her Letters and Journals*, Vol. III, (New York: Harper & Bros., 1885), pp. 30–31.

PART III

CHAPTER 1

1. George Eliot, "Brother and Sister," published with revised edition of *The Spanish Gypsy*, 1874.
2. Colette, *Journal à rebours* (Paris: Librairie Arthème Fayard, 1941).
3. Colette, *Paysages et Portraits* (Paris: Flammarion, 1958).

CHAPTER 2

1. Jacques Gauthier-Villars, *Willy et Colette, un couple parisien de la Belle Epoque, ou Willy vu par son fils* (Paris: Les Oeuvres Libres, Fayard, October 1959).
2. Willy, *Souvenirs littéraires . . . et autres* (Paris: Editions Montaigne).
3. Henri Abert, "Willy," in *Les Célébrités d'aujourd'hui* (Paris: Sansot, 1904).
4. Claude Chauvière, *Colette* (Paris: Firmin-Didot, 1931).
5. Ibid.
6. Sylvain Bonmariage, *Willy, Colette et Moi* (Paris: Editions Charles Fremanger, 1954).

CHAPTER 3

1. Colette, *Lettres de la Vagabonde*, ed. Claude Pichois et Roberte Forbin (Paris: Flammarion, 1961).
2. Ibid.
3. Ibid.
4. Colette, *Paysages et Portraits*, op. cit.
5. Colette, *Lettres de la Vagabonde*, op. cit.
6. Ibid.
7. Colette, *Lettres à Marguerite Moreno*, ed. Claude Pichois (Paris: Flammarion, 1959).
8. Ibid.
9. Colette, *Paysages et Portraits*, op. cit.
10. Letter in André Lang collection, Bibliothèque Nationale.
11. Colette, *Lettres à Hélène Picard*, ed. Claude Pichois (Paris: Flammarion, 1958).
12. Colette, *Lettres à Marguerite Moreno*, op. cit.

CHAPTER 4

1. Colette, *Lettres à Marguerite Moreno*, op. cit.
2. Ibid.
3. Colette, *Lettres au Petit Corsaire*, ed. Claude Pichois et Roberte Forbin (Paris: Flammarion, 1963).

CHAPTER 5

1. Maurice Goudeket, *Près de Colette* (Paris: Flammarion, 1956).
2. Colette, *Paysages et Portraits*, op. cit.
3. Ibid.
4. Colette, *Paris de ma fenêtre* (Geneva: Editions du Milieu du Monde, 1944).
5. Colette, *Paysages et Portraits*, op. cit.
6. Ibid.
7. Colette, *Journal à rebours*, op. cit.
8. Ibid.
9. Ibid.
10. Ibid.
11. Ibid.
12. Ibid.

CONCLUSION

1. Virginia Woolf, *A Writer's Diary* (London: The Hogarth Press, 1953).
2. Colette, *Paysages et Portraits* (Paris: Flammarion, 1958).
3. Robert Graves, *The White Goddess* (New York: Vintage Books, 1958), first edition published 1948.
4. Ibid.
5. Ibid.
6. Erik H. Erikson, *Identity, Youth and Crisis* (New York: W. W. Norton, 1968).

INDEX

Adam Bede, 104, 114, 138, 142-45, 147, 150-52, 173, 174, 258

Adelphi, The, 21, 77-78, 80, 87, 165

Athenaeum, The, 21, 59, 60, 68-69, 93

"At the Bay," 25, 51, 70, 100, 105, 107, 258

Austen, Jane, 3, 83, 93, 107, 179

Baker, Ida Constance ("LM"), 28, 31-36, 44-45, 51, 57, 59, 61-66, 68, 69, 72-75, 86, 102-103, 105-106, 108

Bashkirtseff, Marie, 29, 73

Beauchamp, Annie, 24-26, 31, 64-65, 67, 99

Beauchamp, Harold, 24-26, 33, 64-65, 67, 99

Beauchamp, Kathleen. *See* Mansfield, Katherine

Beauchamp, Leslie Heron ("Chummie"), 25, 28, 33, 39, 49-52, 58, 70, 99, 100, 115, 172

Beauvoir, Simone de, 249

Belbeuf, Marquise de ("Missy"), 210-11, 213-16

Bennett, Arnold, 37-38

Blackwood, John, 141-44, 147, 149, 151, 155-56, 168, 174

Blake, William, 9, 198

Bodichon, Barbara Leigh Smith, 123, 138, 140, 143, 145-46, 149

Bowden, George, 31-32, 42, 58

Bray, Charles and Cara, 116-21, 125, 135-36, 138-39

Brontë sisters, the, 3, 142, 154, 178-79

Carco, Francis, 37, 43, 47-49, 56, 209-10, 222

Carlyle, Jane, 4, 6, 129

Carlyle, Thomas, 133, 138

Chapman, John, 120-25, 133-36, 138-40, 142-43

Chekhov, Anton, 28, 32, 48, 59, 73, 78, 90, 99

Chéri, 224-25, 229-32, 245, 251

"Chummie." *See* Beauchamp, Leslie Heron

Claudine series, 15, 192, 194, 201-209, 211, 213-14, 224-25, 237, 243, 246, 248

Cocteau, Jean, 203, 228, 239
Coleridge, Samuel Taylor, 36, 58
Colette, Adèle-Sidonie ("Sido"), 187-97,
    199-202, 206, 216-18, 220-21, 225,
    234-36, 244-45, 249
Colette, Jules-Joseph ("the Captain"),
    187-97, 198-200
Colette, Sidonie-Gabrielle, 4, 9, 10, 12,
    15-16, 48, 182, 185-251, 256,
    258-60
  childhood, 187-97
  life with Goudeket, 227-36
  life with Jouvenel, 213-26
  life with Willy, 198-212
  works, 237-51
Cross, John, 157-58, 170, 259

Daniel Deronda, 120, 133, 151, 154-56,
    167, 173, 175, 178-81
De Quincey, Thomas, 4-5, 58
Dickens, Charles, 143, 164
Dickinson, Emily, 3, 21
Dostoevsky, Fyodor, 45, 48, 50, 52, 60,
    73, 77, 85, 179

Eliot, George, 3-4, 6, 9-12, 14-16,
    111-83, 189, 196, 221-22, 225, 233,
    240, 246-47, 251, 255, 258-60
  childhood and youth, 113-25
  life with GHL, 138-58
  meets GHL, 132-37
  works, 170-83
Eliot, T. S., 60, 90, 255, 260
Erikson, Erik, 3, 13-14, 136, 190, 259-60
Evans, Chrissey, 114, 120, 124-25,
    146-47
Evans, Christiana Pearson, 114-16, 147,
    189, 191
Evans, Isaac, 114-15, 117-18, 125, 138,
    146-47, 157, 189
Evans, Marian. See Eliot, George
Evans, Robert, 113-14, 116-18, 120,
    135, 140, 147

Felix Holt, 151-52, 173, 175
Fitzgerald, F. Scott, 6, 42

Fitzgerald, Zelda, 6, 8, 42
Freud, Sigmund, 9, 13, 155, 167, 169,
    176-77

"Garden Party, The," 95-96, 105-106
Gauthier-Villars, Henri ("Willy"), 10,
    16, 193, 198-212, 214, 218, 221,
    240
Goethe, Johann Wolfgang von, 128,
    132, 136, 139, 165
Goudeket, Maurice, 10-11, 15-16,
    227-36, 238-40, 245-46, 250-51,
    261
Graves, Robert, 255-59
Gurdjieff, 72-73, 77, 107

Hardy, Thomas, 12, 175
Huxley, Aldous, 60, 68, 84

In a German Pension, 33, 40, 42, 68, 105

James, Henry, 68, 174
"Je ne parle pas français," 49, 56, 59, 68
Jouvenel, Colette de, 218, 221
Jouvenel, Henry de, 10, 16, 193, 213-26,
    227-28, 245
Joyce, James, 10, 12, 85, 260

Keats, John, 7, 22-23, 57-58, 84-85, 108,
    141
Koteliansky, S.S., 47-48, 54, 62, 71,
    73-74, 92

La Maison de Claudine, 195, 236-38
La Vagabonde, 15, 211, 213, 224
Lawrence, D. H., 10, 12, 38, 42-47,
    52-54, 60, 66, 79, 81-88, 93,
    98-103, 104, 106, 164, 260
Lawrence, Frieda, 42-43, 47, 53-54, 58,
    79, 84, 101-103
Leader, The, 125, 130-31, 160
Leavis, F. R., 82-83
Lewes, Agnes Jervis, 125, 129-30, 142,
    150, 171

Lewes, George Henry, 4, 10, 11, 15-16, 104, 111-83, 226, 233, 261
  childhood and youth, 126-32
  life with GE, 138-58
  meets GE, 132-37
  works, 159-69
LM. *See* Baker, Ida Constance

Mansfield, Katherine, 3-4, 9, 11-12, 14, 16, 19-109, 116, 123, 139, 148, 155, 163, 171-74, 182, 192, 196, 209-10, 218, 221, 225-26, 247-48, 250-51, 255, 258-62
  childhood and youth, 21-34
  life with JMM, 40-75
  works, 89-109
Martineau, Harriet, 123, 138
Marx, Karl, 122, 155, 166-67
Middlemarch, 152, 154, 172-73, 179
Mill, John Stuart, 122, 126, 132
Mill on the Floss, The, 114-15, 144, 147, 174, 177, 179, 182, 191
"Missy." *See* Belbeuf, Marquise de
Moreno, Marguerite, 210, 219-20, 228-30
Morrell, Lady Ottoline, 42, 54
Murry, Betty Cockbayne, 79-81, 86, 88
Murry, Colin Middleton, 35, 79-80
Murry, John Middleton, 9, 11, 15-16, 19-109, 127, 139, 162-66, 173-74, 226, 231, 255, 261
  childhood and youth, 34-39
  life with KM, 40-75
  subsequent life and works, 76-88
Murry, Mary Gamble, 81-82, 88
Murry, Richard, 59, 87, 91-92
Murry, Violet le Maistre, 79, 81

New Age, The, 32-33

Orage, A. R., 32, 34, 71-72

Plath, Sylvia, 6-7, 101
Post-Impressionists, 37, 91, 242, 248
"Prelude," 25, 49, 56, 59, 68, 70
Proust, Marcel, 60, 85, 187, 224, 243

Rhythm, 34, 37, 40-42, 44
Romola, 127, 147, 149-51, 175
Russell, Bertrand, 60, 198

Sartre, Jean-Paul, 7, 242, 249
Schwob, Marcel, 209-10
Shakespeare, William, 13-14, 22, 57, 75, 77, 80, 85, 179
Shaw, George Bernard, 12, 38
Shelley, Percy Bysshe, 58, 127, 130, 164
"Sido." *See* Colette, Adèle-Sidonie
Silas Marner, 147-49, 151, 170, 255
Spencer, Herbert, 122-25, 134, 143
Stephen, Sir Leslie, 171-74
Strauss, David Friedrich, 119-21, 123, 132

Webb, Sidney and Beatrice, 123-24
Westminster Review, 121-23, 140
"Willy." *See* Gauthier-Villars, Henri
Woolf, Leonard, 6, 60
Woolf, Virginia, 6-7, 54, 60, 68, 85, 86, 88, 90-98, 103, 106, 148, 171-74, 248, 255
Wordsworth, Dorothy, 4, 6, 8, 58
Wordsworth, William, 58, 143, 147-48, 163, 255